# Finding Locke's God

Also available from Bloomsbury

*Intellectual, Humanist and Religious Commitment*, by Peter Forrest

*Kant's Transition Project and Late Philosophy*, by Oliver Thorndike

*Religious Language, Meaning and Use*,
by Robert K. Bolger and Robert C. Coburn

*Spinoza in Twenty-First-Century American and French Philosophy*,
edited by Jack Stetter and Charles Ramond

# Finding Locke's God

*The Theological Basis of John Locke's Political Thought*

Nathan Guy

BLOOMSBURY ACADEMIC
LONDON • NEW YORK • OXFORD • NEW DELHI • SYDNEY

BLOOMSBURY ACADEMIC
Bloomsbury Publishing Plc
50 Bedford Square, London, WC1B 3DP, UK
1385 Broadway, New York, NY 10018, USA
29 Earlsfort Terrace, Dublin 2, Ireland

BLOOMSBURY, BLOOMSBURY ACADEMIC and the Diana logo
are trademarks of Bloomsbury Publishing Plc

First published in Great Britain 2020
This Paperback edition published in 2021

Copyright © Nathan Guy, 2020

Nathan Guy has asserted his right under the Copyright, Designs and Patents Act, 1988, to be identified as Author of this work.

For legal purposes the Acknowledgments on p. viii constitute an extension of this copyright page.

Cover design by Maria Rajka
Cover image: Locke handwriting © Chronicle / Alamy Stock Photo

All rights reserved. No part of this publication may be reproduced or transmitted in any form or by any means, electronic or mechanical, including photocopying, recording, or any information storage or retrieval system, without prior permission in writing from the publishers.

Bloomsbury Publishing Plc does not have any control over, or responsibility for, any third-party websites referred to or in this book. All internet addresses given in this book were correct at the time of going to press. The author and publisher regret any inconvenience caused if addresses have changed or sites have ceased to exist, but can accept no responsibility for any such changes.

A catalogue record for this book is available from the British Library.

A catalog record for this book is available from the Library of Congress.

ISBN:  HB:     978-1-3501-0351-1
       PB:     978-1-3502-5005-5
       ePDF:   978-1-3501-0352-8
       eBook:  978-1-3501-0353-5

Typeset by Integra Software Services Pvt. Ltd.

To find out more about our authors and books visit www.bloomsbury.com and sign up for our newsletters.

*For Katie*

# Contents

| | |
|---|---|
| Acknowledgments | viii |
| Abbreviations | x |
| Introduction | 1 |

**Part 1  In Defense of the Religious Turn**

| | | |
|---|---|---|
| 1 | The New Perspective on Locke: The Religious (Re)Turn in Locke Scholarship | 15 |
| 2 | Life in the Areopagus: Secular Echoes, Religious Refrain | 31 |
| 3 | Locke and the Latitudinarians: Locke's Religious Experience and Theological Influences in the Context of Seventeenth-Century England | 51 |

**Part 2  From a "Religious" to a "Theological" Turn: Tracing Locke's Theological Argumentation**

| | | |
|---|---|---|
| 4 | The God of Christianity and the Foundations of Morality | 77 |
| 5 | Natural Law, the Law of Nature, and a Theology of Creation | 105 |
| 6 | Revelation, Reason, and Scripture | 131 |
| | Conclusion | 151 |

| | |
|---|---|
| Notes | 153 |
| Bibliography | 219 |
| People Index | 237 |
| Subject Index | 240 |
| Locke's Works Index | 243 |

# Acknowledgments

*To form a young gentleman as he should be ... [involves] an art not to be learnt nor taught by books. Nothing can give it but good company and observation join'd together.*
—John Locke, *Some Thoughts Concerning Education* (1692), 93.

I am extremely grateful for the "good company" of family, educators, colleagues, and friends who have shaped not only my thinking but also my life. The initial impetus to read Locke came nearly a decade ago through a series of engaging lectures and conversations at the London School of Economics and Political Science (LSE). Alex Voorhoeve, Luc Bovens, Katrin Flikschuh, and Paul Kelly all had a hand in raising my interest, while my friend and classmate Garnett Genuis encouraged me to turn my interest into a larger project. The idea for this book began to take shape a few years later while conducting research in the Theology faculty of the University of Cambridge. I found myself surround by "good company" who modeled a perfect blend of erudition, generosity, and refined grace. I think especially of Andrew Davison, Douglas Hedley, Janet Soskice, and the late and lamented John Hughes. My gratitude belongs to St. Edmund's College, Cambridge, not only for providing an ideal living and learning environment for three wonderful years but also for awarding me the John Coventry Prize for my work.

The funding for my years in England came through the generosity of Harding University's executive committee. My special thanks belong to this "good company" of executives, especially David Burks, Bruce McLarty, and Mike Williams.

Returning home from the UK, I enjoyed the "good company" of kind and generous souls who volunteered their time to aid me in my further research and preparation. I wish to thank the able librarians at Harding University (especially Justin Lillard, Holly Tidwell, and Emillia Cline), the students of my Locke Seminar; my colleagues Mac Sandlin, Jim Bury, and Jordan Guy for their careful and critical eye; and two graduate students from Harding School of Theology who lent their invaluable assistance: Lance Hedrick and Jackson House.

In preparing my research, I had the good fortune to present my findings and hone my argument through various presentations at Pepperdine University,

Faulker University's Jones School of Law, Heritage Christian University, and Harding University. To all those involved in providing these opportunities (especially Layne Keele, Joshua Fullman, Jeremy Barrier, Danny Mathews, Tim Willis, and Dale Manor), I extend a sincere "thank you."

Two Locke scholars who read portions of my work and offered feedback have also immensely blessed me. Early in the process, Victor Nuovo gave me both encouragement and critical feedback. In the penultimate stages of book preparation, Greg Forster offered his assistance. Greg's careful reflection and incisive comments helped make this a better book. For their generosity and assistance, I am grateful.

I also wish to thank Colleen Coalter (Senior Commissioning Editor at Bloomsbury), Helen Saunders and Becky Holland (Editorial Assistants), and two excellent copy editors—Shanmathi Priya Sampath and Sudha Soundrapandiyan—for bringing this dream to completion.

Finally, to my family, I thank you. My parents and brothers have been encouraging and supportive every step of the way. It was in the initial stages of dreaming up this project that I met the love of my life. To my wife, Katie, I owe much of my happiness and all of my love. Here's to you, babe.

Nathan Guy

# Abbreviations

1st T     John Locke, "First Treatise of Government" [1690], in John Locke, *Two Treatises of Government*, a critical edition with an introduction and apparatus criticus, ed. Peter Laslett, 2nd ed. (Cambridge: Cambridge University Press, 1967, rep. 1988), 137–263. Citations are by numbered paragraph.

2nd T     John Locke, "Second Treatise of Government" [1690], in John Locke, *Two Treatises of Government*, a critical edition with an introduction and apparatus criticus, ed. Peter Laslett, 2nd ed. (Cambridge: Cambridge University Press, 1967, rep. 1988), 265–428. Citations are by numbered paragraph.

COR     John Locke, *The Correspondence of John Locke*, ed. E. S. de Beer (Oxford: Clarendon Press, 1976–1989), 8 vols. Citations are by volume and page number.

E     John Locke, *An Essay Concerning Human Understanding*, ed. Peter H. Nidditch (1689, 1975, Revised edn. Repr., Oxford: Clarendon Press, 1979). Citations are by book, chapter, section, and page number.

L     Letter (to or from John Locke), as found in *COR*. Citations are by letter number.

Laws     Richard Hooker, *Of the Laws of Ecclesiastical Polity*, Preface, Book I, Book VIII, ed. Arthur Stephen McGrade (Cambridge: Cambridge University Press, 1989, rep. 1997).

LCT     John Locke, *A Letter Concerning Toleration* [1689], ed. James H. Tully (Indianapolis: Hackett, 1983). Citations are by page number.

LL     John Harrison and Peter Laslett, *The Library of John Locke* [1965], 2nd ed. (Oxford: Clarendon Press, 1971). Citations are by page number.

LN     John Locke, *Essays on the Law of Nature* [1664]: *The Latin Text with a Translation, Introduction, and Notes, Together with Transcripts of Locke's*

*Shorthand in His Journal for 1676*, ed. and trans. W. von Leyden (Oxford: Clarendon Press, 1954, reissued 1988). Citations are by page number.

QLN   John Locke, *Questions Concerning the Law of Nature* [1664]: *With an Introduction, Text, and Translation*, trans. Robert Horwitz, Jenny Strauss Clay, and Diskin Clay (Ithaca, NY: Cornell University Press, 1990). Citations are by page number.

RC    John Locke, *The Reasonableness of Christianity as Delivered in the Scriptures*, in *The Works of John Locke in Nine Volumes*, 12th ed. (London: C. Baldwin, 1824), Vol. 6, 1–158. Citations are by page number.

ST    Thomas Aquinas, *Summa Theologiae*, trans. Fr. Laurence Shapcote, ed. John Mortensen and Enrique Alarcón, in *Latin/English Edition of the Works of St. Thomas Aquinas* (Lander, WY: The Aquinas Institute for the Study of Sacred Doctrine, 2012), Vols. 13–18.

STCE  John Locke, *Some Thoughts Concerning Education* [1693], ed. with introduction, notes, and critical apparatus by John W. Yolton and Jean S. Yolton (Oxford: Clarendon Press, 1989). Citations are by paragraph.

TIS   Ralph Cudworth, *True Intellectual System of the Universe: The First Part, Wherein All the Reason and Philosophy of Atheism Is Confuted; and Its Impossibility Demonstrated* (London: Printed for Richard Royston, bookseller to his most sacred majesty, 1678).

# Introduction

The portrait of a decidedly "secular" Locke held sway in many places for much of the twentieth century. Though some did not question Locke's personal faith commitments (believing them to have no bearing on his political philosophy), others described Locke as, at best, a deist (if not a closet atheist), whose use of religious language was either incidental or insidious. For these interpreters, Locke's emphasis on both toleration and individual liberty is intended to push theological matters to the periphery of political affairs and has no bearing on the basis of his political thought.[1] However, a recent spate of research questions the assumption that Locke sought to remove theology from his political theory and, instead, claims that the "deeply Christian" Locke establishes his political thought on an essentially theological foundation.

This "religious turn" in Locke scholarship is often associated with the work of Jeremy Waldron, although its roots are much deeper. Nonetheless, Waldron's 1999 Carlyle lectures (and their subsequent publication in 2002) brought the discussion into the larger public arena, where history, philosophy, theology, and political theory meet.[2] A number of works, building on Waldron's keen insights, have issued from the presses in the last decade seeking to further solidify the inseparable bond between Locke's political thought and his theological moorings.[3] In this book, I will argue that the religious turn in Locke scholarship is fundamentally correct but offer both a historically contextual basis for such a move and a programmatic articulation of the theological basis for Locke's approach. Much more needs to be said about Locke's historical and theological context, as well as his theology in general—not least his doctrine of creation. In this book I hope to use Locke's own tripartite foundation of God, the law of nature, and revelation (Christian scripture) as a means to trace Locke's theological position and, in so doing, point out areas of his political philosophy in which his theology provides grounding or makes a profound impact.

## A three-fold foundation

In his 1671 draft of some initial thoughts concerning human understanding, Locke intimates that there exist moral standards, or "rules of good & evill," which are "not made by us but for us." "But," writes Locke,

> because we cannot come to a certain knowledg of these rules of our actions, without first makeing knowne a lawgiver with power & will to reward & punish & without shewing how he hath declard his will & law I must only at present suppose this rule till a fit place to speake of those god the Law of nature & revalation.[4]

In the place where a revised version of this material appears in the finished *Essay*[5] of 1689, Locke prefaces his remarks by declaring the area of moral actions to be of highest importance.[6] Chief among the various "laws" to which our actions are held accountable is "The *Divine* Law," which Locke describes as

> that Law which God has set to the actions of Men, whether promulgated to them by the light of Nature, or the voice of Revelation. That God has given a Rule whereby Men should govern themselves, I think there is no body so brutish as to deny. He has a Right to do it, we are his Creatures: He has Goodness and Wisdom to direct our Actions to that which is best: and he has Power to enforce it by Rewards and Punishments, of infinite weight and duration, in another Life: for no body can take us out of his hands. This is the only true touchstone of *moral Rectitude*; and by comparing them to this Law, it is, that Men judge of the most considerable *Moral Good* or *Evil* of their Actions; that is, whether as *Duties, or Sins*, they are like to procure them happiness, or misery, from the hands of the ALMIGHTY.[7]

In both cases, Locke delineates "God," the "Law (or light) of Nature," and "Revelation" as foundational topics upon which his moral philosophy is founded. Though Locke only mentions these in passing, in this book I will show that the relationship between morality and these three areas of study provides the key to appreciating Locke's entire project. For Locke, a study of moral rules requires a lawgiver (God), the law itself (law of nature), and the ultimate means whereby we derive certain knowledge of, motivation toward, and obligation to keep that law (revelation). It is not surprising, then, that the impetus for Locke's epistemological considerations (eventually culminating in the *Essay*) was a set of questions concerning "the Principles of morality, and reveald Religion"—principles that, as Nidditch rightly notes, "underlay his text" even when not examined explicitly.[8]

## Political philosophy as a theological project

Yet this theological foundation for his moral philosophy also serves as the basis for his central political claims. In the *Second Treatise*,[9] the basic tenet of Locke's political philosophy is that human beings are "all equal and independent," share in "one community of nature," and have dominion over "the inferior creatures," as a result of theological reasons:

> For men being all the workmanship of one omnipotent, and infinitely wise maker; all the servants of one sovereign master, sent into the world by his order, and about his business; they are his property, whose workmanship they are, made to last during his, not one another's pleasure.[10]

Locke bases his view of human equality not only in the mere formal truth that human beings are born "of the same species and rank" and thus reasonably obligated to one another (in a modern humanitarian sense) but also in the claim that humans were created by God, given a particular role in the world, and are morally obligated to Him. Locke employs philosophical arguments for the existence of God and readily uses Christian scripture to lend support to his basic thesis.

Locke's project of moral and political philosophy, then, can easily be described as a theological one. The theological impulse that lay beneath Locke's political project harmonized well with some explicit teachings of a moderating influence in seventeenth-century England. Locke was especially acquainted with teachings and personalities associated with the Oxford Tew Circle, the London Latitudinarians, and the Cambridge Platonists—three sources of influences, which are each credited with developing approaches to theology that stand between Calvinistic puritanism on the one hand and high Anglicanism on the other. These moderates sought a middle ground through an appreciation for common ground among monotheists, the role of reason in articulating a minimalistic set of key religious truths, and an emphasis on the personal and individual character of faith in contrast with any coercion by the state.[11] Though ever independent, Locke's theological perspective is decidedly Latitudinarian with echoes of similar moderating approaches. This background provides a fitting framework for placing Locke's political project within the sphere of a moderating Christian political philosophy.

The manner and extent to which Locke's political schema is shaped by his religious interest has proved to be a fruitful field of study, attracting historians, philosophers, theologians, and political scientists. Among those with theological interests, recent studies in this regard have either focused on Locke's epistemology, reevaluated his use of scripture, or sought to reconstruct his personal faith commitments. But few have attempted to bring these items together in an articulation of the deep theological structure of his entire political system. Placing Locke in the religious context of seventeenth-century Latitudinarians, as well as paying careful attention to his implicit and explicit theological argumentation throughout his writings, this book will seek to provide a more definitive study of how Locke's political methodology stems from a theological basis. In this sense, Locke would better be classed as a heterodox Christian political philosopher than credited with championing the rise of secular methodology in political affairs.

The argument of this book builds on results of previous research. With regard to literary criticism, a critical-realist approach to reading Locke's works is preferable to the Straussian hermeneutic of suspicion, subversion, and charade. In the main, Locke should be interpreted as meaning what he says.[12] There is good reason to suppose coherence and continuity among Locke's various writings, rather than accepting the inverse (i.e., the Laslett thesis).[13] In terms of biography, that Locke was a believing and practicing Christian, albeit heterodox, until the day he died should now be beyond a matter of dispute.[14] Furthermore, Locke is rightly viewed as a natural law theorist, even if one concludes he is far from traditional in his understanding.[15] From these considerations, several authors have noted that his philosophical, political, and moral outlook was influenced (and possibly shaped) by explicitly Christian principles. A sub-point (gaining great traction though by no means the "consensus") is that Locke's ethical outlook is necessarily tethered to theological (and particularly Christian) principles.[16]

However, a bird's-eye view of the religious turn in Locke scholarship would suggest two important moves needing to be made, both of which I attempt to accomplish in my book. First, locating Locke within the context of the Latitudinarians of the late seventeenth century is pivotal to understanding how his deeply held religious beliefs echo forth in every facet of his writing and may also serve as the impetus for how he conceives his work to be a form of Christian political philosophy. Understanding Locke's tolerant Christianity and his appreciation for natural theology may help explain why Locke sounds "secular" in his political argumentation and has wide-reaching appeal among political philosophers and ethicists who do not share Locke's theological persuasion. Second, the religious turn must now give way to a more carefully considered *theological turn* in which the Latitudinarian Locke works out political implications of his views concerning God, the law of nature, and revelation—each theological element being essential to understanding what Locke wishes to do with his political philosophy. This includes identifying Locke's natural law theory as part of a larger theology of creation. As a result, Locke's political philosophy brings forth theologically rich aims, while seeking to counter or disarm threats such as atheism, hyper-Calvinism, and religious enthusiasm.

## The category of "Christian political philosopher"

Locke's interdisciplinary interests and instincts attracted me to his works in the first place. For someone interested in the borders between (and the intersection of) philosophy, theology, and political theory, studying Locke offers tremendous strengths. At the same time, proper vocabulary—especially in terms of singular designation—can seem elusive. Is Locke a "political theologian" or a "theologically-interested political theorist?" Since his work has spread tentacles into the fields of Christian public theology as well as secular political theory, one wonders how Locke conceived of his own place in such matters. We wonder what he is *doing*, what he *thinks* he is doing, and how his work can be employed by those wishing to do more.

Is Locke a "public theologian"? Locke could be classified as such if one were to take a Stackhouse-inspired definition of public theology as "theologically informed discourse aimed at the general public."[17] Locke does this explicitly in *The Reasonableness of Christianity*,[18] implicitly in Book IV of the *Essay*, and both implicitly and explicitly in various places in *A Letter Concerning Toleration*.[19] Miroslav Volf and Rowan Williams offer a clearer, though more restrictive, approach to public theology as "a matter of the church bearing public witness to Jesus Christ, the embodiment of the good life."[20] Leslie Newbigin speaks of public theology as a public witness taking root from within the church, offering a robust theological vision from the church for the world.[21]

If public theology refers less to "theologically informed discourse for the public" (which can be done simply as a member of the public) and more to "public discourse about theology from the church (or *as* the church) for the world," then the claim is too strong to be applied to John Locke. His heterodox theology raises only part of the criticism. In truth, Locke is better seen as one sympathetic to the task of public theology and, as a working philosopher, providing philosophical groundwork for a public sphere enabling such work to take place. He is more a harbinger of public theology than a practicing participant. This is simply not his field of work.

What about calling Locke a "political theologian"? This designation may be closer to the claims of this book, but it still remains a term easily misunderstood. If one can recognize a meaningful distinction between a "political theologian" and a "theologically-inspired political theorist," then the point is made. Oliver O'Donovan sketches a helpful description of the political theologian. She does not restrict "secular" or "religious" vocabulary or reduce the semantic range of terms while dealing on the border between theological claims and the political aims of public life. But the political theologian does operate with a set of lenses that is willing to "push back the horizon of commonplace politics and open it up to the activity of God."[22] For the political theologian, both theology and political theory are always in view—not only as interested parties but as parties always in conceptual dialogue:

> Theology needs more than scattered political images; it needs a full political conceptuality. And politics, for its part, needs a theological conceptuality. The two are concerned with the one history that finds its goal in Christ, "the desire of the nations."[23]

A defensible case could be made that Locke *believes* this. But a much harder case is to prove that Locke *does* this. O'Donovan describes "the alternative to political theology" as one that allows religious and political spheres but wishes to preserve distinction and separation. According to this camp, "religion may and does shape politics through carefully guarded channels of influence that preserve a cordon sanitaire."[24] Against this alternative, writes O'Donovan, political theologians believe

> it is not a question of adapting to alien requirements or subscribing to external agenda, but of letting theology be true to its task and freeing it from a forced and unnatural detachment. Political theology tries to recover for faith in God, Christ and salvation what scepticism surrendered to mechanistic necessity.[25]

Given how Locke has been viewed for a century, it is not surprising that O'Donovan seems to place Locke in this second "alternative" camp, along with Pufendorf and Kant.[26] I believe the case for viewing Locke as an advocate for a clear distinction and separation of religion from political life is overblown, and it is likely that Locke believed in the kind of political theology O'Donovan has in view.[27] This book lends support to the idea that Locke not only believed in this but operated out of convictions sympathetic (and sometimes parallel) to Christian political theologians. In the words of John Perry, the *LCT* shows Locke "reenvisioning political philosophy and political theology in new ways" and "formulating a political theology in which toleration is a sign of one's loyalty to Christ rather than a violation of it."[28] But it is far more debatable to claim Locke *practiced* as a political theologian in his works. The term may include both "political philosopher" and "theologian" but, as it is worded, places Locke on the "theology" side of the divide. Doing this raises more questions than it answers, especially concerning Locke's approach to the Trinity, the Incarnation, and the role of the Holy Spirit, especially as the latter relates to regeneration and sanctification.[29] Something else is needed.

In this book, I settle on the phrase "Christian political philosopher." At first blush, the term sounds too weak, since it could be applied to anyone working in the field of political philosophy who also happens to be Christian. It can also suggest that Locke only does political philosophy with Christian presuppositions, rather than engaging in theological argumentation. However, when given the options, I prefer to bypass attaching endless disclaimers to stronger phrases in favor of filling this designation with robustness. Greg Forster convinced me to start here:

> My hypothesis would be that Locke scholarship's fruitless detour into secularism was largely caused by a failure to think carefully about this distinction. One might say Locke appeared secular to 20th century scholars because they had a category for "Secular Political Philosopher" and a category for "Christian Public Theologian" (e.g., Augustine, Aquinas, etc.) but not a category for "Christian Political Philosopher."[30]

In this book, I adopt Forster's suggestion. Settled between the secular political philosopher and the Christian public theologian stands a third category occupied by Locke: that of the Christian political philosopher, whose arguments not only self-consciously depend upon Christian assumptions but also offer theological argument in favor of and integrally tethered to his political theory.[31] Within his own historical context, Locke is best seen as offering a Latitudinarian political philosophy, one flowing out of particular religious conviction. While Locke does not demand that the civil authorities claim Jesus as Lord, his vision of society evokes a markedly Christian understanding of life in political society, a vision weakened the further one moves away from a particularly Christian perspective.

## Outline of the book

In Chapter 1 I introduce the "religious turn" in Locke scholarship as, in truth, the religious *return* in Locke scholarship. The portrait of Locke as a secular promoter of Enlightenment rationality—incompatible with the Christian natural law tradition—is, in fact, a largely incorrect view. I provide five pivotal historical moves that created this general view in the mid-twentieth century and show why each move was largely unwarranted. I then trace out the main elements of the religious (re)turn in which Locke is read with theological sympathy as a man whose religious views deeply influenced his political perspective. I conclude the chapter by noting five ways the religious return may move forward in its attempt to lay claim to the theological underpinnings of Locke's entire political project.

In Chapter 2 I ask if the religious return is correct, why does Locke often sound "secular" in his approach? With special attention given to the *LCT*, I challenge interpreters (such as Tate) who believe Locke wished to remove theology from the foundations of his political theory. Borrowing a model employed by Locke himself in the *RC*, I claim that Locke adopts an approach similar to St. Paul as recorded in the Areopagus account of Acts 17:16–34. Locke believes "reason" can access much of what "the law of nature" teaches, thus providing a basic "consensus" for a society that includes and tolerates a wide range of belief. His interest in toleration leads him to search for language and arguments that can cross the boundary lines between warring Christian sects and even include those who are not Christians. Religious truths—if forming the basis of moral life and thought—may be articulated in language that will reach the widest audience. In fact, Locke believes what reason dictates is always in accord with divine revelation, which offers a fuller and clearer picture. In this chapter, I note that Locke is stretched to the extreme when seeking to tolerate non-Christian faiths (such as Islam and Judaism), though he believes he manages to find a way forward, based on (1) a limited view of government, claiming a different jurisdiction than that of the church; (2) a particularly wide and generous view of the mercy of God toward virtuous humanity; and (3) an appreciation for the limits of awareness, since some human beings—in need of societal structures—have yet to know or to fully appreciate the truth of the gospel. Far from distancing himself from theology, Locke actually provides a model for Christian political philosophy rooted in theological aims.

In Chapter 3 I begin tracing Locke's theological roots by placing him in his seventeenth-century religious context. While standard biographies note Locke's religious upbringing and his close association with theologically oriented compatriots, few have taken seriously how Locke's own religious commitments motivated him to offer a Latitudinarian political philosophy. Building on the historical perspective offered by Marshall and Spellman (among others), I link Locke's moral and political philosophy with Boyle's teleology, Hooker's ecclesiology, and the philosophical theology provided by Cambridge Platonists. Locke's unique insights often stem from or build upon the Latitudinarian theology with which he was intimately acquainted; his work is less a prototype of Rawlsian pluralistic philosophy and more akin to an early-modern recapitulation of a Christian political philosophy, though from a decidedly open perspective. My own contribution to this discussion is to lay out various strands of influence, which unite in Locke's political writings to form a coherent Christian political philosophy—one that rests on three planks (God, the law of nature, and revelation) to combat potential dangers.

In Chapter 4 I seek to show that, for Locke, a "true idea" of God is essential to establish the basis of moral obligation and the foundation of moral behavior while also serving as a model for legal punishment. This "true idea" of God is oriented around biblical language. God, maker of heaven and earth, creates the world ex nihilo and thus holds ownership over all things. As judge of the living and the dead, He possesses the power to reward and punish on the basis of right living or moral wrongdoing. Yet his very nature serves as the basis for moral right, and the larger portrait of God provides reasonable authentication of his true nature. Throughout Locke's writings, he describes this God not only as the first cause or prime mover but as the God described in the Bible and worshiped by Christians. I conclude the chapter by suggesting that Locke assumes only a "true idea of God" can form the real basis for his moral and political philosophy, and this true idea of God cannot be less than a broadly Latitudinarian perspective. Thus a relatively "thick" conception of God—one consistent with Locke's Christian theology—is necessary to justify the objectives and claims of Locke's moral and political philosophy. Locke's deep suspicion and intolerant attitude toward avowed atheists is a very important clue in mitigating any notion that Locke has a purely secular motive in mind.

In Chapter 5 I move beyond a broadly Christian conception of God to establish a narrower link: Locke's moral and political philosophies are wedded to his theology of creation. This creation theology explains how Locke is a Christian natural law theorist: his theological anthropology includes a necessary teleology, which is rooted in biblical language concerning creation (Gen. 1–2) as well as Christological references to the life of Christ, who serves as the model of true humanity. Locke's natural law theory is part of his larger theology: a view of creation that gives way to a covenantal theology. Contra hyper-Calvinism, human responsibility and accountability become paramount concerns—not only for issues of eternity but for present relations. In the soil of this theology, political issues such as human equality and freedom find root.

In Chapter 6 I narrow the scope even further: not only does Locke's theory require a true idea of God and a particular theology of creation, but it also includes acceptance of and dependence on God's self-revelation and claims made in scripture. Although Locke has a very high view of scripture, it never culminates in fideism; instead, Locke traces the human need for special revelation from God in order to fully grasp one's purpose in life, the God one serves, and the vision for how to carry out God's purposes—all of which leads to ultimate happiness. He traces this need in both his theological writings (such as the *RC*) and, surprisingly, his philosophical works (such as the *Essay*). Although he has a high view of reason, Locke admits human frailty and sinfulness require humility; God has provided knowledge of his will, and authoritative grounds for obligation and motivation, through the sending of Christ, and the codification of God's teachings in scripture. This perspective works itself out in several elements of Locke's moral and political theory. By way of illustration, one can see how the second greatest commandment—to love one's neighbor as one's self—is more than just some intuitive golden-rule principle; it is a binding rule that forms part of Locke's doctrine of property. When one considers how eternal matters are linked to "life together" in Locke's larger theo-political schema, it becomes clear that he draws from scriptural language, principles, and mandates in order to form his moral and political philosophy. Thus, contrary to religious enthusiasm, humanity is given a reliable identifiable and universalizing witness for guidance in matters that extend beyond religious concerns.

Finally, I summarize my findings and suggest that the intuitions of Dunn, Waldron, Nuovo, and others who advocate a religious (re)turn to Locke's moral and political philosophy are correct. I will add, however, that Locke offers a coherent Christian Latitudinarian political philosophy, the foundation of which is set on three planks. Locke's political theory cannot be divorced from this wider theological perspective. I seek to advance the field of study in this area by clarifying Locke's "true idea of God," relating Locke's doctrine of creation to his teleological theory of natural law, and showing how Locke is able to hold a high view of reason alongside a high view of scripture. Thus I show how Locke relies on a Christian conception of God, the law of nature, and divine revelation in scripture in forming his political philosophy.

This research project is valuable for several reasons. First, it provides a historical contribution to Locke scholarship, aiding in the recontextualization of the deeply Christian structure of Locke's political thought. After supporting and clarifying the significance of the religious (re)turn in Lockean studies, this book shows how Locke's religious convictions are borne out of a particular mode of Christian thought. Second, it offers both a philosophical contribution (e.g., locating Locke's place in the history of the natural law tradition) and a philosophical defense for the underlying unifying theme in Locke's philosophical, political, and religious works. Third, this book makes the claim that Locke owns and operates out of a Latitudinarian-inspired theology of creation—a claim that, if verified, would make a helpful contribution to the field of historical theology. Additionally, this book provides groundwork for further contributions to the fields of public and political theology and the role of religion in liberal societies. By critically reflecting on Locke's working perspective, issues involving church/state relations, religious argumentation in public life, and the limits of religious toleration may be further clarified, and Christian positions on these issues may be enhanced.

## An interdisciplinary approach

In this book, I will concentrate on Locke's well-known political works (such as the *Two Treatises* and the *LCT*), philosophical works (such as the *Essay* and *Questions Concerning the Law of Nature*[32]), and overtly religious works (such as the *RC*), while also borrowing from the entire Lockean corpus. The reason for some restriction (regarding more obscure works) is to account for Locke's central lines of thought in his mature political thought, rather than chase ideas that Locke may have initially considered and later rejected. The reason for cross-pollination across disciplines is because Locke, at all times, is offering considerations that are philosophical, political, and theological. Locke published works in all three disciplines at various stages throughout his life, composing some of them (such as the *Essay* and the *RC*) roughly simultaneously.[33]

Through a close reading of Locke's defining works, I offer a philosophical and theological analysis of Locke's political thought offering a coherent platform set upon three planks—Locke's reliance on particular views of God, the law of nature, and revelation. As such, this book is intentionally interdisciplinary. In this book, readers will find a *historical* study centered on the writings of John Locke but with studied attention to and comparison with earlier and later approaches to political philosophy and theology. In this regard, my work includes a *philosophical* investigation of *political* claims, with *ethical* implications, rooted in Locke's own *theological* premises. As a descriptive, historical task, I situate Locke's reasoning within the context of his Christian beliefs. In terms of philosophical and theological analysis, I show how his political project is borne out of coherent theological aims, and I will explain how these aims provide grounding for his political thought. As a result, this book presents Locke as a Christian political philosopher, whose approach reveals important clues about his theological commitments on which his political philosophy depends.

Part One

# In Defense of the Religious Turn

1

# The New Perspective on Locke: The Religious (Re)Turn in Locke Scholarship

## A tale of two portraits

In political theory classrooms around the globe, it is quite common to be introduced to a decidedly secular historical figure by the name of John Locke.[1] As begetter of the Enlightenment, it is argued, Locke championed a strong separation between church and state for the express purpose of distancing and disparaging the power and influence of religious figures and structures from the economic, social, and political life of the citizenry. Breaking with the Theo-political traditions before him, Locke sought to usher in a secular agenda for governance—one that removed concerns about the sacred, for the sake of peace and economic prosperity. By favoring freedom over virtue, the individual over the social, and rights over duties, Locke left the scholastic tradition to follow in the train of Machiavelli.[2] Though Locke's personal religious commitments were sometimes acknowledged, these had little to no bearing on his political agenda. In short, theology had no place in his political theory—one that sought secular means for secular ends in contradistinction to the theological.

This portrayal can be linked to a similar approach to Locke's moral philosophy. By rejecting the doctrine of innate ideas, and supporting the natural ends of hedonistic materialism, it is argued, Locke separates himself from any natural law foundation for his moral philosophy—despite some of his claims to the contrary. Locke's incomplete moral philosophy is either disconnected from his political thought or, if connected, simply continues a nontheological bent concerned with the formation of personal autonomy in view of material prosperity. Subjecting all moral, political, and theological interests to the supreme test of unaided human reason, Locke ushers in the Enlightenment project bound to remove the tethers of private theology (and "matters of eternal interest") from the concerns of public life.[3]

However, a new perspective on Locke has emerged—especially over the last two decades—which paints a decidedly different picture. A life-long Christian with a deep, sincere, and abiding—albeit heterodox—faith, Locke saw matters bearing on eternity as more weighty by far than to any that concern only this life and declared "believing and doing those things in this Life, which are necessary to the obtaining of Gods Favour, and are prescribed by God to that end" to be "the highest Obligation that lies upon Mankind … Because there is nothing in this World that is of any consideration in comparison with Eternity."[4] Believing in a law of nature—consistent with divine revelation in the Christian scriptures—which prescribes how humans are to see themselves in relation to one another, Locke develops his moral and political theory not only in concert with his religious beliefs but upon theological foundations. Humans, and the world they inhabit, are God's property and are "sent into the world by his order and about his business."[5] A Christian conception of God and a doctrine of creation—both forged out of a close reading of "infallible" scripture—provide the lens through which Locke describes fundamental portions of the law of nature, without which Locke's arguments concerning freedom, equality, toleration, moral distinction, and political power (both in terms of making and executing laws) would never get off the ground. Locke's writings on Christianity near the end of his life serve as "a keystone" to interpreting his entire corpus of work, since theology "runs through his whole work like a scarlet thread."[6]

A bourgeoning field of study suggests that Locke's theological interests cannot be separated out from his moral and political philosophy, nor did he intend them to be. While urging toleration among different forms of belief, disparaging the use of force to compel faith, and separating categorically the power of clergy from that of the magistrate, Locke never intended to separate his theory of government from its theological moorings. Instead, Locke's theology can be conceived of as "constitutive" with regard to essential components of his political and philosophical argumentation.[7]

## On the secular trail—and why it is (mostly) wrong

How could two such radically different portraits emerge from the same set of works? Neither the religious nor the secular reading of Locke is a modern invention, and neither has a sole claim to antiquity. For example, one can find philosophers and political theorists traversing the "secular" trail throughout the three centuries separating Locke from the current scene. One can identify five moves, some of which cover the span between Locke's lifetime and our own, that have tended to the reception of Locke as fundamentally a secularist.

## The first four moves: Heresy hunting, neglect, misrepresentation, and amalgamation

The first move occurred within Locke's own lifetime, near the end of the seventeenth century. In a number of important cases, Locke's writings met opposition from clergy *on religious grounds*, while those with more secular interests paraded (or misapplied) Locke's writings in defense of their own causes. It is well known that some of Locke's religious contemporaries raised serious concerns about Locke's orthodoxy, questioning his religious credentials.[8] And when Locke's *LCT* was first published in English, his translator provided a "Preface to the Reader," which introduced the work as one advocating "Absolute Liberty"—a position at odds with the actual stated purpose of the *LCT* as well as the sentiments of the author.[9] In 1696, when John Toland wrote a scathing rebuke against those clinging to the need for divine revelation, he relied on key facets of Locke's epistemology to root his claims.[10]

Failing to appreciate the context in which Locke's works were produced, a "mirror reading" of Locke's detractors—as well as those employing Lockean arguments to suit their own ends—might suggest that Locke's works must either be irreligious or at least a significant threat to any religious basis for moral and political philosophy. But Locke's vehement defense of his writings on theological grounds suggests that his own intention was not to subvert theological bases for political ends but to clarify them. Just as contemporary readers of Locke's *LCT* may easily forget that the work concerns toleration of disagreements *within* Christianity, readers of Locke's early antagonists ought to remain aware of the sense of threat from within, which was often conceived of as far greater than that from without. Locke was considered by some within his own generation as offering heterodox theology; nevertheless, the chief arguments concerned theological positions *present* rather than absent. And, given that Locke was greeted with such a hostile reception in some ecclesiastical quarters, those outside or on the fringes of religion had little reason to separate their own ends from Locke's Christian commitments in their selective use of his works. These actions helped shape a jaundiced approach to Locke, which would survive for centuries to come.

The second move seems to have emerged in the eighteenth century. Given the nearly half-century between Locke's writings and the employment of his works toward new desired ends, it is apparent that the political fruit of toleration, liberty, and equality was advanced (by intent or neglect) without the same level of regard for the theological roots, which connect Locke's moral philosophy to his political ends. The one considered "the most influential philosopher of modern times"[11] was virtually unread in most places of influence for the first quarter of the eighteenth century. According to Jonathan Israel, there was a "remarkable disinclination of leading intellectual figures early in the century to engage seriously with Locke's work," a conclusion he finds "striking."[12] For example, it was not until the 1730s that Locke garnered much influence in France, the Netherlands, Scandinavia, and Italy, and that in the realm of epistemology.[13] Though the *Lochisti* were a potent force in the 1740s, Locke's *Essay* was only placed on the papal Index in 1734, suggesting a lack of any notable influence until that time.[14] A similar story may be told concerning Locke's influence in the Americas. Although Locke is considered the father of the American Revolution, claiming the *Two Treatises* was "causally responsible" for the American political scene of the 1700s is "largely false."[15] As Dunn has ably shown, Locke's *Two Treatises* was not greatly read in the American colonies before 1750, and any significant influences on American revolutionary sympathies "was largely confined to the post-1760 constitutional writings of the highly educated."[16] Interestingly, the book was not nearly as popular in eighteenth-century France or even England as is customarily thought.[17] In fact, what stands out when conducting a historical survey of the *Two Treatises'* reception history is its glaring ambiguity, being used for differing (and sometimes, cross) purposes.

Recognizing the shelf wear on Locke's moral and political works offers a clue to tracing historically the deviation from Locke's original aims through appropriation for new desired ends. Spellman points out that in the mid-1750s, Jean Le Rond d'Alembert's *Encyclopaedia* spoke of Locke as the founder of "scientific philosophy," following in the footsteps of Newton, credited as the father of "scientific physics."[18] Voltaire considered Locke to be "the Hercules of metaphysics," abandoning the methodology and overturning the conclusions of the scholastics and divine right theorists. Conceiving of Locke's works (for nearly eighty years) passing only through the hands of a few educated persons with their own moral and political agenda leads one to conclude with Spellman that, whatever Locke's intentions, his work was shaped for new purposes by "a less devout eighteenth century" that misunderstood Locke's central aims and intentions.[19]

In the nineteenth century, one sees a third "move" take shape. A particular (re)reading of the philosophy of history created an ill-informed sense of key

Enlightenment thinkers, read in the light of new concerns. The industrial revolution, a grand story of societal evolution, and analysis of the many uses of religion for social and economic purposes provided a new paradigm within which any positive appreciation for the permeating influences of religion struggled to survive. This move to gain a critical foothold over what was considered to be the evil influences of religion led to the loss of a historical perspective concerning the God-intoxicated seventeenth-century Western culture.[20] In Spellman's words, the seventeenth was a century "where Augustine's 'City of God' continued to take precedence over the evanescent city of man."[21] Yet given a new paradigm, Christian philosophers of the past were recast as secular champions for a new era.[22] In this, political historians lost sight of the true fulcrum of seventeenth-century social life. Standing above economics, political structure, and personal ethics was the real issue of the age: religion and religious authority.[23] Thus a "secular" mindset was not (and ought not be) the default assumption for how to interpret Enlightenment thinkers, including Locke.

A fourth movement that begins in the nineteenth century but carries over into the twentieth involves a recasting of natural law theory and, to some extent, a forgetfulness of the theological foundations that went before. According to this model, Locke is simply lumped together with certain other thinkers as a chief contributor to an anthropologically (and thus, not theologically) centered natural law theory concerned with individual rights rather than societal obligations in the shared context of a larger created order. The result, still visible in the present day among the most ardent of religious natural law theorists, is an amalgamation of Locke's natural law theory with the claims of his contemporaries, which mask Locke's distinct contributions and hide Locke's own defense of a previous religious tradition.[24]

## The fifth move: Radical skepticism

The fifth move in Locke scholarship occurred in the middle of the twentieth century. It is both the most radical and the least plausible and can be summarized as Straussian-inspired skepticism.[25] In a series of works published in the 1950s, Strauss argued that Locke is simply deceptive, using inconsistency and incoherency as a stratagem to mask the fact that he is a closet Hobbesian.[26] Borrowing the Platonic concept of a "noble lie," and using a reading strategy he applied to other historical figures, such as Maimonides, Strauss claims Locke provides conformist exoteric teaching for the masses and a veiled subversive esoteric teaching for the privileged few.[27] Writing in an environment of severe political persecution, Locke practices "the art of writing" by couching his true beliefs "between the lines" of his own works, allowing "thoughtful men" to tease out the real meaning of a book.[28] "The real opinion of an author is not necessarily identical with that which he expresses in the largest number of passages," writes Strauss, and writers in Locke's position are likely to offer highly ironic statements, which intentionally commit "such blunders as would shame an intelligent high school boy."[29] "The truly exact historian" will take the hint and recognize that Locke's actual views are the exact opposite of what these "large number of passages" might suggest.[30]

Thus, the Bible-quoting, Hooker-referencing, commentary-writing Locke who sought to distance his own teaching from the "justly decried"[31] Hobbes was simply acting out a charade. According to Strauss, Locke may have confessed with his lips an allegiance to theologically based natural law, but his heart (*a la* Hobbes) lay with a radically atheistic notion of natural right.[32] As a champion of replacing virtue with freedom as the chief end of society, Locke's political theory of acquisition is seen as the fruit of subversively amoral Machiavellian thought.[33]

In 1960, Cox continued this line of extreme skepticism, again claiming that only proper principles of interpretation can draw out Locke's hidden meaning—often directly contradicting his explicit statements. Like Strauss, Cox offers the needed hermeneutical schema, one that was apparently not available before these men were able to discover it.[34] Cox praises Locke for his rhetorical acumen and skills of deception[35] before citing cases where Locke says one thing but believes the exact opposite.[36]

Strauss's removal of Locke's meaning from the actual content of his writings left historians and political theorists with room to usher in their own contemporary concerns. Just as Strauss offered an analysis of Locke as part of his negative critique of modern liberalism, others are sympathetic in their portrayal of Locke as a defender of modern liberal values.[37] Yet the "hiddenness of Locke's true meaning" argument can lead to any number of interpretations. In 1962, Macpherson used a hermeneutic of suspicion to provide a Marxist interpretation of Locke. Like Strauss and Cox before him, Macpherson claims "the presence of apparently clear inconsistency is to be treated as a clue" to unstated or "inadequately stated" social assumptions.[38] These social assumptions, shared with Hobbes, included possessive individualism, focused on unlimited acquisition of property within a larger class warfare. Locke sets out to provide the moral basis for this approach. In so doing, Locke marshals forth theological arguments (and calls upon authorities such as Richard Hooker and the Natural Law tradition) as instruments of rhetoric—which ultimately, according to MacPherson, leave

Locke with a weaker (and less consistent) political theory than that of Hobbes.[39] As an open-textured method, this mid-century reading of Locke paved the way for positing Locke as simply a defender of a nontheological secular liberalism.

The extreme skepticism and eisegetical approach of Strauss and those who followed in his train has been decisively answered on several fronts.[40] But, as has been shown, one can find the residual effects in the general approach to political philosophy as well as the history of ideas. On the one hand, among those who believe Locke's philosophy may be studied within the large sweep of history (as addressing perennial problems), it is altogether too easy to slide Locke into a line of tradition that starts with Machiavelli, runs through Hobbes, and on to a contemporary individualistic, freedom-based political theory concerned at base with self-preservation and group consent. On the other hand, for those who believe Locke must be narrowly examined within the strict confines of his own historical context, the ease is to render Locke irrelevant to any contemporary philosophical concerns.[41] These seem to be extremes.

To some extent, all five of these moves displaced Locke's theology in order to present a "truer" reading of his political philosophy. But, this book will argue, historically understood his theological premises are central to the political project and cannot be excised without radically altering the whole.

## The "religious (re)turn"—and why it is (mostly) right

There exists an alternative interpretive tradition that Sigmund describes as "the religious turn" in Locke scholarship.[42] Though this turn is often dated to within the last half century, the evidence suggests that any recent turn to the religious moorings in Locke's moral and political theory is more precisely a "return" for Locke scholarship. The proponents of this view for the last fifty years may be placed within a long stream of tradition, which both assumed a religious basis and, in later times, countered the prevailing winds agnostic or belligerent toward any religious imperative in Locke's argumentation.

### A historical pedigree

For example, Israel notes that a religious reading of Locke's moral and political philosophy is present in Italy in the mid-eighteenth century. Tommaso Moniglia, the Pisan professor of scripture and Church history, published a dissertation "against the fatalisti" at Lucca in 1744. In his treatise, Moniglia saw Locke as a defender of the faith, providing a philosophical foundation for Christian perspectives on the political order.[43] In a later work (published at Padua in 1750s), Moniglia posited a Lockean perspective as the Christian "answer" to defeating the influence of Spinoza.[44] Eighteenth-century England included several notable theologians who "indebted to Locke in various ways, did not see themselves as rationalizers and secularizers, but as upholders of the Reformation, fulfillers of its true meaning."[45]

In terms of academic study concerning Locke's ethical philosophy, a similar story can be discovered. When Curtis penned *An Outline of Locke's Ethical Philosophy* in 1890, he offered what may have been the first monograph on the subject ever published.[46] Curtis rightly brought together the political, moral, and religious strands of Locke's philosophy in an attempt to proffer a coherent "Lockean" line of thought. For Curtis, Locke considered politics a sub-branch of moral philosophy. Though a Hobbesian materialism led the way for a line of thought stretching through Hume, Voltaire, and Rousseau, Curtis argued that Locke should be seen as opposing this approach. Carrying forward a tradition in the vein of Nathaniel Culverwell, Locke's true moral philosophy was inherited by the Scottish school (of Reid) against a hedonistic materialism and in support of theological correlation with the moral aspects of political philosophy.

Nearly thirty years later, Lamprecht took up the neglected subject once again.[47] Like Curtis before him, Lamprecht sought to combine disparate strands of Locke's thought in search of a coherent picture. For his part, Lamprecht found both rationalistic and hedonistic elements in Locke's moral philosophy. But Lamprecht's great contribution was in identifying Locke's dominant aim as providing a practical approach to moral and political philosophy, operating out of (and bringing forward) religious, political, and social traditions before him. Far from breaking with the theological tradition before him in order to bring about a radically new secular ground for his political project, Locke "is rather the ripe fulfillment of the past than the herald of the future."[48]

## The rise of the new perspective: A survey of the literature

The study of Locke's natural law teaching experienced a watershed moment in 1954, when Locke's early *Questions* were published, remarkably, for the first time.[49] However, the initial analysis of these essays was not particularly groundbreaking. According to von Leyden's analysis, Locke appeared to offer a theological grounding for the law of nature, but displayed logical inconsistency and incoherence, and thus failed to offer a rational defense of natural law.

According to von Leyden, Locke's later explorations in the *Essay* "made it difficult for him to attempt a full exposition of natural law or even to believe in it whole-heartedly."[50] Strauss, on the other hand, simply saw in these essays the deceptive hand of a closet Hobbesian.[51] Yet these interpretations were heavily challenged by authors who saw in the *Questions* a clearer and more coherent theological grounding for natural law that required reconsideration of Locke's theological assumptions within his wider political project.[52]

In 1956, Yolton published *John Locke and the Way of Ideas*. Though primarily interested in the reception history of Locke's theory of epistemology, Yolton sets out a religious context for Locke's project in which Locke's arguments were understood by his contemporaries as primarily intended to answer burning questions arising from moral and theological concerns.[53] The religious implications of Locke's *Essay* are neither surprising nor accidental, since a comparison of minor philosophical writings of the period suggests that Locke is engaging in theologically charged argumentation. In fact, Locke employs principles anticipated by earlier philosophers but refuses to follow their lead in pushing the arguments toward skepticism. According to Yolton, this is partly due to Locke's refusal to conceive of a separation in his writings between the philosophical and the theological.

In 1960, Polin further advanced this theological reappraisal of Locke's larger project through a careful study of the relationship between Locke's moral and political theory.[54] According to Polin, Locke's systematic approach to philosophy required him to seek internal consistency for all of his main views and that Locke is generally successful in doing so.[55] Locke does not compartmentalize his ethics apart from his politics but rather grounds both in a view of natural law that comprises a particular view of God, humanity, and the nature of morality. This sense of a natural order mitigates against reading Locke as an extreme individualist or hedonist. In this work, as well as in later writings concerning Locke's views on justice and freedom, Polin presents Locke's works as a unified piece of philosophy, based on theological premises, leading to political conclusions.[56]

When Dunn published *The Political Thought of John Locke* in 1969, he offered the most significant defense of the century for viewing Locke's political project as rooted in theology. By offering a highly contextual analysis of Locke's work, and completely removing any notion of Locke's relationship to modern concerns, Dunn seeks to provide "a more coherent and historically accurate account" of Locke than had previously been offered; at the heart of this re-appraisal is "the theological centrality of Locke's religious preoccupations throughout his work."⁵⁷ Dunn moves beyond a general appreciation for theological insight in Locke's philosophy; instead, he emphasizes "the intimate dependence of an extremely high proportion of Locke's arguments for their intelligibility, let alone plausibility, on a series of theological commitments."⁵⁸ Dunn showed that Locke's political scheme cannot be conceived, understood, or consistently argued if one removes the theological plank holding it together. Dunn's book should not be underestimated in terms of its significance in breaking the Straussian stranglehold on Locke scholarship. As Woolhouse and Stanton suggest, "After Dunn, the question for most Locke scholars was not whether Locke's professions about God and natural law were genuine, but how exactly they related to his political thinking."⁵⁹

As significant as Dunn's work is, it suffers three drawbacks. First, Dunn mischaracterizes Locke's theological commitments as emanating from a particular Calvinist theology and a dependence on the Puritan doctrine of "calling."⁶⁰ Yet Locke's theology is broader and often at odds with Calvinist approaches, and any semblance of "calling" in Locke's religious views is part of a larger theology of creation.⁶¹ Second, Dunn similarly fails to recognize how Locke's treatment of the law of nature offers a coherent claim within a larger theology of creation.⁶² Third, Dunn concludes that Locke's historical situation called for metaphysical presuppositions and theological structures, which are wholly absent from modern political thought, isolating Locke's works as philosophically irrelevant to contemporary concerns.⁶³ Yet what value Locke's political theory may hold for Christian political philosophy and theology is unaffected by Dunn's conclusion.

In 1973, Sparkes published an article in which he rightly uses a theological category in explicitly identifying Locke's "doctrine of creation."⁶⁴ Noting the similarities between Locke and Aquinas, Sparkes emphasizes the pervasive teleological element in Locke's doctrine of creation—one "not elaborated but presupposed ... not hidden, but there on the surface in fragmentary form." Sparkes claims that Locke's law of nature "is the foundation of his political theory. It is not a set of discrete principles, but a system based on the doctrine of the creative activity of God." Sparkes illustrates this point by noting the natural law basis for Locke's doctrines of property and political power. Sparkes criticizes Locke for relegating the law of nature to a system of broad moral principles, rather than incorporating the creative human aspect within his doctrine of creation.

Over the next fifteen years, a number of works proffered theses concerning the essential relationship between Locke's faith and his political theory.⁶⁵ In 1981, for example, Eisenach concluded the following:

> From his earliest concern with the relationship of morality to revealed religion to his last writings on the reasonable Christianity, Locke saw political life as requiring both reason and faith ... Locke's periodic resort to religion, then, is less an act of piety (or failure of analytic nerve) than an integral part of his philosophical and political enterprise.[66]

In 1983, Colman sought to provide a comprehensive investigation of Locke's moral philosophy, scouring the entire corpus of Locke's published works.[67] The result is a coherent and defensible theological ethics.[68] Following Yolton's lead, Colman rightly advanced the claim that Locke's epistemological interests in the *Essay* is in the service of moral theory rather than natural science. Against Aaron, Colman found a consistent moral theory in Locke, though Colman judged this theory to be of poor quality.[69] He made a strong case that Locke's hedonistic tendencies did not force him to abandon his natural law theory in favor of a utilitarian theory; these approaches are harmonious in Locke's thought.[70] Unfortunately, Colman still views Locke as a demolisher of Christian morality as constructed in his own day, offering a utilitarian basis for his natural law theory, depending on God for natural law obligation but not content.[71]

Locke's commentary on Paul's Epistles was published in 1987, adding more fuel to the fire.[72] One year later, Spellman increased awareness of Locke's theology by analyzing Locke's view of sin and depravity. He rightly argued that—contra Calvin—Locke did not accept the heredity of Adam's sin, though he did emphasize the problem of human weakness and inclination toward evil.[73] The early 1990s welcomed a new generation of scholars who interpreted Locke's *Essay* as concerned primarily with moral and religious issues and who declared that Locke's epistemology, philosophy, and political theory must be understood in the light of his religious perspective.[74]

Marshall's masterful 1994 work represented a growing strand of research emphasizing a religious return in Locke scholarship.[75] Focusing primarily on the *Second Treatise*, Marshall shows that Locke was not a dissenting ideologue driven by self-interested secular political interests; rather Locke was driven to toleration by his theological commitments. In contradistinction to the "possessive individualist" portrayal, Locke operated out of central Christian commitments of service, gratitude, and beneficence, and taught these virtues throughout his writings. Marshall does see progression in Locke's thought, though he does not quite go as far as Ashcraft in suggesting the move is one of increasingly radical political activism. Though Marshall portrays Locke as one whose theological and political views change drastically through the course of his life (due to both external circumstance and internal inquisitiveness), Locke remained a devoted member of the Church of England and a serious student of theological matters throughout his life. To Marshall, Locke's theological independence meant he could not adequately be described as a Calvinist, Deist, nor Latitudinarian Anglican. In addition, Marshall provides perhaps the best defense that Locke eventually moved into the ranks of Socinianism, though the debate on this issue is more open than some may acknowledge.[76] Unfortunately, Marshall argued that Locke abandoned naturalist ethics in favor of revelation due to a failed project, trying unsuccessfully to bridge the gap between a hedonistic theory of happiness and a theory of moral obligation built on theological grounds such as love of neighbor.

In the same year, Harris offered an important work in the same religious stream of Locke scholarship.[77] Wishing to establish continuity among Locke's disparate writings on a wide variety of subjects, Harris emphasized the interplay and interdependence of Locke's views. At the heart of this interplay, argues Harris, "Theology is an indispensable element in the constitution of Locke's thought."[78] With Marshall, Harris notes Locke's lack of any theory of moral obligation, which is needed to explain how the laws of nature can be considered morally binding. Against Ashcraft (and in some ways, Marshall), Harris (following Dunn somewhat) portrays Locke as a consistent moderating conservative who was free from drastic changes in his political and theological views.

In 1997, Spellman provided a short but rich sketch of Locke in theological terms, summarizing the approaches of Marshall, Harris, and others, and emphasizing the large extent to which Locke's Christian theological perspective shaped his life and his work.[79] Spellman rightly claims that the "one overriding problem" that shaped Locke's "entire intellectual life" and "united all of his diverse interests … was the clarification and solidification of a traditional Christian world-view during an age when the buttresses of the ancient faith were under severe strain from a number of quarters."[80] Indeed, the main argument of the book is that "the Christian story and it's vigorous, albeit innovative and at times controversial defense, constituted the core of Locke's main work."[81] Locke eschews traditional language but only to "reaffirm the ancient faith" rather than destroy it.[82]

The turn of the century brought about a surge in the religious turn of Locke scholarship. The reaction to Waldron's 1999 Carlyle lectures (and its subsequent 2002 publication) is comparable in scope and influence to that associated with Dunn's 1969 publication. In *God, Locke, and Equality*, Waldron not only solidifies the inseparable bond between Locke's theology and his political theory, he makes the bold claim that Locke's theological basis for human equality is coherent, consistent, and preferable to contemporary nontheological approaches to the subject. Not only is it impossible to "bracket out" Locke's theology from his political conclusions, a logically consistent political theory, which seeks Locke's ends would fare well to retain Locke's theological assumptions.[83]

A second author with a tremendous impact on Locke scholarship at the turn of the century is Nuovo. Stretching from the mid-1990s to the end of the first decade of the new millennium, Nuovo not only wrote key articles on Locke's religious moorings but introduced and edited editions of the *RC* and a collection of Locke's writings on religious topics.[84] In 2011, Nuovo added new contributions to some of his earlier writings to publish a compendium of his approaches to Locke entitled *Christianity, Antiquity, and Enlightenment.*[85] He followed this work in 2017 with *John Locke: The Philosopher as Christian Virtuoso.*[86] Nuovo's investigations yielded a rich analysis of how Locke's Christology, view of scripture, and indebtedness to ancient and scholastic sources charted a course for Locke, the "Christian philosopher and philosophical Christian,"[87] to offer a religiously inspired political project.

In 2003, after surveying the role of Christology in Locke's political philosophy, Nuovo offered a provocative conclusion: "I do not think it is saying too much to assert that he belongs as much to the Christian tradition as does Augustine of Hippo, Thomas Aquinas, or John Calvin," citing him as "a principal founder of modern liberal Christianity" rather than the founder of the sort of secular liberalism often ascribed to him.[88] After a study of Locke's appropriation of St. Paul, Nuovo took note that Locke weaves philosophy, theology, and politics throughout his writings as pieces of a larger whole.[89] He would go on to argue that the seamless thread uniting the various "Locke's" (the philosopher, political theorist, and theologian) is, in fact, a belief in and dependence on Christian revelation. "For Locke," writes Nuovo, "Christian revelation encompassed the whole of reality. It was as real an object of intellectual inquiry as civil society, human understanding, the law of nature or personal identity."[90]

The year 2004 marked the three hundredth anniversary of Locke's death. As a result, a number of conferences took place to commemorate the occasion.[91] The increased interest in Locke provided opportunity for several contributors to further advance the religious reading of Locke and inspire further research in that direction. Since 2004, several monographs have rolled off the presses advancing the religious turn. In 2004, Parker showed Locke's unmistakable dependence on scripture (and a particular theological reading of Genesis) in developing the character of political arguments in the *Two Treatises.*[92] The conclusion, Parker contends, is that Locke sees himself as articulating a political theory that flows out of a thoroughly Biblical paradigm. In her 2006 dissertation, Tetlow conducted a textual analysis of the *RC* and the *Paraphrase*, concluding that the only accurate reading of Locke is one that acknowledges his theological presuppositions form the basis of his political thought.[93] Tetlow rightly locates Locke's major influence in the Oxford Latitudinarians and the Cambridge Platonists and draws (perhaps clearer than anybody) the close relationship between their theological positions and Locke's theological and philosophical assumptions.

The progression in this direction has continued in recent years. Timothy Stanton has also contributed to the religious interpretation of Locke through further defending the view that Locke placed theological assumptions at the center of his political theory and advocated theological argumentation as a means of persuading the populace toward his most cherished desired ends.[94] One of those cherished desired ends—namely, religious toleration—received special attention in 2006 by Marshall and in 2014 by Loconte.[95] Marshall roots religious toleration in an "early enlightenment culture" strongly connected to the Dutch Republic. Tracing Locke's relations in this regard, Marshall notes the religious and theological connections that gave rise to Locke's arguments for toleration. But Loconte takes a step forward, rooting Locke's motivation and argumentation for religious toleration in the Erasmian Christian humanist tradition. Rather than isolating Locke's rationale to instrumentally pragmatic grounds, Loconte also shows how Locke's relationship with English and Dutch reformers helped him form an attitude toward religious toleration that was decidedly Christian and theologically anchored. What Marshall and Loconte are able to show regarding one area of Locke's political schema this book will show with regard to his larger political agenda.

The "religious" reading of Locke has had enough impact to lead some researchers to move to a second phase of research, applying the results of the religion turn to contemporary concerns in political theory. In 2005 and 2011, respectively, Forster and Perry sought to bring this reading of Locke into the larger realm of political theory, suggesting ways in which Locke's religiously committed approach to issues of liberty, equality, and toleration might play out in the contemporary public sphere.[96] Though Forster is more sympathetic than Perry that the contemporary situation calls for Locke's particular solutions, both authors recognize the deeply religious Locke sets out a project that did not seek to divorce theology from philosophy and politics but rather to inform them. These studies are important in the light of the larger debate concerning Christianity's relationship to Western liberal democratic ideals.

## Solidifying a theological portrait: Problems, proposals, and parameters

This book will argue that the religious turn is necessary but needs further to be explored. Locke may have sought to curb political control away from unscrupulous religious leaders, and he may have championed the separation of church and state (for mutual benefit). But it was not his intention to separate a distinctly Christian worldview (which includes ideas about God, humanity, law, morality, and creation) from the ends of his political program. He is offering a pragmatic Christian political philosophy without using distinctly Christian language.

In the chapters to follow, this book will argue that much of Locke's mature political thought is driven by his Christian theological convictions in deeper and richer ways than often assumed even by exponents of the "religious turn." We will begin by placing Locke within the religious contexts of his own day. The excellent groundwork for placing Locke within the circle of Latitudinarian theology laid down early but clarified by Marshall and supremely by Tetlow can be sharpened. For example, precisely how did this background provide not only a general influence but an impetus to provide a political philosophy working out of theological premises shared or advocated by Whichcote, Cudworth, and the like? The answer of this book is that many of Locke's political aims (and theological argumentation to support those aims) are already present in his theological context. This backdrop shows how Locke was able to establish the crucial link between his political ends and his Christian theological commitments.

While several scholars have mentioned different portions of Locke's theological angle, it remains necessary to identify the platform of Locke's moral and political theory as resting on three theological planks (God, the law of nature, and revelation). Each of these planks, in turn, is in need of further elaboration. Though some have assumed any deity can do justice to Locke's religious claims, only a "true" idea of God (as Locke conceives it)—whose character includes goodness, mercy, and justice, who affirms the freedom of human beings made to participate in creation, and whose past and future actions are described in the Bible—can serve as the moral basis for a truly just society. While Colman rightly identifies a coherent moral theory in Locke's philosophy, a clearer theological answer is needed to explain how elements of hedonistic psychology relate to moral accountability within a wider natural law theory[97] as well as how to establish the basis of human equality. For Locke, the answer lies in a larger theology of creation (connected to covenant theology) that grounds any law of nature and provides ultimate ends beyond temporal happiness and higher than any human pleasure or societal unity.

Finally, while much attention has been given to Locke's use of and appreciation for scripture, there still is work to be done on Locke's doctrine of scripture and how that relates to his wider interest. Locke's Latitudinarian framework explains his high view of scripture that lends itself to a kind of biblical conservatism: one that seeks general acceptance of a minimal creed discovered through the "plain" reading of an agreed-upon standard—Christian scripture. In this way, Locke affirms the necessity of revelation at the same time as decrying religious enthusiasm. Locke's reading of scripture allows him to place judgment in the hands of God at the last day—a move that is essential to the logic of his argument for the executive powers of government and allows Locke to advocate a generous liberality and discretion among political and religious leaders whose judgments are, at most, penultimate. Locke's high regard for scripture, and claims concerning the necessity of divine revelation, provide the bridge for understanding how (and why) particular aspects of the call of the gospel find their way into Locke's political theory, and establish the way in which, for Locke, both reason and faith serve to support his political aims.

In truth, only Locke's three planks—laid down in Locke's terms—can carry the weight of Locke's political agenda. Locke's political theory is not a "secular" approach to governance that Christians can accept; it is a coherent Latitudinarian political philosophy intended to support Christian aims (across denominations), which could also be accepted by those outside the Christian faith.

2

# Life in the Areopagus: Secular Echoes, Religious Refrain

## Secular sounds: Tate's challenge to the religious turn

According to Jeremy Waldron, who is perhaps the leading proponent for the religious turn in Locke scholarship, Locke believed it was "not reasonable … to think that you can proceed safely in public discourse or in public life, without accepting the theism which … is an indispensable basis for equality and social stability."[1] For Waldron, "proceeding safely in public discourse" goes beyond philosophical recognition of the theological roots of egalitarianism but extends to the very language used. Given the theological underpinnings in Locke's political philosophy, writes Waldron,

> it may be impossible to *articulate* certain important egalitarian commitments without appealing to what one takes to be their religious grounds … Locke is not just saying that religious argumentation about equality should be permitted in public life; he is arguing that it is indispensable.[2]

This view, however, is not without detractors. John William Tate is a modern Locke scholar who represents an interpretive stream diametrically opposed to public theological appeals or overtly religious argumentation in the political sphere. According to Tate, "Locke understood … that … religion and theology constituted no basis for public deliberation or civil and political agreement, either concerning the role and purpose of government, individual consent to that role, or the obligations arising from these."[3] "Far from 'religious argumentation' being 'indispensable,'" writes Tate, "Locke explicitly tries to exclude it from the justification of civil and political arrangements and the exercise of political authority associated with these arrangements."[4] For Tate, the foundation of Locke's political philosophy is found in shared material interests, far removed from divisive theological commitments.[5] Neither natural law, religion, nor revealed theology can "provide a basis of commensurability" to establish consent-based political justification.[6] Tate summarizes the "secular" interpretation of Locke in the following manner:

> Locke in no way sought to make the normative conclusions of his political philosophy dependent on their theological foundations. Indeed, he sought quite the reverse, given the religious divisions of his time, as he wanted to advance his political philosophy on grounds that a diverse audience (even "pagans") could affirm irrespective of their theological point of view. In other words, not only can we divide Locke from God, but when it came to the justification of his political philosophy, this was in fact Locke's own intention.[7]

Perusing Locke's political writings, one is able to find ample evidence of language lending itself toward this "secular" perspective. For example, in the *LCT* Locke is emphatic that church and state are "most different" and occupy two different spheres, "absolutely separate and distinct," with "just bounds" set between them.[8] The state, charged with care for temporal worldly concerns, is the "Keeper of the publick Peace"; the church, interested in the eternal things of heaven, is "the Oversee[r] of Souls."[9] According to Locke, there is only an "unhappy Agreement that we see between the Church and State" when the boundaries are crossed.[10]

Just as Locke describes the distinct roles for "church" and "state," he also speaks of what is *not* in each jurisdiction. "Churches have [not] any Jurisdiction in Worldly matters."[11] Ecclesiastical authority "ought to be confined within the Bounds of the Church, nor can it in any manner be extended to Civil Affairs."[12] Likewise, the state is not concerned with eternal matters: "All the Power of Civil Government relates only to Mens Civil Interests, is confined to the care of the things of this World, and hath nothing to do with the World to come."[13] Since the magistrate has jurisdiction only over "civil interests," which concern "temporal" things, "it neither can nor ought in any manner to be extended to the Salvation of Souls."[14] Locke's strong and passionate feelings on the matter are expressed most clearly near the beginning of the work:

> The Church it self is a thing absolutely separate and distinct from the Commonwealth. The Boundaries on both sides are fixed and immovable. He jumbles Heaven and Earth together, the things most remote and opposite, who mixes these two Societies; which are in their Original, End, Business, and in every thing, perfectly distinct, and infinitely different from each other.[15]

According to Locke, churches are notoriously divisive and, in prescribing differing interpretations of divine laws upon their adherents, tend toward isolation rather than inclusive.[16] The state, in enforcing civil law, has a vested interest in governing those of differing religions or none.[17] In an earlier work, Locke claims only a "stranger to England" would fail to notice that intra-church squabbles offer "distinctions able to keep us always at a distance, and eagerly ready for ... violence and cruelty," the exact opposite goal of political peace.[18]

Not only does Locke appear to argue for civil and religious authorities to maintain their respective roles, some of Locke's language seems to indicate that civil governance is neither founded on nor intimately connected to religious concerns. For "peace and security" to prevail—indeed, even "so much as common friendship"—society must disabuse itself of the false opinion "that dominion is founded in grace."[19] The problem with appeals to religious views is that people are often in violent disagreement about the binding nature and proper interpretation of such things, when the goal of Locke's political theory is to establish rights on the basis of consent between people of differing theological persuasions.[20] From this premise, Locke comes to two conclusions. First, general shared consent in a diverse society will most likely revolve around topics that increase the guarantee of security and liberty, not religious agreement.[21] Second, on this basis, the role of government is limited to securing opportunity for material interests and does not extend to divisive issues leading to church squabbles.[22] "Though it be true, those powers that are, are ordained of God," writes Locke, "yet it may nevertheless be true, that the power any one has, and the ends for which he has it, may be by the contrivance and appointment of men."[23] These "ends" of civil power are secular in nature and do not extend to "men's souls":[24]

> Commonwealths, or civil societies and government, if you will believe the judicious Mr. Hooker, are, as St. Peter calls them (I Pet., ii. 13) ... the contrivance and institution of man .... You must show them such a commission, if you say it is from God. And in all societies instituted by man, the ends of them can be no other than what the institutors appointed; *which I am sure could not be their spiritual and eternal interest.*[25]

This desire to ground civil obligation in consent concerning shared material interests leads Locke to "privatize" certain faith commitments, separating them from civil concerns, as a way to preserve both church and state. Locke admonishes civil magistrates to treat church claims or matters of religious disagreement as private matters concerning "Indifferent Things" and to adjudicate toleration of them only as they concern "the Publick Good"—not from some privileged divine perspective but based on their civil effects in accordance with "the Civil Right of the Community."[26]

Locke scholars have proposed solutions in an effort to explain Locke's secular-sounding language in juxtaposition to the seemingly intractable religious grounding of his arguments, though many of these are ultimately unsuccessful.[27] It is true that Locke's language can seem inconsistent, but it is worth asking whether Locke's texts are truly polyvalent or if Locke's works are simply, at times, ambiguous enough to allow interpreters to see their own reflection. It is clear that Locke believes in the separation of church and state and that there exist "just bounds" between them. He is clearly concerned about respect for their proper spheres and seems to go to great lengths to cut off cross-pollination *of some sort*. It behooves interpreters, however, to consider what Locke actually means: what are the "just bounds"? What belongs to each category? What cannot traverse the line in the sand? By referencing Locke's opposition to the slogan that "dominion is founded in grace" and that the role of civil government is not concerned with one's "spiritual and eternal interest," Tate assumes a wide and deep separation and argues interpreters are right to "divide Locke from God" with respect to political matters, since Locke wished to create a "secular" civil society freed from divisive religious argumentation:

> It is hardly likely … that a man so aware of the endemic nature of religious disagreement would choose a set of explicit theological concerns (knowledge of God and His purposes for us) as the basis for agreement, justification, or consent within civil society, or as a criterion for political equality, civil rights, or political obligation … Indeed the fact that Locke did quite the opposite is evident.[28]

Contrary to Tate's claim, and consistent with the new perspective presented in Chapter 1, Locke does not intend to remove "knowledge of God and His purposes for us" from the public realm; on the contrary, he believes they are indispensable. Locke employs a method of argumentation that is intentionally broad, while retaining positions that are wedded to theological premises. A careful study of Locke's "secular" sounding language helps remove some of the disparity.

## *A negative response: What Locke does not mean to affirm*

### "Dominion founded in grace"

Twice in the *LCT*, Locke reveals his opposition to the belief that "dominion is founded in grace." Though Tate offers this slogan as a blanket statement of Locke's opposition to theology's role in grounding political affairs, this phrase requires contextual understanding. Throughout the *LCT*, Locke is concerned about the things that make for peace. Chief on his list of that which threatens peace is any notion of oppressive violent force: "There is only one thing which gathers People into Seditious Commotions," writes Locke, "and that is Oppression."[29]

Thus, in the *LCT*, we see the term "dominion" coupled with terms of oppression, force, and warfare. For Locke, "the business of True Religion … is not instituted in order to … the obtaining of Ecclesiastical Dominion, nor to the exercising of compulsive Force."[30] What Locke sees in ecclesiastical dominion of his day is replete with a "Spirit of Persecution" and "unchristian (or 'inhumane') Cruelty."[31] These church leaders were using force when "it is only Light and Evidence that can work a change in Mens Opinions" or produce a truly volitional faith.[32] He wants church leaders to use arguments of reason rather than "instruments of Force"; use of the latter reveals that "whilst they pretend only Love for the Truth, this their intemperate Zeal, breathing nothing but Fire and Sword, betray their Ambition, and shew that what they desire is Temporal Dominion."[33] Locke has to remind his readers that force of arms as a means of evangelism is unchristian: "Nor put he the Sword into any Magistrate's Hand, with Commission to make use of it in forcing men to forsake their former Religion, and receive his."[34]

Locke uses the case of Native Americans, whom he describes as "innocent Pagans, strict Observers of the Rules of Equity and the Law of Nature, and no ways offending against the Laws of Society." Yet, due to their practice of idolatry, some contend that they "are to be turned out of the Lands and Possessions of their Forefathers, and perhaps deprived of Life itself."[35] Locke is describing a severely oppressive environment produced from motives and beliefs that Locke believed were perversions of the Christian gospel. "Then at last," concludes Locke, "it appears what Zeal for the Church, joyned with the desire for Dominion, is capable to produce; and how easily the pretence of Religion, and of the care of Souls, serves for a Cloak to Covetousness, Rapine, and Ambition."[36]

It is in this context that Locke's famous line about "Dominion founded in Grace" should be read:

> No body therefore, in fine, neither single Persons, nor Churches, nay, nor even Commonwealths, have any just Title to invade the Civil Rights and Worldly Good of each other, upon pretence of Religion. Those that are of another Opinion, would do well to consider with themselves how pernicious a Seed of Discord and War, how powerful a provocation to endless Hatreds, Rapines, and Slaughters, they thereby furnish unto Mankind. No Peace and Security, no not so much as Common Friendship, can ever be established or preserved amongst Men, so long as this Opinion prevails, That *Dominion is founded in Grace*, and that Religion is to be propagated by force of Arms.[37]

In this passage, "dominion" is synonymous with "invad[ing] the Civil Rights and Worldly Goods of each other," while "grace" appears to be used by some as a foil, a mere "pretence of Religion." Given the background information, it is likely that Locke conceives of "this Opinion" as having two parts: (1) that the right to invade the rights and goods of the masses is given to church leaders (of the ruling state-sponsored church), and (2) that, consequently, those leaders can and should use oppressive force and warfare to force religion on the masses.

Locke uses the same phrase later in the *LCT*, again explicitly showing the context of "unchristian cruelty" in the form of oppression.[38] Oppression may be found at the hands of religious people, but that is "upon pretence of Religion" not as a consequence of principles professed by "true religion."[39] It is "upon the pretence of Religion" that these leaders "persecute, torment, destroy, and kill other men."[40] Instead of peaceable toleration as Christianity would demand, "the Heads and Leaders of the Church, moved by Avarice and insatiable desire for Dominion, [made] use of the immoderate Ambition of Magistrates" to root out those they found disagreeable, who "are to be outed of their Possessions, and destroyed."[41] Such attitudes go against Christian teaching as well as reason.[42] Intolerant oppression of this nature and this magnitude is "contrary to the Laws of the Gospel and the Precepts of Charity" as well as "contrary to all the Laws of Equity, both Humane and Divine."[43] According to Locke, "those that ought to be the Preachers of Peace and Concord … continue, with all their Art and Strength, to excite men to Arms, and sound the Trumpet of War," thus proving themselves to be "Disturbers of the Public Peace" and promoters of "Tyranny in the Commonwealth."[44]

It is clear, then, that the slogan "dominion is founded in grace" evoked an unhealthy and unchristian ambition for seditious acts intended to oppress others by the most extreme measures. Locke fully opposes this obvious threat to peace, but it is completely unwarranted to infer from Locke's antipathy for this slogan (in his own context) that he meant to exclude "God and theology" from civil life and public discourse.

## Locke's views on religious argumentation in public political discourse

Believing that "religion and theology constituted no basis for public deliberation" in Locke's political theory, Tate claims Locke "explicitly tries to exclude" religious argumentation from any justifying role with regard to civil arrangements.[45] If such a sentiment is strictly confined to how a magistrate enforces a civil law, or the publicly declared basis for using force to coerce private devotion, the point is well taken. But as a sweeping statement against the use of religious arguments in persuading the populace to accept the grounds of a civil action, this position is at least dubious; as a historical judgment concerning John Locke, it is simply false. Two clear indications that Locke not only allowed but favored "religious argumentation" in making one's case are that (1) he explicitly claims such, and (2) he engages in this very thing in the *LCT*. Thus, in word and in deed, Locke rejects the extreme secularity imposed upon him by later interpreters.

Locke advocates the use of careful reasoned argumentation as a way to persuade the populace. The use of "arguments" is "the only right Method of propagating Truth, which has no such way of prevailing, as when strong Arguments and good Reason, are joined with the softness of Civility and good usage."[46] But this applies to religious people on religious and secular matters: "Oh that our Ecclesiastical Orators, of every Sect, would apply themselves with all the strength of Arguments that they are able, to the confounding of mens Errors! But let them spare their Persons."[47]

Locke is clear that "the Care of Souls does not belong to the Magistrate."[48] But he narrows the scope of this claim: "Magisterial Care … consists in prescribing by Laws, and compelling by Punishments. But a charitable Care, which consists in teaching, admonishing, and persuading, cannot be denied unto any man."[49] Indeed, the magistrate *as magistrate* ought not to legislate conformity of beliefs with his own; but as a man, as a member of the brotherhood of humanity, he bears a responsibility to persuade others toward the truth, even in matters of "religious" concern:

> It may indeed be alledged, that the Magistrate may make use of Arguments, and thereby draw the Heterodox into the way of Truth, and procure their Salvation. I grant it; but this is common to him with other Men. In teaching, instructing, and redressing the Erroneous by Reason, he may certainly do what becomes any good Man to do. Magistracy does not oblige him to putt off either Humanity or Christianity. But it is one thing to perswade, another to command; one thing to press with Arguments, another with Penalties … Every Man has Commission to admonish, exhort, convince another of Error, and by reasoning to draw him into Truth.[50]

There is nothing more important than the eternal fate of one's soul; the fact that "the care of each man's Salvation belongs only to himself" prohibits "Force and Compulsion" but not persuasion. As Locke notes, "any one may employ as many Exhortations and Arguments as he pleases, toward the promoting of another man's Salvation."[51]

In addition to declaring his support for religious argumentation in persuading others in public discourse, Locke offers religious arguments for civil order in separating the roles of church and state. Near the beginning of the *LCT*, Locke makes three arguments for why "Care of Souls" does not fall to the civil authorities. In all three arguments, Locke employs religious argumentation. Locke's first argument for why the care of souls is not committed to the civil magistrate is that such was not committed (and could not be committed) to him by God. The idea that a civil ruler could "compell" others to his religion by force is inconsistent with the fact that "no Man can … conform his Faith to the Dictates of another."[52] This is true for two reasons: the first is based on the nature of faith; the second is based on the nature of God. "Faith is not Faith without believing," writes Locke; to ignore this, and offer something other than what we believe is "well pleasing unto God," creates difficulties for ourselves and shows contempt for our creator.[53]

Locke's second argument on this topic also employs religious argumentation. The care of souls "cannot belong" to a civil ruler because "his Power consists only in outward force: but true and saving Religion consists in the inward perswasion of the Mind, without which nothing can be acceptable to God."[54] His third argument is that even if force were "capable to convince" others to faith, "yet would not that help at all to the Salvation of their Souls."[55] Each country would believe whatever teaching is embraced by the leader and thus each would "owe their eternal Happiness or Misery" to the accidents of geography—a conclusion, Locke asserts, "which heightens the absurdity, and very ill suits the Notion of a Deity."[56]

Halfway through the *LCT* Locke is in the midst of serious reflection on the duties of toleration and why his audience ought to accept this doctrine. He offers a paragraph that purports to address "the *principal Consideration*, and which absolutely determines this Controversie."[57] Locke begins with this suggestive sentence: "Although the Magistrates Opinion in Religion be sound, and the way that he appoints be truly Evangelical, yet if I be not thoroughly perswaded thereof in my own mind, there will be no safety for me in following it."[58] To what safety does Locke refer? Rather than temporal common goods, Locke has in mind eternal security and thus makes a thoroughly religious argument:

> No way whatsoever that I shall walk in, against the Dictates of my Conscience, will ever bring me to the Mansions of the Blessed. I may grow rich by an Art that I take not delight in; I may be cured of some Disease by Remedies that I have not

Faith in; but I cannot be saved by a Religion that I distrust, and by a Worship that I abhor. It is in vain for an Unbeliever to take up the outward shew of another mans Profession. Faith only, and inward Sincerity, are the things that procure acceptance with God.[59]

It appears obvious, then, that Locke does not oppose using sound and reasoned arguments (in public or private) that are intended to persuade the populace. Given the religious scruples of his audience (and his own), employing religious argumentation is seen as a fitting way to accomplish the just aims of deliberation in a tolerant yet truth-seeking society.

## *Summarizing what Locke does not mean to affirm*

This study helps clarify how terms such as "secular" and "religious" apply to Locke's conception of political life. Locke affirms a "secular" sphere in the sense that the magistrate operates outside the jurisdiction of church affairs. He is also against particular church authorities assuming that ecclesiastical leadership implies civic control. Rather than offering an anti-religious (or even "neutral") approach, Locke believes these distinctions protect faith and honor God and are consistent with the teachings of divine revelation.

It is fairly clear, then, what Locke is *not* saying. Locke does not envision a "secular" society in the sense of one that is devoid of religious people (at all levels of society) using religious language in articulating their views of how society ought to seek, protect, and maintain goods for the good of society. Likewise, Locke does not believe that it is wrong to affirm a theological ground for government. It is also clear what serves as Locke's chief concern: delineating the difference between coercion and persuasion. The key for Locke is that the magistrate cannot coerce a populace to engage in religious matters, but he does bear the responsibility to enforce civil action. As this book will show, some of the foundational aspects of civil action—such as one's obligation to obey laws, the right for the magistrate to enforce proper punishment, and the selection of virtues to be rewarded and vices to be punished—revolve around theological assumptions. Thus Locke does not seek to separate God from political life. A more developed analysis of Locke's positive contribution to the Theo-political problem, especially with regard to the "secular" sphere, is now able to be made. After considering how Locke approaches the need for (and the limits of) "secular" reasoning and action, this chapter will consider the practical import of Locke's views as evidence of a burgeoning Christian political philosophy.

## Sizing up the marketplace: Clarifying Locke's method and approach

### Three important distinctions

It is important to consider three crucial distinctions that can help interpreters place Locke's teaching in its proper context. First, one must be careful not to confuse ontological categories and epistemological ones. It is in this vein that Tate makes a crucial distinction in his exegesis of the two weight-bearing theological passages in the *Second Treatise*.[60] The ontological basis of human equality rests with our nature as beings created by God and thus under His rule, having nothing to do with any range property or threshold concerning the level of one's epistemological capacity for abstract thought.[61] However, any aim at moral persuasion necessarily appeals to one's epistemological awareness, and the moral imperatives under his rule are part of what it functionally means to be "human" in any political context.

Second, a distinction must be made between means of motivation and the grounds of obligation. According to Yolton and Singh, Locke makes this distinction himself. One's obligation to obey the law of nature has its foundation in God; self-interest considerations (led by pleasure and pain, rewards and punishments) provide the motivation to abide by one's obligations.[62] Yet separation of concepts does not preclude overlap. Locke at times offers some of the same arguments for motivation as he does for obligation, leading scholars in two very different directions. Forde claims Locke confuses the two categories and never satisfactorily solves this in the *Second Treatise*.[63] On the other hand, Drury contends that Locke wishes to include obligation within motivation, placing God as the source for both.[64] Regardless of the differences, these scholars rightly note that motivation and obligation are different concepts, as well as the fact that both distinction and correlation are possible.

Finally, when assessing Locke's language, one must not confuse "religious argumentation" (i.e., citing scripture or church edicts as a final authority or seeking to persuade one's audience by appeals to their religious sensibilities) with reasoned "secular" argumentation that is consistent with mature theological reflection (and that may, indeed, cite religious authorities as supporting planks). Tate makes his fundamental error at just this point.[65] Tate excludes "religious argumentation" from (1) the justification and exercise of political arrangements, (2) grounds upon which individuals are *able* to agree, and (3) the interests for which society and government were created in the first place. If one were discussing an attempt to play on the conscience of one's "zealous votaries," with reference to religious habits, food restrictions, or times of worship, Tate would accurately describe Locke's position.[66] But Locke does not wish to exclude from persuasive public discourse all arguments that make authoritative reference to God, natural law, or revelation, as this book seeks to show.

## Locke as tolerant and pragmatic

The "secular" language of Locke described above shows that his approach to politics includes a fair degree of pragmatism. Locke does not envision a completely Christian society or a mass conversion as prerequisite for a stable economy. As a student of history, with an avid interest in cultural anthropology, Locke acknowledged his familiarity with varieties of cultures and nations that operated with civility even in ignorance of the full scope of truth with regard to Deity and natural law.[67] Although no one before Christ, according to Locke, provided a complete and systematic list of God's requirements for humanity, this did not preclude their ability to form themselves into societies and seek profoundly efficient governance.[68] This should lead one to conclude that Locke intends for his political theory to work in a nonhomogenous society—which inevitably will involve some scale of compromise, areas of common interest, and privatization of hopelessly conflicting opinions. This led Locke to his doctrine of toleration.

Locke is widely recognized for his views on religious toleration, and rightly so. Honest disagreement exists in theological matters, and Locke's own personal experience with religious bigotry and inevitable conflict taught him that a diverse society cannot pin its political hopes on a shared theological agenda in the style of denominational loyalty. While the term "theology" can have a wide or narrow context, it is in this sense of the word—referencing novel divisive religious points of doctrine—that Locke indeed wishes to limit any reliance or dependence of his political agenda on theology.[69] Locke, the sincere practicing Christian, writes the *LCT* to express "my Thoughts about the mutual Toleration of Christians in their different Professions of Religion."[70] In Locke's view, toleration is not only politically advisable but is "the chief Characteristical Mark of the True Church."[71] Locke has no stomach for making mandatory any certain religious practice or belief that "are much rather Marks of Men striving for Power and Empire over one another, than of the church of Christ."[72] But it is important to consider the kinds of things Locke has in mind. He wishes to advocate a level of toleration among Christians that takes into account disputable matters—such things as "the introducing of Ceremonies, or ... the establishment of Opinions, which for the most part are about nice and intricate Matters, that exceed the Capacity of ordinary Understandings."[73] He makes this clear in *Two Tracts on Government*:

> He must confess himself a stranger to England that thinks that *meats* and *habits*, that *places* and *times* of worship etc., would not be as sufficient occasion of hatred and quarrels amongst us, as *leeks* and *onions* and other *trifles* ... and be distinctions able to keep us always at a distance, and eagerly ready for like violence and cruelty as often as the *teachers* should alarm the *consciences* of their zealous votaries and direct them against the adverse party.[74]

One can be a Christian without these things, writes Locke, while one cannot be about "the Business of True Religion" without "Holiness of Life, Purity of Manners, and Benignity and Meekness of Spirit."[75] "No man can be a Christian without *Charity*," adds Locke, "and without *that Faith which works*, not by Force, but by *Love*."[76]

Locke also wishes for Christians to exercise a level of toleration toward non-Christians, which is in accord with Christianity itself: "Let any one have never so true a Claim to all these things, yet if he be destitute of Charity, Meekness, and Good-will in general towards all Mankind, even to those that are not Christians, he is certainly yet short of being a true Christian himself."[77] Locke directs his ire toward "those that persecute, torment, destroy, and kill other Men upon pretence of Religion," since such actions "are certainly more contrary to the Glory of God, to the Purity of the Church, and to the Salvation of Souls, than any conscientious Dissent from Ecclesiastical Decision, or Separation from Publick Worship, whilst accompanied with Innocency of Life."[78]

Within context, then, Locke's "secular" language about toleration finds a proper home. One can speak of "Locke's desire to avoid reliance on theology where possible ... wish[ing] to construct a morality with minimal reliance on theology ... in part to avoid unnecessary confrontations with Christianity."[79] But this is only true if one remembers the Christian context in which Locke promotes his views of toleration and the kind of "disputable matters" Locke has in mind when calling for (what modern commentators describe as) a separation between politics and "theology."[80]

## Appreciating epistemological limits: Seeking common ground

Locke is also epistemologically modest—far more than some might suppose. In the *RC*, Locke reminds his readers that the wisdom of God is greater than that of humans, and his reasons may, in fact, be past finding out. For Locke, any "rational man, or fair searcher after truth" would recognize the truth and importance of such epistemic humility.[81] The frequent recognition of reason's limits stands out in the latter half of the *RC*. Humans are "poor, frail creatures," the "frail offspring" of God.[82] Locke applies these epitaphs to the field of epistemology. "It is not requisite on this occasion," writes Locke, "to enlarge on the frailty of our minds, and weakness of our constitutions; how liable to make mistakes, how apt to go astray."[83] This language is also present in the *LCT*, where Locke acknowledges "the pravity of Mankind," which requires some sort of social governance to deal with "poor sinful men."[84] In addition, the vast majority of people do not have the capacities to understand "sublime notions" or "mysterious reasoning" offered up by some other religious men, let alone the things of God.[85] By itself, this argument would challenge any notion that Locke grounds the law of nature in man's reasoning capacities; the latter is simply not able to handle the weight.

Not only does reason have its limits, but human beings differ with regard to cognitive abilities and access to knowledge. Not all human beings are able to "know" profound truths equally, and one is only responsible for the information available to them.[86] In addition, there are differing standards of "proof" required for particular truths; for example, nonbelievers need to be instructed by appeal to that which would count as authoritative—rather than expecting them to believe based on Christian authoritative structures.[87] What seems common teaching among Christians will appear as the "dream of a crazy brain" to the nonbeliever, and thus Locke calls for proper appeal to proper sources with careful regard for one's audience.[88]

But Locke not only has important things to say about reason's limits; he is also concerned about its proper role. Locke has such high regard for those who live their lives "according to the Rules of Vertue and Piety," and such disregard for those who use their knowledge to "persecute, torment, destroy, and kill," that his discussions of morality (in the *LCT* and the *RC*) often describe the "simple" as superior to the "wise"—suggesting that proper regulation for civil society ought to focus on duties rather than philosophical bases for those duties.[89]

Instead of assuming that all humans ought to draw from their vast resources and accept the theoretical grounding for political obligations as well as proper motivations, Locke is much more adamant that civil society focus on common agreement covering basic needs and general welfare. Locke recognizes that most people learn of their social obligations by paying attention to habits, customs, and social mores. His high praise for such methods of instilling virtue in others (especially children) ought not lead one to assume Locke is a "natural egoist."[90]

As West rightly notes, Locke's pragmatism and respect for normal patterns in civic social life only enhance his broad appeal for a civil society that finds common ground within the everyday norms of life.[91] But Locke explicitly rejects "the norms of a given culture" as providing ultimate grounds of obligation, since then we would have no means to adjudicate between conflicting norms among various cultures.[92] Cultural norms may serve as a means of learning but not as an ultimate source of moral knowledge. Locke's high appeal to common life presumes one that, in general, embraces the truths of "virtue and piety"—not just anyone's list of virtues but true virtue as God's revelation and natural law ascribes.[93]

## Summarizing Locke's method and approach

In this way, we may summarize the points earlier discussed in an effort to frame Locke's "secular" language, given his deeply Christian commitments. There is no doubt that Locke personally believed in "one truth, one way to heaven."[94] He also believed that truth—whether naturally deduced or supernaturally revealed—is grounded in the nature and will of God. He considered "knowledge of God" to be "the most natural discovery of human reason"[95] and that "the taking away of God, tho but even in thought, dissolves all."[96] But even knowledge of God is not innate, and some will never fully come to a knowledge of this or other great truths.[97]

In addition, what is true on an ontological level need not be fully acknowledged by every citizen in order to maintain a happy and productive civil society; indeed, to press matters over which reasonable human beings are not able to agree can have adverse effects. Where there exists no impartial means of adjudication, endless division inevitably follows.[98] What is called for, on the civic level, is a kind of toleration very much in accord with Christian principles: one that allows human beings to grow in their understanding, differ on their interpretations, and live in accordance with their own judgments. However, civic peace and harmony requires not shared personal beliefs but proper actions with regard to the welfare of others. By means of acquired habits and social customs, one may discover certain obligations toward a neighbor that are right and just; reference to faith is not necessary to inspire motivation in such cases and can have just the opposite effect. If a society—in the absence of shared religious beliefs—is able to operate according to the life of virtue expressed in scripture in which neighbors show charity to one another, why enforce certain doctrines that would lead to civil unrest?[99]

But none of this ought to be interpreted as a "secular" model of governance in the style of modern liberalism, even if both models share similar aims.[100] Locke's regard for outliers fits with the Christian call to be concerned for "the least of these"; but those who make civil laws, and those who seek to enforce civil laws, are not allowed to make and enforce laws of their own devising based on self-interest. A law that does not conform to the law of nature is not a law; rewards and punishments must be in accord with those actions that receive ultimate reward or ultimate punishment in the next life. There is such a thing as "injustice" even in the state of nature, and justice is not simply a state in which everyone gets along. A civil society cannot reward bad behavior or punish good behavior; laws must be in accordance with the divine rules established by the ultimate lawmaker.

Locke recognizes that appealing to habit and custom may work for the bulk of humankind, but those with higher rational faculties and a penchant for philosophical reflection will need a greater reason for behaving morally; to such persons Locke only and always offers reasons either grounded in or consistent with the nature and will of God.[101] As Forde notes:

> It appears that the more rational a man is, the more providence becomes necessary to support his morality … [T]hose who think for themselves, who understand the true principles of rational action, need instead a reason for behaving morally … Providence is the only reason offered to such individuals by Locke's philosophy.[102]

Hobbesian self-interest may be universal, but Locke describes it as childish—the lowest common denominator from which human beings ought to grow.[103] Thus Locke advises parents to teach their children better so that habit and social custom will include virtue, not simply self-interest. And, as one would expect, Locke includes Christian instruction (and the use of scripture) as a means by which virtue can be instilled in children.[104]

Thus it is clear that religious values, religious argumentation, and religious grounding are not foreign to Locke's political philosophy; his willingness to suspend religious language for the sake of civil peace is a far cry from modern liberal neutrality. Locke believes that "reason" can access much of what "the law of nature" teaches, thus providing a basic "consensus" for a society that includes and tolerates nonbelievers. Though he employs "secular" reasoning and "bridge" language (that is not peculiarly "Christian"), he believes his teaching is always in accord with divine revelation, which offers a fuller and clearer picture.[105]

## The problem with atheists: Why Locke's "secularity" has religious limits

### The exclusion of avowed atheists

Locke is willing to extend toleration far beyond his own bounds of comfort. Though expressing deep concern at various points, Locke concludes that civil society ought to tolerate Jewish, Muslim, and possibly Catholic religious beliefs and practices.[106] Locke even specifically includes the "Pagan" among those who "ought [not] to be excluded from the Civil Rights of the Commonwealth, because of his Religion."[107] All of this is consistent with Locke's views in the RC. But when it comes to avowed atheists, Locke has reached the end of the branch:

> Those are not at all to be tolerated who deny the Being of a God. Promises, Covenants, and Oaths, which are the Bonds of Humane Society, can have no hold upon an Atheist. The taking away of God, tho but even in thought, dissolves all. Besides also, those that by their Atheism undermine and destroy all Religion, can have no pretence of Religion whereupon to challenge the Privilege of a Toleration.[108]

It remains to ask why tolerate others but not atheists? The goal of civil toleration is to "promote universally the Civil Welfare of all ... except only of such as are arrogant, ungovernable, and injurious to their Brethren."[109] As long as "one Man does not violate the Right of another, by his Erroneous Opinions, and undue manner of Worship, nor is his Perdition any prejudice to another Mans Affairs," toleration should be granted.[110] As long as a person's opinions "do not tend to establish Domination over others ... there can be no Reason why they should not be tolerated."[111] Neither the "gospel" nor the "church" provide reason to exclude anyone from civil life on the basis of religion, and "the Commonwealth, which embraces indifferently all Men that are honest, peaceable and industrious, requires it not."[112]

Those who read Locke with a "secular" lens seek a secular solution to this conundrum. Tate, for example, believes that proscribing atheists from civil society is due only to civil consequences that result from an unwillingness to forswear oaths. Atheists could not swear by the Almighty God—and, since oaths were at the center of political obligation, it meant atheists could not covenant and thus form the bonds of human society.[113] According to Tate, "Locke viewed atheism as no different from any of the other proscribed religious beliefs and practices ... all of which he proscribed for their civil consequences."[114]

But Locke places atheism in a category all by itself. In the opening to *A Vindication of the Reasonableness of Christianity*,[115] Locke speaks against "the Capital Crime of Atheism" in the strongest words possible:

> I cannot but approve of any ones Zeal, to Guard and Secure that great and Fundamental Article of all Religion and Morality, That there is a God: But Atheism being a Crime, which for its Madness as well as Guilt, ought to shut a Man out of all Sober and Civil Society.[116]

"Madness" and "guilt" are hardly synonymous with recusal of an oath. Besides, atheists deny the "fundamental article of all ... morality," not by failing to take oaths but by failing to believe in that which ontologically binds oaths in the first place. Thus, even when talking only on the level of oaths, civil consequences that result from failure to take such oaths are only part of Locke's concern.

Locke's problem with atheism is much deeper than this. Consider each of the specific reasons given in Locke's seminal passage cited above for being intolerant of atheists, in reverse order. First, perhaps Locke is simply concerned with atheists who use their atheism to "undermine and destroy all Religion," thus sowing discord. But this will not do, since Locke addresses the *LCT* to seek peace among those who use their beliefs to "persecute, torment, destroy, and kill other Men upon pretence of Religion."[117] There is no indication that, since some Catholics or Protestants have done so, all Catholics or Protestants are to be banished; just the opposite is true.

Second, consider what Locke gives as the reason for why covenants and oaths cannot bind the atheist: "the taking away of God, tho but even in thought, dissolves all." If Locke was explicit that he only had in mind formal covenants made in public ceremonies, there might be reason to consider Tate's claim. But Locke's language appears more universal. The phrase certainly is not illimitable, since common sense and experience would show that atheists are able to read, understand, and keep laws. But what "the taking away of God ... dissolves" is any ultimate obligation to keep any promises or any justifiable reason to accept another man's right to require justice in my actions. This would be true even in the state of nature where no such formal oaths are made.

Finally, consider Locke's initial blanket statement: "those are not at all to be tolerated who deny the Being of a God." When placed alongside the laundry list of people and beliefs that "ought" to be tolerated, Locke's isolating language concerning atheists is indeed stark. Locke wants to tolerate all who are "honest, peaceable and industrious" and exclude only those that are "arrogant, ungovernable, and injurious to their Brethren."[118] It stands to reason that, for

Locke, atheists may fail to qualify in the former list and might legitimately be placed with the latter.

Throughout the *LCT*, Locke often explains how his particular civil rules are either in harmony with Christian teaching or at least do not in any way contradict Christian teaching. When it comes to the fertile field of a society that is, at least, penetrable by the gospel message, Locke is able to find wide room for toleration. God-fearing pre-converted members of society are treated with civility and dignity, and given opportunity—not only to be industrious in civil life but to discover the law of nature and the teachings of God.

It seems plausible, then, to imagine that Locke does not have in mind one with weak rational capacities who is unable to articulate a clear vision of God or those who, recognizing the existence of Creator, fail to properly seek Him out. Locke is describing those who—in the face of undeniable evidence—wantonly and arrogantly reject the existence of a Creator and thus do not (and cannot) accept an ultimate authority over their lives. This removes the very ground for telling truths, keeping promises, and submitting to laws that go against one's self-interest; it also means the more clever ones, upon pains of questioning, will never be able to reach a firm reason for keeping societal norms. The very notion of rewards and punishments—especially long-lasting ones—cannot be legitimately held without recourse to the ultimate judge in heaven or the ultimate rewards and punishments upon which temporal sentences are based.[119] A little leaven leavens the whole lump, and the avowed atheist is one who, in theory, cannot be implicitly trusted, will not be governed, and whose influence may very well be injurious to society. Belief in God is a prerequisite for understanding the nature and force of law, thus faith *in some form* is necessary to be an industrious member of civil society. Even Locke's "pagan" is one who must be allowed to "pray unto and worship God," thus more akin to the "justified heathen" of the *RC* than to an avowed atheist.[120]

In a sense, then, the atheist voluntarily fails to qualify as a candidate for obedience to law, which places him—by his own decision—outside the scope of the moral community of equals. Locke begins a sentence in the *LCT* this way: "No man in his wits (I had almost said none but an Atheist)."[121] Humans disagree about the details on when, where, or how to approach the Creator, but "all men know and acknowledge that God ought to be publickly worshipped."[122] If we grant that Locke is speaking distributively (in recognition of his other statements acknowledging not all men will properly deduce the existence of God), there is reason to assume Locke has in mind "all reasonable men," those with "wits," who would serve in important roles within a given society. The failure to acknowledge

God intentionally—to emphatically affirm the universal negative "there is no God"—is an offense to reason and disqualifies one as a "moral man."[123]

**Summarizing Locke's intolerance toward atheism**

For Locke, a Christian view of a tolerant society is one in which differing Christians and even non-Christians are able to find peace and harmony with regard to promoting the general welfare. Civil laws are based on consent and seek to avoid "indifferent" matters of religion that lead to friction and factions. This is a society in which members are at least theoretically potential subjects of the kingdom—where the gospel may spread and thrive and where virtue may be practiced even where the gospel is not to be found. Locke is careful to use reasoned argument and "open" language to appeal across a wide spectrum for civil concord. But lying behind this view of a tolerant society is an undeniable reliance on the existence and beneficence of a Creator, who establishes law and keeps covenant with his creatures. The full picture of this God and his promises is found in Christian revelation, but one need not have the total picture to serve the needs of a fellow man in an effort to contribute to a just and fruitful society. Yet this is not a "secular" picture of one who wishes to "remove God and theology" from civil society. Those who explicitly deny God's existence are not to be tolerated, since they reject the very grounds upon which the laws of civil society are based.[124] Those who make and enforce laws do so on the presupposition that law is divinely sanctioned, that human laws are in accordance with divine truths, and that rewards and punishments are aligned with virtue and vice as taught by the law of nature, which is, in fact, the law of God.

## A bi-furcated legacy? Teasing out elements of Locke's Christian political philosophy

What are we to make, then, of what Forde calls Locke's "bi-furcated legacy," given that Locke proposes a theologically grounded political theory that he wishes to be free from theological controversy?[125] How has his political theory survived and thrived in the hands of those who fail to notice any fundamentally theological considerations? Equally important, how can his ideas serve any lasting contribution to Christian political philosophy? In this regard, an "Areopagus" motif provides a helpful framework for appreciating Locke's positive contribution.[126] Adopting "secular" language to teach "natural" truths that are consistent with revelation is not foreign to Christian approaches to political philosophy. In Locke's view, this approach is theologically appropriate, philosophically possible, and politically desirable.

Even those who deny the theological imprint on Locke's political philosophy agree that Locke's worldview included God at its center. It is apparent in Locke's writings that when "nature teaches" something, it is God teaching that thing through nature (i.e., God's truth able to be deduced from reflection on nature). Likewise, when "reason teaches" something, it is only because such truth is ascertained by means of one's reasoning faculties. All knowledge is rooted in God, just as the law of nature is, in fact, the law of God as revealed through nature.

It should not be surprising, then, that Locke does, on occasion in his writings, substitute the term "nature" for "God."[127] What "nature" teaches is the command of God. Locke might as well substitute the term "reason" for God, since "tis [God] that commands what reason does."[128] This style of argument is adapted from biblical language, especially that involving the Apostle Paul.[129] In the RC, Locke references Romans 1:19–20, where "what may be known about God is plain"; even "God's invisible qualities" are "clearly seen, being understood from what has been made." Paul "reasoned" with his audience on a daily basis (Acts 17:2, 17; 18:4, 19). In Romans 2, Paul contrasts lawless believers with the righteous Gentiles who do "by nature" what God's law commands (Rom. 2:14). Forde rightly notes that Locke's minimal use of "God" and increased use of "reason" or "nature" is "parsimony," which "allows Locke to develop his argument with minimum controversy and maximum appeal."[130]

In addition, several schools of modern political theology bear Locke's imprint, including the most unlikely suspects.[131] On the political front, Perry and Forster offer constructive ways to apply at least part of Locke's vision of liberalism in contemporary life.[132] Christopher Insole's approach to "principled neutrality" also provides a philosophical defense for the sort of liberalism Locke has in mind.[133] In both cases, these authors operate with both a firm allegiance to Christian faith and an appreciation for the kind of civic life exemplified in the writings of Locke.

It is true that attaching secular sounding practical teaching to undeniably theological moorings can be misleading. But if one is able to identify (1) a particular historical religious context in which Locke's approach finds a home and (2) a deep structure that unites the various strands of Locke's teaching, the appearance of contradictory bifurcation may lessen or even disappear. These, in turn, will serve as the focus for the remainder of this book.

# 3

# Locke and the Latitudinarians: Locke's Religious Experience and Theological Influences in the Context of Seventeenth-Century England

In seventeenth-century religious history, the Great Tew Circle in Oxford and the Cambridge Platonists are each credited with developing a theological approach for the moderately inclined. Standing between Calvinistic puritanism on the one hand and high Anglicanism on the other, those of Oxford and Cambridge sought a broader ecclesiology, religious toleration, and appreciation for commonality among those who differ. While those of the Cambridge school are better known for their metaphysical claims grounding these areas of interest, both of these movements led directly to the formation of Latitudinarianism in the latter part of the century.[1]

Locke was deeply familiar with each segment of this moderating influence and counted proponents among his friends.[2] He frequented churches that touted this message, lived among its adherents, and collected writings in its favor. Locke did not engage in serious biblical and theological reflection until the last two decades of his life, commencing when he met the Cambridge Platonist Damaris Masham and her Latitudinarian friends. At the time of his death, Locke's library held over one hundred books written by these voices of moderation, including a sizeable number of books from the Oxford Tew Circle, Cambridge Platonists, and other Latitudinarian preachers in restoration London.[3]

Though ever independent, Locke's theological views are born out of a context, and reflections on Locke's religious environment provide a fitting framework for placing Locke's political project within the sphere of a moderating Christian political philosophy. His circle of influence, which included Latitudinarian and dissenting voices, provided Locke with a broader practical theology while his encounters with the Cambridge Platonists offered him a deeper philosophical theology. In addition, each in their own way provided a theological framework for Locke's moral and political thought.[4]

## Locke, the life-long (heterodox) Christian

By any charitable measure, John Locke was a sincere Christian. After all, he believed Jesus to be the messiah, held a deep and abiding allegiance to the Old and New Testaments as divine revelation, and was a life-long member of the Church of England.[5] His training is full of diverse Christian influence, and his writing (both public and private) reveals a keen religious sensitivity of a deeply Christian character. It may be true, as Tate notes, that "few scholars have ever doubted" the sincerity with which he held his "deep religious faith" in Christianity.[6] But it is imperative to show more precisely how Locke's Christianity helped define him and his ideas.

### Locke's religious training (1630s–1650s)

Locke's early life was steeped in religiosity, yet within the story of his birth resides the seeds of a tolerating spirit waiting to bloom. On the day of his birth, Locke was christened by Samuel Crook, rector of All Saint's Church parish in Wrington. A Cambridge-educated Calvinistic puritan, Crook was independent-minded, gaining a reputation for doubting the efficacy of infant baptism and a tendency to ignore the rubric of the prayer book. Locke's mother, Agnes, whom Locke once described as "a very pious woman," was a devotee of Dr. Crook, and Locke's religious upbringing was severely Puritan, probably Calvinist, with leanings toward Presbyterianism.[7]

Locke's father, John, was a strong advocate of the people's sovereignty and political representation through Parliament. When the philosopher was only nine years old, Parliament, which had only recently been called after an eleven-year hiatus, issued the Grand Remonstrance challenging the King's authority and fitness to rule. Locke's father joined the Parliamentary army, and Locke's earliest years were formed in the context of a great Civil War between this army and King Charles I. The economic situation in Somerset reflected national tension: suicide-inducing poverty for many, yet ever-increasing wealth for a few. This reality, coupled with religious and political strife, served as the storm center for Locke's earliest memories.[8]

Locke's teenage years were spent at Westminster School, where his curriculum strongly emphasized Latin, Greek, and Hebrew. His schedule included 5:00 a.m. daily ablutions. Sunday's involved far more than attending service in the Abbey; the students engaged in memorizing the catechism in Greek, copying and translating the gospels, and composing verses based on their reading of the Greek text or the morning homily. Locke found much to dislike at Westminster, from the method of punishment, to the kind of extreme scholastic training in Latin. However, the religious and political environment proved to be quite influential in providing further experience of disparate views, tension, and dissent.[9]

In 1652, Locke went up to Christ Church, Oxford, in pursuit of a BA degree. Like all colleges at Oxford and Cambridge, the curriculum was rooted in Aristotelian scholasticism, and Locke was trained extensively in logic, metaphysics, and the classics.[10] In many ways, these studies only furthered Locke's aversion to the disputational, peripatetic school of philosophy, which Locke thought led only to fighting over useless questions, generating more heat than light.[11] But one cannot fail to appreciate how knowledgeable of and conversant with scholastic training Locke would have been. Consistent with a style of education never divorced from religious underpinnings, seventeenth-century Oxford also provided an education in theology. The move from Westminster to Christ Church meant that Locke continued his 5:00 a.m. ritual in the required attendance at morning chapel. According to Cranston,

> Oxford men of Locke's generation had to hear at least two sermons a day, and remember them. All undergraduates, and Bachelors of Arts as well, had to go every Sunday evening between six and nine o'clock to "give an account to some person of known ability and piety ... of the sermons they had heard," and later they had also to pay nightly visits to their tutors "to hear private prayers and to give an account of the time spent that day."[12]

Yet, again, in keeping with Locke's constant exposure to varying levels of dissent in religious matters, it is not surprising to learn that the tutor to whom Locke was responsible was a twenty-six-year old former Westminster man who was fiercely independent in matters of religion.[13] It is also important to note that Parliament issued a ruling in 1653 requiring Oxford colleges to expel any undergraduates who were not "good puritans."[14] Biographers Cranston and Woolhouse note that Locke's survival says more about Dean John Owen's tolerant sensitivity than John Locke's religious orthodoxy.[15] But in terms of influence, Locke's survival further evidences the kind of expansive and tolerant spirit *within a deeply Christian context* Locke was able to imbibe.

In fact, Locke's connection with John Owen is interesting. Locke would have heard Owen's preaching for a considerable amount of time, stretching from his entrance into Christ Church in 1652 through his MA, which culminated in June 1658. Owen preached a gospel of toleration rooted in biblical teaching, which gave no authority for the repression of dissenters. A Cromwellian, Owen believed the role of government was to promote peace, not impose religion.[16] Though Locke did publish a Latin verse honoring Cromwell's peace treaty with the Dutch during this time,[17] it would be years before Locke would echo Owen's views, which now appear strikingly "Lockean."

## Locke's religious choosing (1660s–1680s)

In Locke's mid-twenties and thirties, he moved beyond a student receiving a religiously rooted education to a fellow and tutor responsible for providing it. Appointed as a lecturer in Greek, a tutor, and Censor in Moral Philosophy, Locke took his duties seriously. In a letter penned to one of his graduating pupils, Locke encourages the lad to maintain "a courage that may defend and secure your virtue and religion."[18] To his students, Locke would recommend a devotional work both Anglican and orthodox by Richard Allestree, entitled *The Whole Duty of Man*.[19] In the summer of 1659, Locke wrote to his father expressing his own lack of faith in mankind but included a note of confidence that "serenity" belongs to "every one that remembers there is a god to rest on, and an other world to retire into."[20] This decision to operate out of a theological grounding is evidenced in Locke's life, mentoring, lecturing, and writing. It was also the general perspective of virtually all of Locke's closest associates. Writing of Locke's relationships during the late 1650s and early 1660s, Marshall notes that "among Locke's close friends of this period only one did not become a cleric in the Church of England and that was because he inherited a fortune."[21]

In Locke's first writing intended for publication, he offered a defense of monarchical power and discretion rooted in a theological paradigm of God's right to impose laws.[22] Locke prepared the work for publication at the instigation of his friends who expressed confidence that his work would "doe God and the church a peice of seasonable service."[23] In a second early essay on toleration, Locke further argued that the magistrate may impose matters "indifferent" in worship, offering three main arguments—the final of which is purely theological: it is the will of God that mankind should form themselves into political communities; this requires everyone to release their claim to independent liberty and render obedience to their leaders.[24] Locke's argument relies heavily on distinctions drawn from scholasticism and shows how indebted Locke is to his formal training. According to Woolhouse, "Locke was now, whatever his earliest religious affiliation had been exactly, clearly committed to the Church of England in its re-established form."[25] But this only reveals part of the story. Locke believes that true religion is a matter of personal assent and differentiates between what a magistrate may impose (concerning duties that must be obeyed) and what no one, save the individual, is able to offer (the assent of the heart). Even in Locke's more royalist-leaning writings, he shows an underlying sense of the sacrosanct personal faith, which is untouchable by even magistrate rule.

In these *Two Tracts on Government*, Locke speaks of a "law of nature," which is given by God. In response to questions raised by Gabriel Towerson, and in preparation for his lectures as Censor of Moral Philosophy, Locke composed several Latin essays, which remained unpublished until 1954.[26] In these early essays on the law of nature, Locke argues that God exists, is the creator and benefactor of creation, and has made rules to govern human conduct. Humans, therefore, have an obligation to know, worship, and obey God, which includes how to relate to one's fellow creatures; knowledge of God and his will is available through general revelation, which is the law of nature.

When Locke completed his year of service as Censor of Moral Philosophy (on Christmas Eve, 1663), he offered the traditional outgoing speech (given as a funeral dirge) in which he "did remind the scholars of the importance of 'the hall where men learn to debate' as well as 'the temple where men learn to pray,' of being a philosopher as well as a theologian."[27] Even when Locke's interests moved toward medicine, his thoughts were never far removed from theology. Locke forged a friendship with Fellows of the Royal Society (including Robert Boyle) who were Baconian advocates, acknowledging God as the author of twin revelations: natural and written.[28] Boyle himself was an avid Christian and not only combined biblical studies with scientific investigation but encouraged others to do the same.[29]

Locke's thirties and forties were filled with international travel, which, combined with forming new friendships abroad, afforded him opportunity to evaluate issues of religious toleration and governmental authority in new contexts. On Locke's first visit to the Continent (in December 1665), Locke sent letters to his friend Strachey describing his participation in various religious services[30] and a letter to Robert Boyle expressing his pleasant surprise at the success in Cleves of religious toleration among Calvinists, Lutherans, and Catholics.[31]

In 1667, when Locke was in his mid-thirties, he began a long and important relationship with Anthony Ashley Cooper (the Lord Ashley), who served as Locke's patron. Ashley was a fervent advocate of religious toleration.[32] In the same year, Locke composed a manuscript essay known as the "Essay concerning Toleration."[33] Locke expended a considerable amount of intellectual energy in preparing this work, writing at least four drafts.[34] In this transitional work (between the *Two Tracts on Government* of 1660–1661 and the later *LCT* of 1689), Locke shifts his emphasis concerning religious imposition by a magistrate to the limits of such imposition. Since the end of government is to promote peace, and given that various religious bodies could exist peacefully within the same society (as Locke's experience in Cleves had shown), the magistrate ought to avoid religious imposition concerning indifferent matters that affect only the individual. The individual is responsible to God and must obey their conscience—even if it leads one to disobey the magistrate. He is clearly averse to Papal allegiance (which replaces consent to the societal laws) but wishes to avoid creating "secret malcontents" rather than "friends to the state," though they be not "sons of the church."[35]

In 1668, Locke began attending the Anglican congregation of St. Lawrence Jewry, in London, when the Cambridge Platonist Benjamin Whichcote took over as Vicar. The same year, Locke was elected a Fellow of the Royal Society, but rather than attending to the eleven-person committee to which he was appointed, Locke formed a smaller circle of friends to meet regularly in his room at the Lord Ashley's Exeter House. Locke penned or contributed to a number of writings on a wide range of topics over the next two years, including having a hand in the *Fundamental Constitutions of Carolina*.[36] These writings prescribed religious toleration but mandated belief in God. According to the *Constitutions*, "No man shall be permitted to be a freeman of Carolina, or to have any estate or habitation within it, that does not acknowledge a God, and that God is publicly and solemnly to be worshipped."[37] "Natives of that place ... who ... are utterly strangers of Christianity, whose idolatry, ignorance, or mistake gives us no right to expel or use them ill" are to be given religious liberty so that "civil peace may be maintained amidst the diversity of opinions." While Catholics are not mentioned by name, the work goes on to proclaim "heathens, Jews, and other dissenters from the purity of Christian religion" are fully expected to be tolerated as members of society, while those considered orthodox "by good usage and persuasion, and all those convincing methods of gentleness and meekness suitable to the rules and design of the Gospel" do their part in hopes that dissenters may "be won over to embrace and unfeignedly receive the truth."[38]

Whether Locke penned these words is unknown, but a comparison with his own words in the *LCT* of 1689 reveals remarkable similarity.

In the early months of 1671, Locke's little club met in his chamber at Exeter house to discuss "the principles of morality and revealed religion."[39] Something in the meeting prompted Locke to explore the nature of human understanding, and he returned to the next meeting with "hasty and undigested Thoughts" on the matter.[40] These thoughts were either recorded or (more likely) elaborated in the summer months, when Locke penned what is now known as Draft A for the *Essay*.[41] Locke notes that moral standards guiding our actions are

> not of our owne makeing but depending upon something without us & soe not made by us but for us & these are the rules set to our actions by the declard will or laws of another who hath power to punish our aberrations ... But ... we cannot come to a certain knowledg of these rules of our actions, without first makeing knowne a lawgiver with power & will to reward & punish & without shewing how he hath declard his will & law.[42]

God has declared his will, Locke notes, through "the Law of nature" as well as "revalation."[43] In the latter half of 1671, Locke begins with a fresh manuscript to pen what is now known as Draft B of the *Essay*.[44] Locke not only reiterates the paragraph above (with minor alterations)[45] but adds that our knowledge of God's existence is "more certain" than our knowledge of any existence other than our own.[46]

In 1675, Locke leaves to spend several years in France, and his foreign experiences, like before, profoundly affect his views on religion—both deep and wide. Locke noted the peaceful coexistence of Protestants and Catholics, read widely the best religious and philosophical books available (especially concerning the history of the French Protestant movement and the writings of Pascal), met famous men such as Pufendorf and Leibniz, and struck a friendship with Nicolas Toinard who shared with Locke an interest not only in science but in the scriptures.[47] Locke would later write to Toinard that "when you feel the desire to learn the English language, you have only to follow my method and read every day a chapter of the New Testament, and in a month's time you will become a master."[48]

However, Locke's reading of the New Testament at this time (as throughout his life) was not simply to gain proficiency of foreign languages or to ingratiate himself with Toinard. In a letter penned near the close of 1678, Locke wrote that "we are not placed in this world to stay here for ever, or without any concernment beyond it" and therefore "the much greater good of another world" and "our concernments in an other world" demand our attention, as well as "frequent addresses ... of thanks prayer and resignation" to the "author of our being." As Locke notes, "We are borne with ignorance of those things that concerne the conduct of our lives in this world," so it follows that "enquiry, study, and meditation is necessary."[49]

The year 1681 served for Locke as a year of religious centering. On Sunday, 26 June, Locke recorded a journal entry in which he describes politics as a subcategory of moral philosophy; the central aims of theology are implicit throughout.[50] This theological grounding of the political and moral realms would only be enhanced in the latter part of 1681, when Locke met and began a long-term friendship with Damaris Cudworth (better known as Lady Masham), the daughter of Cambridge Platonist Ralph Cudworth. A philosopher in her own right, Damaris proved to be of significant influence on Locke. Locke was nearly fifty years old at the time, but this encounter marked the beginning of Locke's sustained theological inquiry. The two exchanged letters for several years before Locke took up residence as a paying guest at the home of Lady Masham and (her husband) Sir Francis Masham.[51] He continued his theological pursuits while living in the Masham home until his death in 1704.

In 1684, during Locke's visit to Amsterdam, Locke recorded in his journal an unusually high proportion of notes on theological matters.[52] This is probably due to his meeting Philip van Limborch who served as Professor of Theology at the Remonstrant's seminary.[53] In similar fashion to the Latitudinarians and the Cambridge Platonists, the Remonstrants were known as purveyors of rational religion and people of the minimal creed; the emphasis was on moral living, leaving personal conscience to determine one's answers to questions of faith. It is not surprising that Van Limborch was in correspondence with Ralph Cudworth as well as other Cambridge Platonists.[54] Van Limborch was also busy writing his *Theologia Christiania* (1686), which, in many ways, is similar to the central claims Locke would make later in his *RC*.[55] Years after their initial encounter, Van Limborch recalled that

> [Mr. Locke] introduced himself to me, and we afterwards had many conversations about religion, in which he acknowledged that he had long attributed to the Remonstrants doctrines very different from those which they held, and now that he understood what they really were, he was surprised to find how closely they agreed with many of his own opinions.[56]

By April of this same year, Locke was engrossed in reading Arminian and Remonstrant works uniting freedom and grace in contradistinction to the predestinarian Calvinist theology that was so antipathic to his own sensibilities.⁵⁷ At the end of July, Locke attended an Armenian worship service and noticed their open communion for all Christians and charitable attitude toward differing opinions.⁵⁸

On a later trip to France, Locke met a group of Huguenots, whose views of ecclesial primitivism and voluntary contract Locke found favorable.⁵⁹ A long career of interest in religious toleration followed, though never removed from a peculiarly Christian vision. As late as 1688, while living in the home of the liberal Quaker Benjamin Furly, Locke sought (and failed) to establish the "Society of Pacifick Christians," which sought to welcome members of contrary opinions, practice charity toward all, and hold Christ alone as "master," with the scriptures as the only "infallible" guide.⁶⁰

What this evidence suggests is that Locke did not simply receive religious training but actively sought to live out a genuinely religious life. His intellectual pursuits were never divorced from his theological interests, and his activities during the most formative years of his independent life bear the hallmark of a man seeking to unify social, political, and religious scruples, which collectively energized his soul.

## Locke's religious teaching (from 1689 to his posthumous writings)

As this book will show, Locke's principal writings—not only his distinctively religious works but his practical and political books as well—arise from and contribute to a theologically rooted central core. When Locke anonymously published his *Two Treatises* in 1690, he not only challenged Robert Filmer's religious foundation for the divine right of kings but, in the second book, sought to construct a new and better foundation that was every bit as religiously grounded as Filmer conceived of his own project.⁶¹ In the *LCT*, the English version of which was published anonymously the previous year, Locke is extremely clear on the importance of religious matters, not only for himself but for others, declaring "observance of these things is the highest Obligation that lies upon Mankind … Because there is nothing in this World that is of any consideration in comparison with Eternity."⁶²

A third work (published in 1689) did contain Locke's name in the byline and secured his fame. The *Essay* was released to both high acclaim and sharp criticism. It is true that some of Locke's epistemological reflections would challenge religious arguments in a variety of ways, including Locke's take on the doctrine of substance and innate ideas. However, in Book IV of the *Essay*,

Locke affirms that from God's existence we may infer necessary attributes as well as certain principles of morality, which flow from his nature,[63] and describes "faith" along with reason as two "way[s] of discovering truths to men."[64] Locke speaks of the authority and veracity of scripture in the loftiest terms, declaring that "everything said in the text [is] infallibly true,"[65] though humans are prone to error and disagreement in their interpretation of it.[66] Borrowing language from John Smith (whom Lady Masham suggested Locke read in 1683), Locke claims there are truths that are "above reason," incapable of being deduced, given through revelation—thus making revelation indispensable for those seeking to know and appropriate truth.[67]

In 1697, Locke penned *Of the Conduct of the Understanding*.[68] In this work, originally intended to serve as a new chapter in further editions of the *Essay*,[69] Locke lays out a clear vision of his high regard for theological matters, declaring "Theology" to be "one Science ... incomparably above all the rest" since it deals with man's "true end; i.e. the Honour and Veneration of the Creator, and the Happiness of Mankind."[70] In addition to explicit references (in his political works) to the importance of theological reflection and religious conviction, Locke also authored works devoted in its entirety to religious matters; these include the *RC* (1695) (along with vindications of the same) and the *Paraphrase* (published posthumously from 1705–1707).

As Locke neared the time of his death, his religious teaching increased and occurred in private as well as public. In 1703, Richard King asked Locke's advice concerning "the shortest and surest way for a young Gentleman to attain a true Knowledg of the Christian Religion" as well as morality.[71] Locke's answer is simply to study the "Holy Scripture," especially the New Testament, since the subject matter of this revelation from God concerns "Truth, without any mixture of Error."[72] In the same year, Locke offered similar advice when he dictated to Samuel Bold a short piece entitled "Some Thoughts Concerning Reading and Study for a Gentleman."[73] The sentiment was one which, according to his wishes, would shortly appear on his tombstone in 1704; instead of extoling Locke's virtues, the epitaph reads, in part: "an example of virtue, you have already in the Gospels."[74]

## Summary of Locke's Christian background

There are at least three important things that may be gleaned from Locke's religious biography. On the broadest level, Locke's upbringing, education, social climate, writings, and friendships took place within the "God-intoxicated" environment of the seventeenth century. This fact alone would caution any interpretation of Locke that renders him ignorant of or wholly indifferent to religious concerns. But more specifically, Locke extended his interest in religious matters throughout his life, and the evidence shows that Locke's religious sensitivity was coextensive with his political, social, and practical concerns. There is a "whole of life" quality to Locke's pursuits that would caution any interpretation of Locke that seeks to ferret out Locke's religious interests in a way that renders them tangential to or disconnected from his epistemology, moral philosophy, or political theory. Finally, Locke's religious interests do not simply "happen" to be Christian; they are deeply rooted in a particular conception of God and Creation that arises from a particular biblical perspective with an emphasis on the moral teachings and the example of Jesus in the gospels. Any true interpretation of Locke and his writings must move beyond Locke's "Christian heritage" to speak of Locke's theological motivation, theological claims, and theological construction of his moral and political theory.[75]

Locke is not alone in this endeavor. As I will seek to show below, Locke is not merely influenced by others but consciously joined in the shaping of a particular Christian view of the world that was known as Latitudinarianism in seventeenth-century England.

## Locke's moderating influences

### A theologically grounded teleology: Robert Boyle

Locke's scientific mentor, Robert Boyle,[76] believed investigative pursuits ought to seek out final causes rooted in the fact that nature has a teleology, given by God; recognition of this is not only one's duty (as an act of piety) but also necessary for truly understanding nature.[77] For Boyle, this led to a manifestly theological appreciation for creation,[78] and the greater degree of scrutiny (such as by the professional natural philosopher), the greater the perception that all nature is ascribed to God, and thus God is worthy of praise and adoration by creatures made for that very purpose.[79] Boyle recognizes the study of natural philosophy to be a moral requirement, since by this study one seeks to know God and comes to understand God's intentions.[80] Thus the pursuit of natural philosophy is, for Boyle, the "Philosophical Worship of God."[81]

But for Boyle, reflection on teleology accords with human flourishing, and thus philosophical investigation within a theological context not only leads to piety but to happiness. Boyle's description of the contemplative natural philosopher experiencing the greatest happiness is decidedly more Aristotelian than Locke's portrayal of the pursuit of happiness,[82] but Boyle anticipates Locke when he suggests that the desire for what is most pleasing naturally leads to revealed theology.[83] In a pregnant passage that bears striking similarity to Locke's own reasoning, Boyle writes the following:

> When we duly consider the very different ends to which many of God's particular works, especially those that are animated, seem design'd ... we cannot but think it highly probable, that so wise, and so bountiful a Being, has never left his noblest visible creature, man, unfurnished with means to procure his own welfare, and obtain his true end, ... And, since man is endow'd with reason, which may convince him ... that God is both his maker, and continual benefactor, ... since finding in his own mind a principle, which tells him, he owes a veneration ... to the divine author of his being, and his continual and munificent benefactor; ... and since, lastly, his reason may assure him, that his soul is immortal, and is therefore capable and desirous of being everlastingly happy, after it has left the body; he must in reason be strongly inclined to wish for a supernatural discovery of what God would have him believe and do. ... And thus the consideration of God's providence, in the conduct of things corporeal, may convey a well-disposed mind from natural to reveal'd religion.[84]

Carlin traces Boyle's reasoning in this passage in the following way: "natural philosophy leads one to knowledge of the divine, which in turn gives pleasure to the natural philosopher, and motivates ('strongly inclines') her to engage in revealed theology in order to learn how to secure eternal bliss."[85] Only by reaching the ultimate, final end of teleological investigation—namely, revealed theology—can a person come to know and value "Divine Truths" of "a much higher and nobler Order, and of an Inestimable and Eternal Advantage," including "the assiduous discovery of God and Divine Mysteries" in Heaven.[86] What is interesting is that, for Boyle, the awareness of God's purposes *naturally* leads one toward the actions necessary to achieve eternal happiness.[87] In other words, human happiness is part of the natural order of creation, which, in turn, depends on acquiring true knowledge of God and his attributes.[88]

In Boyle, Locke found a fellow virtuoso who borrowed from empiricist but also rationalist foundations, made systematic connections between philosophy, theology, science, and moral theory, and who recognized a theologically grounded teleological view of nature as fundamental for pursuing final ends in all relevant areas of study.[89]

## A broader ecclesiology: Richard Hooker, the Tew Circle, and the Latitudinarians

In addition to his theologically grounded teleology, Locke and his contextual partners formed a broad and generous ecclesiology. A number of influences converged in seventeenth-century England to bring about a theological outlook especially designed for those with a rationally oriented, tolerating spirit. Those following this stream of thought were opposed to dogmatism, offering within the Church of England (and Christendom at large) what Cranston describes as "the religion of the minimal creed."[90] Key terms to describe this group are *minimization* and *moderation*. Gilbert Burnet characterized those who would later be known as Latitudinarians in the following way:

> They wished that things might have been carried with more moderation. And they continued to keep a good correspondence with those who had differed from them in opinion, and allowed a great freedom both in philosophy and in divinity: from whence they were called men of latitude.[91]

This is not *all* they were called. Gilbert claims their moniker changed from "men of latitude" to the "Latitudinarians" only when "men of narrower thoughts and fiercer temper fastened [the label] upon them."[92] They sought a mediating position between traditionalists and Unitarians, which meant they were susceptible to serving as objects of suspicion from all sides. Those uncomfortable with such a mediating position called them Socinians, deists, or even atheists.[93] But the Latitudinarians rejected labels and the party spirit associated with them. Their aversion to dogmatism meant that one could not raise their ire against the logical conclusion of a particular line of thought since, as Cranston notes, "a particular of Latitudinarians was that they did *not* push things to their logical conclusion. They would not have thought of doing anything so immoderate."[94]

Since its inception, the Anglican Communion had been the proper place for this moderating spirit to flourish.[95] As Tetlow remarks, the Church of England had, for over a century, possessed a "hybrid nature," which "facilitated both flexibility and stability."[96] But a desire to keep a wide communion needed to be paired with a well-reasoned theological grounding for such toleration. The later Latitudinarian movement found this theological reasoning best expressed in the writings of Richard Hooker.

### *Richard Hooker: A case study*

According to Cranston, "one direct influence not in dispute" is Richard Hooker (1553–1600).[97] Locke was a huge admirer of Hooker, an Anglican divine who was a favorite of the Latitudinarians.[98] In fact, the entire Latitudinarian movement deeply embraced Hooker's memorable words, "Think ye are men, deem it not impossible for you to err."[99] Though not a political liberal himself, Hooker's theology provided an informed foundation for a political liberalism that valued tolerance precisely for theological reasons.[100]

In the late sixteenth century, a traditional Catholicism and a radically reforming Calvinism were pulling the Anglican Communion in opposite directions, though—as Insole notes—both offered a vision of "a unified church founded upon a systematic and comprehensive conception of the good."[101] In writing *Of the Laws of Ecclesiastical Polity*,[102] Hooker is perhaps one of the earliest defenders for a via media between Rome and Geneva.[103] The puritanical element in the Elizabethan church was manifesting itself among radical Presbyterians who desired to "purge the earth of all manner evil" by removing all Catholic remnants with the national church, reforming the doctrine and practices along perceived scriptural lines, and thus pave a clear path for "a new world afterward, wherein righteousness only should dwell."[104]

According to Insole, Hooker defines the root of the Puritan problem as twofold: (1) a failure to appreciate the limits of human wisdom and the weaknesses of our will, and (2) an improper tendency to conflate the visible and invisible church.[105] Just as there may be nominal church members who will not inherit the kingdom of God, there may be members of God's fold outside the recognition of the national church. Hooker views not only the church but also the entire world as a *corpus mixtum*, containing both good and bad elements, and thus impossible for humans to adjudicate the precise borders of the kingdom until Christ makes such judgments at the end of time.[106]

Hooker chides Puritanical self-righteous confidence when they rupture ties with other believers based on the naive assumption that a particular form of church government is clearly taught or condemned in scripture—"no church ever hav[ing] found out" what scripture taught on this subject, or "no church ever perceiving the word of God to be against" the type of government they despise.[107] On the other hand, Hooker also challenges a misplaced confidence in tradition as a given truth rather than a presupposed assumption. Hooker lists "our belief in the Trinity, the Coeternity of the Son of God with his Father, the proceeding of the Spirit from the Father and the Son, [and] the duty of baptizing infants" as just a few examples of teachings "in scripture nowhere to be found by express literal mention" but rather "deduced ... out of scripture" by a "collection" that, due to the limits of human wisdom, is not certain but "probably and conjecturally surmised."[108] Even teachings that are found directly expressed in scripture are only thought to be binding on humans if one presupposes "the sacred authority of Scripture."[109] Human beings are limited and frail, working with assumptions and lacking the clarity that can only come with divine perfection. In this light, Hooker advocates a humble reluctance to push one's own views to the breaking of fellowship, a humble acceptance of disagreement, and willingness to allow Christ, at the end of time, to render judgment on and set the borders of the kingdom.

Yet Hooker does not believe that all actions and decisions are thus relativized by differing presuppositions. For Hooker, there is a "law of reason or human nature" to which all humans are accountable, which can be known apart from divine revelation.[110] Simply "by the light of their natural understanding" all humans "evidently know, or at leastwise may know" this eternally binding law, which distinguishes virtue from vice, good from evil.[111] To illustrate his point, Hooker references the Golden Rule:

> Do as thou wouldest be done unto, *is a sentence which all nations under heaven are agreed upon. Refer this sentence to the love of God, and it extinguisheth all heinous crimes: refer it to the love of thy neighbour, and all grievous wrongs it banisheth out of the world.*[112]

From this beginning point, notes Insole, Hooker presents a theological rationale for government that not only is modeled after but actively participates in the governing actions of God.[113] For Hooker, when human beings come together to form societies, and they (individually or representatively) set up and yield themselves to imperfect but expedient human laws, they are in fact sharing in the divine self-limitation of God. Though God rules the world by an "eternal" law, He by "his wisdom hath stinted the effects of his power" in certain ways, such as in allowing human agency to play a role.[114] All laws are subject to the eternal law, but while natural laws "ordereth natural agents," the law of reason "bindeth creatures reasonable in this world," and divine law is known in no other way "but by special revelation from God," the act of governmental law-making (which Hooker calls "human law") involves a sense of delegation, where "out of the law either of reason or of God, men probably gathering to be expedient, they make it a law."[115]

Political authority, then, is from God but mediated through his reasonable creatures who, by societal consent, may invest it in Prince, Parliament, or whatever societal structure they deem appropriate.[116] The model, then, is not a hubristic societal seizing of God's authority for one's own prideful political ends but a gracious act of self-limitation, modeled after the divine.[117]

For Hooker, *consent* is a theological virtue and a necessary one for just government.[118] It need not matter whether a human law arises "by vow unto God" or by "contract with men"; if agreed upon by societal consent, the act of making and yielding submission to the law is a theologically rich act for creatures imaging God on earth.[119] Judging from Locke's own notes, it was this doctrine of consent that most attracted him to Hooker's thinking, yet the theological basis underpinning his notion of consent finds a home in Locke's writings as well.[120]

### The Great Tew Circle and the Latitudinarians

The road leading from Hooker's broadening theology to Latitudinarianism passes through Oxford. In the first half of the seventeenth century, Oxford was home to the "Great Tew Circle," a gathering of notable theologians such as John Hales (1584–1656), William Chillingworth (1602–1644), Jeremy Taylor (1613–1667), and Henry Hammond (1605–1660).[121] By the 1660s, Latitudinarianism was a recognized theological outlook in churches throughout England, where such men as Isaac Barrow (1630–1677), Gilbert Burnet (1643–1715), and Edward Fowler (1632–1714) called for the kind of generous spirit and wide ecclesiology found in the writings of those at Great Tew.[122] Locke was intimately familiar with these men and their writings, and I elsewhere trace these connections in finer detail.[123] Here, however, I would like to highlight four key areas where Locke's ecclesiological approach owes a considerable debt to this group and betrays remarkable agreement with its leading defenders.

First, Locke shares with Latitudinarians and those of Great Tew a great respect for religious toleration—for those outside the Anglican Communion as well as for those within it. In *Discourse of the Liberty of Prophesysing*, Jeremy Taylor makes an impassioned plea for nonviolent persuasion over any kind of religious coercion, detailing the horrid violence used in the pursuit of heresy.[124] In so doing, Taylor lays out an early case for toleration of religious diversity, a key theme of Locke's *LCT*.[125] In *The Religion of Protestants*, Chillingworth decries "the imputation of atheism and irreligion upon all wise and gallant ment that are not of your own religion," leading to "uncharitable and unchristian judgment" upon fellow believers with differing religious views.[126] In this, Chillingworth anticipated Locke's own language in the *Second Vindication*.[127] When Locke sought for words to pen in the *Second Treatise* to explain the kind of charity all humans owe one another in the circle of equality, he consciously or subconsciously echoed a sermon on peaceful coexistence by Isaac Barrow. Just consider the chart below:

| Isaac Barrow | Locke's 2nd T: 5–6 |
|---|---|
| Since "[w]e were all fashioned according to the same original idea, (resembling God our common Father,) | "For Men [are] all the Workmanship of one ... wise Maker ... |
| all endowed with the same faculties ... [w]e are obliged ... upon account of common equity ... | And being furnished with like Faculties, sharing in one Community of Nature, there cannot be ... *Subordination* among us ... as if we were made for one Anothers uses ... Every one ... is *bound to preserve himself*, and ... *to preserve the rest of Mankind*." (2nd T: 6) |
| [to] pay the same love, respect, aid, and comfort to others, which we expect from others."[128] | "This *equality* of Men ... Hooker ... makes it the Foundation of that Obligation to mutual Love amongst Men." (2nd T: 5) |

Second, Locke shared with this group the belief that proper religious toleration *within* the believing community involved distinguishing fundamentals from non-fundamentals of the faith. Taylor speaks of "the important distinction between fundamental and non-fundamental doctrines" as the only antidote to the immoderate spirit in which "every opinion is made an article of faith, every article is a ground of quarrel, every quarrel makes a faction, every faction is zealous and all zeal pretends for God."[129] Taylor offers up the familiar (though often misunderstood) minimal creed "that nothing is required to be believed by any Christian man but this, that Jesus is the Messiah"—a claim that will be echoed by Locke in the *RC*.[130] Chillingworth also wishes to distinguish issues over which Christians may disagree from "fundamentals," which are both "necessary" and "plain in Scripture."[131] Chillingworth does not offer a "catalogue of fundamentals" but instead speaks of repentance, belief in Scripture and the gospel, and a life lived in conforming obedience and refraining from sin—a view also advocated by Hammond.[132] Locke reveals his sympathies with this approach in his *Vindication of the Reasonableness of Christianity*.[133]

Third, both Great Tew and the later Latitudinarians of which Locke drew inspiration believed the tolerant spirit that distinguished essentials from nonessentials must make its final appeal to scripture itself. Taylor is explicit that only the New Testament can claim the right be the final arbiter for Christian faith. According to Taylor,

> If we have found out what foundation Christ and His apostles did lay, that is, what body and systems of articles simply necessary they taught and required of us to believe, we need not, we cannot go any further for foundation, we cannot enlarge that system or collection.[134]

"Scripture," writes Chillingworth, "is all true," and thus "it is sufficient for any man's salvation that he believe the Scripture" and endeavor to obey it. "He that does so," continues Chillingworth, "may be secure that he cannot err fundamentally. And they that do so cannot differ in fundamentals."[135]

Fourth, Locke shared with the leading lights of this association the view that belief in the scriptures must also be accompanied by a moral life. Such a view can be seen in Taylor and Chillingsworth as cited above but also in Gilbert Burnet who, like Locke, railed against the "faith alone" doctrine of the fideists.[136] Christianity is a moral religion, and the call for purity of life is at its core. Human sin, according to Burnet, was less an intellectual malady as it was a moral failure.[137]

In these four areas, among others, Locke reveals a kindred spirit to those advocating a broader ecclesiology within the widening stream of liberal Anglicanism housed at Great Tew and among the later Latitudinarians.

## A deeper philosophical theology: The Cambridge Platonists

Situated roughly between the early men of generosity at Great Tew and the later Latitudinarians was another influential group who Burnet describes as a "set of men at Cambridge" who "studied to assert and examine the principles of religion and morality on clear grounds, and in a philosophical method."[138] "All these," continues Burnet, "and those who were formed under them, studied to examine farther into the nature of things than had been done formerly."[139] This group included philosophically minded theologians and theologically motivated philosophers who became known as the Cambridge Platonists. Members such as Benjamin Whichcote (1609–1683), Ralph Cudworth (1617–1688), Nathaniel Culverwell (1619–1651), Damaris Cudworth Masham (1659–1708), and Henry More (1614–1687) sought a middle ground between "superstition on the one hand, and enthusiasm on the other" and supported a moderating inclusivism.[140] In this, they were similar to the train of thought discussed previously. According to Colie, the connection is even stronger:

> The tradition … of Richard Hooker, of rational theologians like Falkland, Chillingworth, and Hales worked on in England within the English Church,

temporarily in retirement during the Interregnum, to emerge with particular force among the Cambridge Platonists.[141]

Whereas the dominant force of Hooker, Great Tew, and Latitudinarian preaching upon Locke concerned personal piety, societal liberty, and ecclesial polity, the Cambridge Platonists brought to the table an interest in metaphysics, providing philosophical grounding for a moderating theology rooted in a rational justification of claims.[142] The elevation of human reason did not remove Divine truths but rather provided a mechanism for the proper use of natural theology to demonstrate God's existence, providential care, and moral guidance. From these truths, they claimed, one could also deduce hope for one's own immortality.[143] Scripture affirms, explains, and builds on these truths, but a person could recognize God, live in concert with God's will, and form the basis of a healthy society as a result of these truths derived by human reason. While sincere reflection would lead all people to some sort of natural moralistic religion, careful and sustained reasoning would ferret out improper religious action not in accordance with the nature of God deduced through natural theology. It is also true that human reasoning has its limits, leading us to seek and appreciate Divine revelation if and when reason determines something to *be* Divine revelation.[144]

Several authors—including myself—have detailed the biographical connections and conceptual links between Locke and the Cambridge Platonists.[145] What is often underappreciated, however, is how pervasive these links appear in the corpus of Locke's published works. In this section, I will list several of Locke's major works, noting in a summary fashion how strands of philosophical theology commonly associated with the Cambridge Platonists are either already present in Locke's thought or else influence and shape Locke's thinking and writing.

### *Essay concerning human understanding*

One of the first objections that might be raised with respect to any link between the Cambridge Platonists and Locke concerns the difference between the former's rationalism and the latter's supposed empiricism. But, as Wolterstorff suggests, "the center of gravity" in the *Essay* is not his discussion about the origin of ideas in Book II (which has long been "the traditional school-book interpretation of Locke") but his theory of entitled belief in Book IV.[146] As Wolterstorff remarks:

> The traditional neo-Hegelian interpretation of Locke as an empiricist is based on emphasizing Books I and II and all but ignoring Book IV. When Book IV is

given its due and intended weight, it becomes clear that Locke is one of the great rationalists of the Western philosophical tradition.[147]

It is in Book IV—"the center of gravity"—where Locke explicates the central role of Reason in relation to belief, and it is not a coincidence that the verbal and conceptual links with the Cambridge Platonists are most evident here.

Locke refers to reason as "the candle of the Lord," a quote from Proverbs 20:27, and a favorite designation among the Cambridge Platonists.[148] Throughout Book IV of the *Essay*, Locke speaks of reason as "the prime intellectual virtue" (*E*: 4.17.2: 668; 4.18.5: 692; 4.18.8: 694; 4.18.10: 696), which is also the position of Whichcote.[149] In a series of aphorisms, Whichcote spoke of reason as a religious endeavor:

> The *Rule* of Right is, the Reason of Things; the *Judgment* of Right is, the Reason of our Minds, *perceiving* the Reason of things … to go against Reason is to go against God … Reason *discovers*, what is Natural; and Reason *receives* what is Supernatural … Reason is not a shallow thing; it is the *first* Participation from God: therefore he, that observes Reason, observes God.[150]

The Cambridge school felt that while some truths may be "above reason," none are "against Reason."[151] When Locke began exchanging letters with Damaris Cudworth Masham in 1681, he was quite skeptical of any claims to divine knowledge that was "above reason," as if only a reference to some enthusiastic vision. However, over the next eight years, Damaris would pen several letters to Locke in defense of truths "above reason."[152] Defending the writings of Cambridge Platonist John Smith, Damaris claimed there was a via media between enthusiastic vision and pure natural reason where God could make himself known to those possessing "Puritie of Life."[153] Locke appears to have been persuaded, since Book IV of the *Essay* (which was published in 1689) speaks approvingly of "truths above reason" (*E*: 4.18.7: 694; 4.18.9: 695).

The problem of religious enthusiasm was a frequent topic among the Cambridge Platonists. Whichcote, for example, claimed "Enthusiasm is the Confounder, both of Reason and Religion: therefore nothing is more necessary to the Interest of *Religion*, than the prevention of *Enthusiasm*."[154] Locke's concern over enthusiasm led him to add a chapter entitled "Of Enthusiasm" to the fourth edition of the *Essay*, published in 1700 (*E*: 4.19: 697–706). In this chapter, Locke expressed reservation for the excesses of enthusiastic claims, comparing them to the opposite extreme seen in the excesses of atheistic claims (*E*: 4.19.12: 703). Interestingly, Henry More made the same analogy, claiming enthusiasm and atheism grew out of the same branch.[155]

In chapter 10 of Book IV, Locke sets out to demonstrate the existence of God, following an approach reminiscent of Ralph Cudworth.[156] Both are concerned with deriving a "true idea of God" and suggest that God's attributes are those that flow from Divine perfection—including goodness, wisdom, and power.[157] For both authors, God's existence is as demonstrable as a geometric theorem.[158] In defense of this claim, both offer a cosmological argument.[159]

## *The Second Treatise of Government*

Recall that Barrow's London sermon on peaceful coexistence uses similar language that would reappear in Locke's *Second Treatise*. But Barrow is not the only contemporary thinker whose ideas and language find a home in this work. Ralph Cudworth's deeply theological work provides not only a philosophical ground but also a conceptual schema for some crucial aspects of the *Second Treatise*. For example, Cudworth argues that the goodness of God leads him to rule by a rational, rather than arbitrary, will and accord freedom to his creatures.[160] In other words, God's wisdom and power cause him to act as justice demands, but all of this is to be understood through the lens of his goodness, whereby he acts and allows his creatures to act of their own free will.[161] As a result, Cudworth saw that humans individually, and governments collectively, can share in the divine life by taking part in what is just and good, while respecting the exercise of free will—as God allows "all rational creatures" to act with "self power."[162]

Locke acknowledges (in bare outline) what Cudworth defends with theological precision. In the *RC*, Locke notes that God's goodness is central to His nature (*RC*: 129), and, in the *Essay*, he combines the Godly attributes of wisdom, power, and goodness suggestively, perhaps in support of their interrelationship (*E*: 2.7.4: 129; 2.9.12: 148). In the opening section of the *Second Treatise*, Locke specifically combines love of neighbor (as a chief sign of goodness) with the kind of personal liberty and social tolerance demanded in a society that respects free will (*2nd T*: 4–6).[163] In this passage, it is not surprising that Locke invokes God to make his claim secure.

What Locke declares, Cudworth defends. "God and Nature create the state," writes Cudworth, in that "were there not a natural conciliation of all rational creatures, and subjection of them to the Deity, as their head," there could be no "superiority and subjection, with their respective duty and obligation."[164] When a government seeks to operate out of a system of justice, it will inevitably make laws, but a just society must assume obligation to the demands of justice (as a result of being creatures of a Deity) for any human laws to accord with nature and conscience. Something is not made just or morally obligatory by a will or command; instead, a just law is one that enforces what is already obligatory on account of the goodness of God and natural justice.[165] Like Locke, Cudworth thought that humans were social beings with a tendency to form themselves into communities. But this was not only because they belonged to "one community of nature" but because they were "rooted in the one divine mind."[166]

### *Reasonableness of Christianity*

Writers from Great Tew, the Cambridge school, and later Latitudinarian circles were suspicious and critical of "dogmatic" Calvinism.[167] Henry Hammond of Great Tew published his *Practical Catechism* in 1644, arguing that a covenantal relationship with God could better be expressed as a system of contractual duties and corresponding obligations rather than a sacramental gift bestowed only on the elect.[168] He followed this work with his *Pacific Discourse*, published in 1660, challenging the Calvinistic notions of irresistible grace and limited atonement.[169] Benjamin Whichcote of the Cambridge Platonists also spoke out against the doctrines of original sin and predestination.[170] Locke offered his own blistering critique of these same central Calvinistic claims in the *RC*.[171]

It was Ralph Cudworth, however, who not only shared Locke's concerns but offered a robust philosophical and theological platform for raising such concerns. For Cudworth, Calvinism's doctrine of predestination reduces God's nature to that of essential power; without goodness and wisdom to guide and direct, God's power is irrational, and God is "*Arbitrary Will Omnipotent*," rather than a holy being "*Bound or Obliged to the Best*."[172] That some are predestined to do evil, and to suffer the eternal end of evil, means that God's power is not directed by His goodness; yet power without goodness cannot last, nor can it serve as any standard for objective morality. On this score, there is no longer "good" or "evil," neither virtue nor vice, and humans do not bear the guilt of moral evil whose sole cause is God.[173]

Instead, writes Cudworth, we must conceive of God's essential nature as that of goodness and love. Through wisdom, God's power is offered in accord with His providential care, not some blind arbitrary will.[174] In the *RC*, Locke appears to rest the bulk of his ire against Calvinism on just this theological plank, noting God's providence (not just his power) as central to His nature and challenging Calvinism's rejection of God's rational wisdom and goodness.[175] Locke's belief that Christianity is a moral religion requires that God's actions accord with what wisdom and goodness would suggest, since all humans are called to emulate God in their moral lives.

One last strand connecting the Cambridge Platonists and the *RC* concerns the discerning of truths by reason or by revelation. Though a proponent of rational faith, John Smith taught that one should favor the "Truths of Divine Revelation" over the "less clear and legible" truths derived from reason alone.[176] Contrary to how Locke is often understood in contemporary scholarship, he seems to affirm this point in the *Essay* as well as the *RC*.[177]

## Other works (and other connections)

Ideas reminiscent of Great Tew, the Latitudinarians, and the Cambridge Platonists appear in virtually every main published work by Locke. Tillotson advocated miracles as the last word of defense to authenticate the teachings of the Bible, just as Locke argued in his *Discourse on Miracles*.[178] Both Whichcote and Cudworth speak of God's eternal law and the nature of obligation in ways that suggest a similar mind to the young Locke who wrote *Essays on the Law of Nature*.[179] Cudworth even receives positive mention in *Some Thoughts Concerning Education*, where Locke recommends, as a means to good education, reading Cudworth's approach to ancient philosophy.[180]

But a deeper connection may be found in fundamental ideas, which appear like a golden thread running throughout Locke's works. The emphasis on free will and liberty of conscience appears straightforwardly or in the background of Locke's theological, political, ethical, and philosophical works. That humanity owes to truth both mental assent and conformity of life is more than simply a religious perspective for Locke (in the sense of faith in accordance with moral living); the thought appears in his philosophical, political, and ethical writings as well.

To give one final example, consider the role of "happiness" in Locke's works.[181] In his theological, ethical, political, and philosophical works, Locke portrays happiness as one's ultimate end but understood as a reference to that perfect state of happiness in eternity.[182] All of life must be conformed in such a way as to achieve blessed happiness and avoid eternal misery at the hands of a just God. Yet before Locke penned these words, Cudworth also claimed that human happiness is defined teleologically and that seeking happiness means one should filter all of life through an eternal lens.[183] In his 1647 sermon before the House of Commons, Cudworth declared the following:

> But it is a piece of that corruption that runneth through humane nature, that we naturally prize truth, more than goodness; knowledge, more than holinesse. We think it a gallant thing to be fluttering up to heaven with our wings of knowledge and speculation, whereas the highest mystery of a divine life, and of perfect happinesse hereafter, consisteth in nothing but mere obedience to the divine will. Happinesse is nothing but that inward sweet delight, that will arise from the harmonious agreement between our wills and God's will.[184]

## Summary and conclusion

A study of Locke's biography, his published works, and his theological influences suggests that theology remained a central concern throughout his life. From his early youth, to the day he died, Locke imbibed a spirit of ecclesial liberty with philosophical grounding best represented among the Latitudinarians. The Latitudinarians were not always in agreement, and Locke differed with them at several points. But the ability to disagree *while in* fellowship is what attracted Locke to their moderating theology. The conclusions of this chapter suggest both intentional and unintentional—conscious and unconscious—overlap between Locke's central claims and areas of Latitudinarian concern. His connections are not coincidental but reveal a network of influence that helped shape Locke's political and philosophical reflections throughout his life.

This chapter has attempted to place Locke within the seventeenth-century Latitudinarian context wherein his theological planks, as well as his political aims, took shape. From his early youth, to the day he died, Locke imbibed a spirit and engaged in a network where theological discourse bled into philosophical and political aims. The moderating influences of Hooker, the Tew Circle, the Cambridge Platonists, and Locke's larger Latitudinarian environment provided theological grounds for Locke's own political ends. A high view of scripture, respect for religious toleration, and an expectation of morality are just the tip of the iceberg. In the chapters that follow, this book will detail Locke's three theological planks, including his emphasis on a "true" idea of God rooted in scriptural language, acknowledgment of a law of nature arising from his theology of Creation, and the necessity of revelation in forming a true understanding of God's will in religious terms. Locke's political ends are also linked to three theological concerns, including his aversion to atheism, hyper-Calvinism, and religious enthusiasm. All three of his theological planks, coupled with his three theological concerns, underpin his philosophical and political aims, such as human equality, religious toleration, individual liberty, just government, and the separation of church and state.

Part Two

# From a "Religious" to a "Theological" Turn: Tracing Locke's Theological Argumentation

4

# The God of Christianity and the Foundations of Morality

In the next chapter, I will set out Locke's doctrine of creation as a theological appropriation of natural law. Yet this approach to natural law necessarily presupposes several Christian doctrines, including the existence of God. Locke makes this point explicit in the fifth essay of his *Questions*:

> Even if God and the soul's immortality are not moral propositions and laws of nature (*leges naturae*), nevertheless they must be necessarily presupposed if natural law (*legis naturae*) is to exist. For there is no law without a law-maker, and law is to no purpose without punishment.[1]

However, Locke does not merely presuppose a first cause or some nebulous higher power with a penchant for punishment; he makes clear that his moral and political philosophy relies upon a "true Idea of God." "[He] that has a true Idea of God," writes Locke, "of himself as his creature or the relation he stands in to god and his fellow creatures and of Justice goodnesse law happynesse &c. is capable of knowing morall things or having a demonstrative certainty in them."[2] Locke's positing of God is far from incidental: the existence, nature, and attributes of the God described in scripture form the basis for Locke's theory of moral obligation, serve as the model for political governance, set the bounds for just and true ends, and provide the essential justification for punishment.

## Is Locke's God the Christian God?

But whether this "true Idea of God" is a Christian one has long been a hotbed of contention among scholars. Orthodox Christian theology, though monotheistic, understands God to refer to the Trinity—a term not found in the Christian scriptures but serving as shorthand for the claim that God is Father, Son, and

Spirit. One can conceive of the God of Christian tradition as the one whose attributes are enumerated in the first four ecumenical councils. On this account, Locke's description of God falls short. His apparently intended avoidance of Trinitarian language and refusal to borrow such from the creeds led to charges of Socinianism.[3] Though Locke borrows descriptions of God's essential attributes and character from the Bible (blending them with philosophical language derived from Hellenistic sources), it could be argued that reducing vocabulary about God to language found in scripture will not yield the robust depiction of God that results from the language of the councils (developed precisely because of competing descriptions of God put forth by advocates citing biblical language).[4] Despite these objections, I believe Locke's "true Idea of God" is, and was intended to be, broadly speaking, a Christian one.

## Understanding the prosecution's case

It is fairly common for Locke scholars to claim Locke is heterodox, especially in terms of his Christology and views on the Trinity.[5] In Locke's own day, Edward Stillingfleet (1635–1699) offered a series of blistering critiques of Locke on this score, garnering several fiery responses.[6] In his first book, the Bishop of Worcester argued that all Trinitarians are unified on three issues: (1) there are three distinct persons in the Godhead, (2) the unity of God is not impaired (since there are no separate or separable substances in God), and (3) divine essence is given to the Son from the Father and to the Holy Spirit from both.[7] According to Philip Dixon, Stillingfleet's book "broke new ground" in suggesting Lockean epistemology, with its confused discussion of what constitutes a "person" or a "substance," leads to trouble with Trinitarian claims, removing "key components in the traditional exposition of the mystery."[8] In his two follow-up works, Stillingfleet argues that even if Locke did not seek to wreak havoc on the doctrine of the Trinity, his epistemology aided and abetted those who do—making him both suspicious and accountable.[9]

For some, Locke's silence seems deafening. In all of his published works, including his replies to Stillingfleet and others, Locke appears "conspicuously silent" on the doctrine of the Trinity.[10] "While Locke protested that he never denied the doctrine of the Trinity," writes Wainwright, "he never took the trouble to affirm it."[11] Given that Locke seem willing to enter into other contentious debates, his silence is even more interesting.[12] Dixon lists several reasons why Locke would remain silent on his heterodox beliefs, including a concern for safety, given that Aikenhead hanged for blasphemy in 1697.[13]

But Locke's lack of affirmation may also be matched with implicit denials. There are four such examples usually cited. First, in the *RC*, Locke expresses distain for religious requirements, which include theological "niceties" learned in the academy.[14] Second, in his correspondence with Limborch, Locke includes his disgust for doctrines that speak of unity and plurality in a way that implies more than one all-powerful Being exists.[15] Third, in his final reply to Bishop Stillingfleet, Locke considers the following two propositions: (1) "there are three persons in one nature" and (2) "there are two natures in one person."[16] Locke then states, "I deny that these very propositions are in express words in my Bible."[17] Finally, in an unpublished notebook entitled "Adversaria Theologica," Locke lists several objections to the Trinity (and other matters), which, according to some scholars, were Locke's own Socinian thoughts.[18]

## A charitable defense

On the other side of the dispute, some Locke scholars challenge or outright deny that Locke was guilty of heresy in this regard.[19] Locke never explicitly denied either belief in the Trinity or the theological doctrine of the Trinity, alleged examples notwithstanding. For example, Locke's language decrying required religious "niceties" one learns in the academy contains very similar phrasing to a passage in *STCE*, which occurs, interestingly, right before Locke praises the Apostle's creed.[20] Locke goes on to recommend Dr. Worthington's catechism, "which has all its answers in the precise words of the scripture," as daily reading for children—but only after a child "can say the Lord's prayer, creed, and ten commandments by heart."[21] In response to the charge that Locke's arguments imply or lead to a denial of the Trinity, Catharine Cockburn argued that one cannot believe Locke's one article of faith—that Jesus is the Messiah, the Son of God whose miracles came by the Spirit's power—without ascribing to the implicit Trinitarian claims therein.[22]

Victor Nuovo has argued persuasively that the *Adversaria Theologica* is not a collection of Locke's own Socinian thoughts but rather notes taken predominately on Limborch's *Theologia Christiana*, which Locke received in 1794.[23] Locke would have resonated with the strong anti-Calvinism motivating Limborch's work, but a comparison of Locke's note-taking style suggests it is unwise to read into his notes any agreement with Limborch's challenge to Trinitarian doctrine or orthodox Christology.[24]

Lack of affirmation is not evidence of denial. It is difficult to arrange Locke's theological beliefs into an organized systematic account, which is as Locke would have it.[25] Locke was chiefly concerned with biblical language for Christian teaching, limiting required shibboleths (for acceptance of God's covenant of grace) to the one complex affirmation that Jesus is the Messiah and recognition of Christianity's moral challenge.[26] His Latitudinarian leanings can account for his great reluctance to requiring more than biblical language and claims, and his anti-Calvinism can explain his special interest in Limborch's work. But this does not lead to the conclusion that Locke was anti-Trinitarian or a thoroughgoing Socinian. "Locke's theological program is clearly not Athanasian," writes Nuovo, "but it is, with certain anomalies, arguably biblical."[27]

It is also unfair to accuse Locke of guilt by association, since he held acquaintances and friendships across the theological spectrum, recommending books that argued for a wide variety of beliefs. Some of Locke's readers even used Lockean language and epistemology to argue *for* Trinitarian doctrine.[28] The case against Locke as an anti-Trinitarian has some support but seems insufficient to firmly establish the charge against him.

## Locke on the offense? Constructing a possible affirmative case

It is one thing to say that the evidence for condemning Locke as an anti-Trinitarian is unconvincing. But it is quite another thing to affirm Locke as a Trinitarian advocate, operating out of a robust Christian doctrine of God. For the purposes of this book, I wish to affirm Locke has every intention to ground his theological commitments in the God described in scripture and would oppose the notion that any "true idea of God" could deny the biblical depiction of His nature or attributes. Using biblical language, Locke affirms the one God who is known in scripture as Father, Son, and Spirit.

First, Locke affirms the basic tenets of the Apostle's creed and all scriptural truths concerning God.[29] This means affirming "one God," as well as affirming the Father, Son, and Spirit. It means affirming that baptism is in the singular name of the Father, Son, and Spirit. It means affirming all the passages used in support of Trinitarian doctrine. In the absence of clear proof to the contrary, it would be fitting to assume that any Christian who affirms the Apostle's creed (which is structurally Trinitarian), and all scriptural truths concerning God, accepts in broad outline that affirming the Father, Son, and Spirit is to affirm the one God of Christian tradition.

Second, Locke denies any charge that he fails to believe in the Christian God. In his replies to Stillingfleet, Locke denies that in writing the *Essay* he was remotely interested in attacking or undermining the doctrine of the Trinity.

He even states that if his views on "person," "nature," and "substance" are incorrect, that would only mean he fails as a philosopher, not as an orthodox Christian.[30]

Third, Locke affirms his belief in mysterious Christian doctrines. Stillingfleet's concern about removing all mystery from the Christian religion was appropriately directed against John Toland (1670–1722), who claimed "we hold that Reason is the only Foundation of all Certitude," since "there is nothing in the Gospel contrary to Reason, or above it; and that no Christian Doctrine can properly be call'd a Mystery."[31] But this is just as certainly not a fair criticism of Locke, who both affirms truths "above reason" and affirms that revelation can and does provide truths that are not gleaned from reason alone.[32] Locke thinks faith includes a rational assent to what is intelligible and does not require an irrational assent. But suprarational truths are possible, and there is a difference between the sum total of what one believes and what one ought to be *required* to believe.

Not only was Locke a life-long member of the Church of England, he believed his depiction of God to be consistent with the one proclaimed from pulpits. His distaste for creeds is rooted in a deep concern, shared with Chillingworth, Hammond, Taylor, and Limborch, that "detailed doctrinal tests" are more divisive than unifying.[33] However, this distaste did not weaken his acceptance of truth proclaimed in creeds, as long as they were consistent with biblical claims. Locke chose to avoid the terminology resulting from theological discussions throughout church history in favor of New Testament language. "His aim," writes Wainwright, "was to explain the Christian message as it had been communicated by Jesus and the Apostles."[34] Locke's language, then, may be due to a sort of Biblicism rather than secret heresy.

In Joanne Tetlow's important work on Locke's theological context, the question whether Locke was Trinitarian served as "an underlying theme."[35] "Despite Locke's affinities with heterodox thinkers," concludes Tetlow, "I interpret Locke as Trinitarian in an unorthodox form, although he never affirmed this, and he took great pains to defend his writings as not undermining the doctrine of the Trinity."[36] I concur with her assessment.

In addition, Locke's political philosophy is self-conceived as a Christian project rooted in Latitudinarian theology, and, as such, he is compelled to speak of God's character (and political aims, which flow from his character) in ways consistent with that of Whichcote, Cudworth, and other explicitly Trinitarian thinkers. While Locke's Christology is a functional one, he accepts the full authority of Christ, his preexistence, resurrection and return, and affirms Jesus's authoritative teaching concerning the nature, character, will, and activity of God.[37] In this way, as Nuovo has argued elsewhere, Locke rightly belongs in the "Christian tradition," offering a "Christian philosophy."[38]

## Establishing the existence of God

### Argumentation, not assumption: Appreciating the "why"

Locke speaks of God's existence with the language of mathematical certainty: "Tis as certain that there is a God as that the opposite Angles, made by the intersection of two strait Lines, are equal. There was never any rational Creature, that set himself sincerely to examine the truth of these Propositions, that could fail to assent to them."[39] "That *there is an eternal, most powerful, and most knowing Being*" is a "certain and evident Truth";[40] indeed, "the most obvious Truth that Reason discovers ... and ... its Evidence [is] (if I mistake not) equal to mathematical Certainty."[41] That God existed from all eternity is "past doubt";[42] for any man to deny Him (and the duties assigned from Him) is to "boldly quarrel with their own Constitution."[43] There are few ideas, if any, "as ... agreeable to the common light of Reason, and naturally deducible from every part of our Knowledge, as that of a God is."[44] If anyone would just inquire into the constitution and causes of things, the mere inquiry "would easily lead him to the Notion of a God."[45] Yet for all this certitude, Locke is compelled to move beyond a mass appeal to general assumptions and to make a series of arguments in favor of God's existence.[46] These proofs leave something to be desired, and better arguments have been made (before and after Locke). But his proof is not as important as the fact that he believes God's existence is in need of defense. *Why* he feels compelled to make these arguments is more important than the quality of the arguments themselves.

Atheism (in the modern sense) was not an inconceivable threat in Locke's own lifetime; Smith, Cudworth, and More had each written treatises on the subject.[47] Yet Locke repeatedly expresses his disdain for scholastic disputes concerning basic maxims or ideas held in common by the bulk of mankind. Some might think it understandable were Locke to simply reference the obvious existence of God and thus the absurdity of atheism. But God, for Locke, is essential for his moral and political philosophy. The mere possibility of atheism is a threat to the entire system.

This is true for at least three central reasons, all of which will be further analyzed when explicating Locke's view of the nature of humanity as part of his doctrine of creation. First, Locke's definition of humanity includes possession of the kind of rationality that leads to an awareness of God. Locke conceives of mankind, generally speaking, as those beings "having the notion of God"[48] or at least the only kind of beings on earth possessing "light enough to lead them to a Knowledge of their Maker."[49] Second, Locke's theory of moral obligation is rooted in God's role as lawmaker. Knowledge of God brings with it "the influence that the discovery of such a Being must necessarily have on the Mind of all."[50] That "influence" is largely moral. Men have been fitted with faculties not only to acquire "Knowledge of their Maker" but also "the sight of their duties."[51] This emphasis on duties is key to appreciating the teleological aspect of man's nature, since "all things requisite to the end of such a Being" includes "attain[ing] the Knowledge of God, and other things that concern him," including moral duties.[52] Third, Locke's theory of moral behavior, which underpins his political theory, is itself rooted in the twin beliefs that God determines the standard by which "good/right" and "evil/wrong" are to be judged and the ground for governmental structures that provide reward and punishment in accordance with those judgments.

For Locke, God's existence cannot simply be assumed; it must be established. Whether considering the three reasons given above, or with reference to Locke's method for discovering natural law, his dependence on revelation, and his justification for belief in miracles, Locke's philosophy fundamentally depends on God's existence.[53] Our ability to believe things about God, ourselves, and the world around us that are incapable of demonstration is only plausible on the grounds of this assurance.[54]

## Locke's arguments for God's existence

In Book IV of the *Essay*, Locke offered a cosmological argument for the existence of God.[55] Locke intentionally laid out his argument in simple terms, both comprehensible and able to be followed by the common person.[56] However, Locke's cosmological argument has not fared well in the judgment of some prominent philosophers and historians.[57] The same can be said for his argument from the cause of mentality.[58] Even his appeal to the arbitrary and inscrutable actions of God has been appreciated within Locke's seventeenth-century context (given the theistic impulse involved in defending the new approach to atomism) but ultimately has been judged by most interpreters to be—in the words of McCann—"what seems to us a crippling defect in the theory."[59] The negative reaction concerns not only what Locke says but what he fails to say—or rather, what his arguments fail to support. His set of logical arguments lacks some classical options (such as the ontological argument) and traits such as the essential goodness of the "true God" Locke wishes to defend do not seem to naturally follow from those he does employ.[60]

There are five points worth making concerning Locke's arguments for the existence of God. First, critics of Locke have not always understood him properly. When Hume offered his famous critical evaluation of the causal principle (in just four pages), he incorrectly posited Locke as one of four interlocutors who (supposedly) set out to show the causal principle to be "demonstrably certain."[61] After responding to Hobbes and Clarke, Hume offers a third argument attributed to Locke—"Whatever is produced without any cause, is produced by *nothing*, or, in other words, has nothing for its cause" to which Hume adds, "but nothing can never be a cause." Hume does not offer a citation, and the two passages cited by later editors (E: 4.10.3: 620; 4.10.8: 622) do not set out to prove the causal principle.[62] But even if we allow that Hume recognized an underlying assumption, an implicit suggestion, or a necessary inference in Locke's argument, the recognition is, in fact, a misrepresentation. As Khamera has noted, Hume makes two crucial mistakes: first, he creates a "Lockean" argument to prove the causal principle, which Locke, in fact, does not make; second, he locates a fatal flaw in the argument based on the reification of "nothing" as a viable cause—which represents another move foreign to Locke's argument.[63]

As another example of misunderstanding, Zuckert once made the incredible claim that "it is Locke's view that reason is not in possession of ... rational knowledge of the existence of a revealing God."[64] Zuckert reasons the following way: to assume "that which cannot be conceived, cannot be" (attempting to summarize yet inexcusably butchering *E*: 4.10.10) contradicts Locke's larger strain of argument against determining the measure of things according to what "the narrow measure of our capacities" can comprehend.[65] However, rather than retreating (as Locke does) into a humble acceptance of things beyond our grasp, Zuckert paints Locke as irascibly moored to a logical minimalism. For Zuckert, "Since Locke lacks rational knowledge of a revealing God, Locke knows of no authentic revelation, including of course the Hebrew and Christian Scriptures."[66] This conclusion—wildly at odds with the whole tenor of Locke's philosophical and theological project—will be directly contradicted in Chapter 6 of this book.

Second, even if Locke's arguments fall short of philosophical proof, the general trajectory of his line of argument has strengths that later philosophers sought to retain, enhancing the case by supplementing better arguments in support of the same conclusion.[67] Third, Locke did not believe that simply positing a logical argument for the existence of a powerful deity did sufficient work to yield proof *in and of itself* for the Christian God.⁶⁸ In context, Locke's cosmological argument sets out to provide "certainty" that "there is an eternal, most powerful, and most knowing Being," and several other essential attributes may be delineated once his existence is established.⁶⁹ But, as I will argue in Chapter 6, Locke believed that divine revelation was essential for establishing the full identity, character, and will of God. Yet Locke held that reasonable reflection on what may be gleaned by philosophical analysis concerning God's existence and character was fully compatible with the truths revealed in scripture. Locke, at times, assumes biblical characteristics of God, which are not necessarily derived from his philosophical arguments. This move need not represent a philosophical flaw as much as establishing a necessary connection among two different arguments—(1) that the existence of a powerful deity may be established by a cosmological argument, and (2) revelation provides a true account of the this deity's character.

Fourth, as this book will show, Locke offers an implicitly *political* argument for the existence of God that is not fully appreciated. According to Locke, if one wishes to defend fundamental human dignity, liberty, and equality—or if one wishes to claim the legitimacy for making and executing laws within a hierarchical system, which allows punishment for oppressors or law violators in view of human dignity, liberty, and equality—one must first posit the existence of God.

Finally, there is a rhetorical element in Locke's exposition. Locke does believe in the God of Christianity (or, at least a God described in biblical terms), yet he deliberately uses the philosophical language of classical theism to appeal to a broader humanistic audience. Locke wishes to describe God in terms compatible with Plato. The fact that some of Locke's necessary descriptors—such as *creatio ex nihilo*—are not compatible with Plato only enhances the notion that Locke is wishing to present a particular understanding of God in language as broad as the facts will allow. Locke employs the language that suits his purposes, thus, in some ways, taking the debate out of the modern era.

## The "true" God: Locke's Christian conception of God

### God's biblical (and theologically satisfying) attributes: Good, personal and revealing

In the service of grounding his moral and political theory, how generic did Locke intend his "god" to be understood? When Locke's early Latin *Questions* were translated and published in 1954, von Leyden famously "helped" frame a "truly theistic conception" of Locke's work by constantly replacing *deus* with *Deus*, capitalizing personal pronouns, and translating the Roman superlative *Deum Optimum Maximum* ("God, Best and Greatest")—used in pagan worship to Jupiter—as "Almighty God."[70] Horwitz rightly chastised von Leyden for these moves, once noting rather humorously, "Locke corrected the amanuensis, and then von Leyden corrected Locke."[71] For Horwitz, whether Locke intended his references to designate the God of Christianity remains an open question, the answer of which he finds doubtful.[72] He is not alone in this assessment. Some Christian theologians, of persuasions at times both critical and sympathetic to Locke's general outlook, have recoiled at what is often assumed to be a deistic view of God.[73] For some authors, Locke seems to present a "calcified" rather than a "crucified" God.[74] There are certainly elements in Locke's writings that lend themselves to this picture, and the general tenor of Locke's project (with arguments for God based on reason alone, and attributes of God holding pride of place rather than His divine names) may indeed be found among non-Christian approaches to describing the prime mover.

However, the use of classicizing titles in Locke is deliberate and should not be offered as proof that Locke was a deist. Locke's conception of God is fundamentally Christian; in common with many great theologians of antiquity, including Aquinas, Locke shared the notion of a natural knowledge of God. In addition, Locke offers three clues that militate against the claim that he was a deist. First, Locke provides a description of God throughout his writings that explicitly delineates a version of deity rooted in biblical language and literature—so much so that this vision of God (even perceived through nature alone) cannot be far removed from a Christian conception. Second, Locke's founding principles for his political vision, articulated in the opening paragraphs of the *Second Treatise*, require a certain kind of deity that includes interactive providence, revelation, and mission that is rooted in Christian concepts. Third, Locke's political arguments throughout his writings include implicit (and, sometimes, explicit) Christian assumptions concerning the deity, which are integral to his case. The first two points will now be covered. The final point will be discussed in a later section.

In the *RC*, Locke acknowledges that there exist false notions of deity from which starting point flows improper thinking. One's "own sense" can (and does) "determine against the vain philosophy, and foolish metaphysics of some men."[75] In a number of places, he singles out polytheism and idolatry as examples intimating improper notions of God, leading to improper philosophical ethics.[76]

Polytheism fails to acknowledge the "one true God," while idolaters, by their "gross imagination," disregard the "invisible" nature of God, which is "not like to any visible objects nor represented by them."[77] A central tenet of proper reflection on deity is to acknowledge "but one eternal and invisible God, the maker of heaven and earth."[78] Without this distinct understanding, all people (including pious polytheists) are not only "in a state of darkness and errour" but are "without God in the world."[79]

This distinction between false notions of God and holding a "true Idea of God" is not a novel emphasis appearing only in Locke's explicitly Christian writings. On the contrary, Locke raises this issue in a number of places, including the *Essay*.[80] In his discussion of educating children, Locke insists on the primacy of instilling a "true" notion of God as the foundation of virtue, and in a private journal entry of 1781 Locke includes having a "true Idea of God" as a prerequisite for "knowing moral things or having a demonstrative certainty in them."[81] This would suggest that Locke should either provide a list of God's essential attributes (appealing to philosophy), invoke God's properly essential names (appealing to theology), or appeal to a method whereby one may deduce either of the two. Locke, in fact, attempts all three.

In the *RC*, Locke tells his readers that "the honour and attributes of that infinite Being"[82] are revealed in scripture but are consonant with reason and, thus, necessarily arise from reasoned reflection on God's nature.[83] Addressing matters of soteriology, Locke advises that "we must, therefore, examine and see what God requires us to believe now; for the belief of one invisible, eternal, omnipotent God, maker of heaven and earth, &c. was required before, as well as now."[84] The "&c." is an extremely important insertion; Locke is alluding to the fact that God's necessary attributes need not be clearly delineated since they flow from his nature. What is interesting to note is that Locke says virtually the same thing in the *Essay*, when he claims "all" essential attributes of God can be "easily deduced" from God as creator of all that is.[85] Locke's description of God's basic incommunicable attributes in the *RC*—in terms of supremacy, eternality, omnipotence, wisdom, and infinity—is consistent with his description of God in his political and philosophical writings.[86]

But Locke does not, and indeed cannot, stop with incommunicable attributes; the moral lawgiver must also possess necessary moral attributes, which speak to "the purity of his nature."[87] God possesses "justice" by which he deals "fairly" with his creatures.[88] God is able to render justice because he—and he alone— is the ultimate judge.[89] With righteousness, God will judge all men and offer eternal reward for some, eternal punishment for others.[90] Yet God's justice is not confined to the afterlife, and whatever circumstances faced in this life, or sentences meted out in the next, such justice is consistent with his "goodness," which includes his "bounty" or "bountiful" nature, expressed through kindness, compassion, tenderness, and mercy (including "tender mercies").[91] Locke also references God's "faithfulness,"[92] which, in concert with the aforementioned attributes, helps explain his "wonderful providence."[93]

Some of the most personal, Christian, and theologically rich reflection on the nature of God is found in passages where Locke emphasizes the way in which God acts toward and responds to humanity. The portrait of God expressed above reaches its culmination set against the needs and limitations of his creatures:

> The works of nature show his wisdom and power; but it is his peculiar care of mankind most eminently discovered in his promises to them, that shows his bounty and goodness; and consequently engages their hearts in love and affection to him. This oblation of an heart, fixed with dependence on, and affection to him, is the most acceptable tribute we can pay him, the foundation of true devotion, and life of all religion.[94]

God's beneficence is not only known by members of the Christian religion; His merciful kindness extends to all mankind:

> Yet God had, by the light of reason, revealed to all mankind, who would make use of that light, that he was good and merciful. The same spark of the divine nature and knowledge in man, which making him a man, showed him the law he was under, as a man; showed him also the way of atoning the merciful, kind, compassionate Author and Father of him and his being, when he had transgressed that law. He that made use of this candle of the Lord, so far as to find what was his duty, could not miss to find also the way to reconciliation and forgiveness, when he had failed of his duty.[95]

Such adoring praise language is not confined to Locke's explicitly religious works. The same language may be found in the *Essay* as well as *Thoughts*. Locke's God is one with knowledge of particulars—unlike the deity offered by Plato or Aristotle; he is one to engage in genuine relational devotion, who knows our weaknesses and responds as a "kind and merciful Father," "from whom we receive all our good," and "who loves us and gives us all things." As such, children should develop "a love and reverence of this Supreme Being ... and *pray* to him and *praise* him as the Author of his being and of all the good he does or can enjoy."[96] Locke's God is far from the cold, distant caricature often called the deistic God of the philosophers.[97] Locke's God is personal and revealing.[98] Locke is conflating what can be drawn from natural reason with descriptors drawn from revelation.

This only enhances the suspicion (defended in Chapter 6) that God's revelation of Himself (and "His business") in scripture is of signal importance to Locke.

## Maker of heaven and earth: *Creatio ex nihilo* and the nature of God

The doctrine of *creatio ex nihilo*, developing over a thousand-year period, is one shared by many in Jewish and Muslim as well as Christian traditions.[99] At its heart, *creatio ex nihilo* is a metaphysical claim that goes beyond cosmological theories about the origin of the universe; according to the doctrine, "all that is" radically depends "on God's free choice to create and sustain."[100] The implication for this doctrine is that God is clearly a God on whom everything depends. The teaching was rejected by Aristotle as nonsense and was not favored by Neoplatonists who preferred emanationism.[101] Yet, as Soskice notes, "*Creatio ex nihilo* has the odd distinction of being a *biblically compelled* piece of metaphysical theology."[102] Since the doctrine involves biblical language, identifying Locke's position concerning *creatio ex nihilo* would help to clarify his theistic inclinations, as well as further solidify Locke's theological perspective.

In an article criticizing Locke (in comparison with Aquinas), Soskice emphasizes that the heart of a Christian doctrine of creation is the radical freedom and autonomy of God manifested in *creatio ex nihilo*.[103] This signal element in Jewish and Christian writers is lacking in the stories of the prime mover provided by Hellenistic philosophy, for the language of a "first cause"—in the absence of space and time—is manifestly incoherent.[104] As David Sedley observes, the doctrine of *creatio ex nihilo* is not a product of Greek philosophy where the universally shared assumption was that even a divine maker would construct out of already-existing material.[105] The natural theology provided by the ancient Greeks, as Soskice suggests, furthermore does not deliver the personal, revealing God of Christian teaching. Locke, she suggests, wishes to align himself with Greek natural theology but seems to think by doing so he can derive the God of Christian scripture.[106] Soskice thinks that an attempt to derive a Greek-inspired natural theology divorced from revelation cannot fully yield the personal, revealing God of Christian tradition on whom all things radically depend.[107] Instead, in keeping with Aquinas, reason must be aided by revelation, which provides the proper naming of God (not just delineating his attributes) in ways that describe and define his free and personal nature. Soskice makes a compelling case for the essentiality of biblical language and a biblical schema for a Christian conception of God, especially concerning a doctrine of creation.

While Locke draws much of his language and conceptual schema from Hellenistic philosophy, his decidedly Christian vision of God compels him to accept both *creatio ex nihilo* and God's radical autonomy. In his sixth essay of *Questions*, Locke makes his belief in *creatio ex nihilo* emphatic and foundational:

> For, in the first place, since God is supreme over everything and has such authority and power over us as we cannot exercise over ourselves, and since we owe our body, soul, and life—whatever we are, whatever we have, and even whatever we can be—to Him and to Him alone, it is proper that we should live according to the precept of His will. God has created us out of nothing and, if He pleases, will reduce us again to nothing: we are, therefore, subject to Him in perfect justice and by utmost necessity.[108]

It is probably not a coincidence, as von Leyden points out, that Locke's language here mirrors that of Aquinas, who writes: "But all that man is, and can, and has, must be referred to God; and therefore every action of man, whether good or bad, acquires merit or demerit in the sight of God, as far as the action itself is concerned."[109] Locke reaffirms his belief in *creatio ex nihilo* in the *Essay*.[110] Locke differentiates between "makers" (such as humans) who produce from preexisting matter and God the "creator" who fashioned the universe from nothing.[111]

Thus, the doctrine of *creatio ex nihilo*, which speaks to creation's ontological dependence on God, is affirmed by Locke. Keith Ward has ably shown how this doctrine—which maintains an absolute distinction between Creator and creation—fundamentally separates thinkers in the line of Aquinas from those who, like Hegel, fuse God and world into one reality.[112] Locke undoubtedly follows the scholastic tradition in following the implications of this doctrine with respect to God's "otherness." In Locke's writings, God is described as one unlike anything else in the world (rather than the largest thing at the end of a cosmic chain). Locke wishes to distinguish the creator from the creation in drastic terms. While it's true that Locke does, at times, speak of infinity and eternity in terms of endless addition (most likely for illustrative purposes),[113] Locke places God alone in the category of "infinite" Beings and states "nothing finite bears any proportion to infinite."[114] In his formulation of the doctrine of substance, Locke says that to use "substance" in the same sense to speak of God and finite spirit would "be a very harsh doctrine."[115] God's necessarily perfect nature means he is "the first incomprehensible Being."[116] The reason God is incomprehensible is not simply a class distinction in which finite humanity runs out of room when adding thoughts concerning God. Rather, Locke has in mind a category distinction. God is not "like" humanity: "there being some proportion between mine and another man's understanding," writes Locke, "but none between mine and God's."[117] The difference between God and everything else is one of nature, not proportion.[118]

The doctrine of *creatio ex nihilo* carries other profound implications concerning the nature of God. McFarland builds a gradual case for "God's richness" implicit in the doctrine—beginning with God as transcendent, living, productive, present, and limitlessly free, carried through to reflection on the radical dependence of all creation upon God, which brings the notion of essential goodness front and center in McFarland's discussion of God's providence.[119] McFarland concludes that "the confession that God created … from nothing is at bottom a claim that it makes sense to trust God … More precisely, in teaching creation from nothing, Christians affirm that in all things God is acting for creatures' good."[120] McFarland admits that "there is nothing self-evident about this belief" but that the Christian may find within the doctrine itself the ground for holding "the conviction that no creature exists except as God gives it being: sustaining, empowering, and guiding it to the end that God intends for it."[121] "And if asked why God does this," he continues, "their answer must be clear: it is simply and solely because God sees every creature as good. There is no other reason, no other motive, no other factor in play. Nothing."[122]

These observations by McFarland provide insight into Locke's depiction of God's nature and character. Locke feels free to borrow a conceptual schema from the language and stories of scripture since the God described in such language and stories is consistent with the attributes that flow philosophically from the Christian doctrine of *creatio ex nihilo*. Locke's God is transcendent, living, productive, present, and limitlessly free. Since all of creation is radically dependent on God, any tales of thriving—success, opportunity, felicity—must originate in the good pleasure of the will of God. In addition, the very notion of transcendence leads to the transcendentals of unity, goodness, and truth.[123] This argument rooted in *creatio ex nihilo* militates against the claims that Locke's philosophy does not provide an account for God's goodness.

In fact, Locke's progression from *creatio ex nihilo* to God's goodness is deep in the Western tradition.[124] Aquinas, for example, begins with creation, and from reflection on creation flows aspects of perfection such as infinity, intellect, will, and personhood with respect to God but also love, joy, and liberality.[125] After all, creation itself is a free gift; thus the very act of creation implies goodness, providential care, and love. In similar style, Locke appears to believe that God's goodness necessarily follows from creation as one aspect of God's perfection; he hints at this in the *Essay*:

> We apply to that first and supreme Being, our *Idea* of Infinite ... to his Power, Wisdom, and Goodness ... I do not pretend to say how these Attributes are in GOD, who is infinitely beyond the reach of our narrow Capacities: They do, without doubt, contain in them all possible perfection.[126]

Although Locke's language here could sound like a kind of perfect being theology that collapses into a sort of Christian deism, when taken together with his other comments this quote is in keeping with the larger Christian tradition in its depiction of God. Locke offers *creatio ex nihilo* as a unifying doctrine, drawn from Christian theology, but capable of incorporating diverse viewpoints and open to dialogue across the religious spectrum.[127]

## Judge of the living and the dead: Possessing the power to reward and punish

When Locke declares that God's existence must be presupposed for natural law, he specifically refers to the necessity of punishment for any law to be effective.[128] The notion of final judgment, with pursuant reward or punishment in an afterlife, is directly related to "the great Ends of Morality and Religion" and is, for Locke, quite certain:

> All the great Ends of Morality and Religion, are well enough secured, without philosophical Proofs of the Soul's Immateriality; since it is evident, that he who made us at first begin to subsist here, sensible intelligent Beings, and for several years continued us in such a state, can and will restore us to the like state of Sensibility in another World, and make us capable there to receive the Retribution he has designed to Men, according to their doings in this Life.[129]

Locke's emphasis on a God who renders rewards and punishments appears across the Lockean corpus. In the *LCT*, Locke addresses concerns about true worship practice and doctrinal purity; "The Decision of that Question," writes Locke, "belongs only to the Supream Judge of all men, to whom also alone belongs the Punishment of the Erroneous."[130] God is "the Supreme Magistrate ... who will retribute unto every one at the last day according to his Deserts."[131] Elsewhere in his political writings, Locke reinforces his belief in God's role as supreme judge, reminding citizens locked in a legal dispute that the ultimate appellate court is not on earth but rather in heaven.[132]

Locke's philosophical and religious writings repeatedly reference eternal rewards and punishments meted out by the supreme judge of all men.[133] While this chapter will later show the direct connection between eternal rewards and Locke's moral and political philosophy, the prevalence of such references suggests that, for Locke, a God who holds such power to render everlasting judgments plays an important role in cultivating a "true" idea of God and in rendering a meaningful foundation for ethical obligations in his political philosophy.

It is interesting to note that Locke's arguments for the existence of God do not lead to a proof of an afterlife with rewards and punishments. Yet his assumption of an afterlife plays a central role in the development of his political philosophy. In a minor essay written in 1677, as well as in his later published writings, Locke reveals his belief that an afterlife was "probable" and that humans have sufficient reason to follow the dictates of reason that attach to this probability.[134] Whether Locke ultimately gathers his notion of the afterlife from reasonable reflection on the law of nature, or from revelation in scripture, it is clear that the notion of a God who will reward and punish in the afterlife is central to his "true" idea of God.

## The Christological connection

When one compares language concerning God shared across the range of Locke's works—religious, political, and philosophical—it is hard to imagine that Locke intends the "God" who grounds his moral and political theory to be anyone other than the God proclaimed in Christian scripture. On this account, Locke's Christology can serve to lend credibility to the larger argument of this chapter in identifying Locke's God.[135] What emerges from this discussion is that Locke smuggles into his depiction of God several Christian assumptions that one could not get outside of the Christian circle.

First, Locke presents Jesus as the final judge—a position Locke elsewhere ascribes to God alone.[136] God's name appears fifty-eight times in the *Second Treatise*, and "heaven" fourteen times. In this regard, Locke mentions on several occasions that, after making one's appeal to the highest judge in the land, one can make her ultimate "appeal to heaven," though such a person ought to make sure she has right on her side, since every person (including Locke himself) will one day answer to the "supreme judge of all men" on that great judgment day, knowing the judge will render to each according to what they have done.[137] Though the language employed here is reminiscent of St. Paul's discussion in Romans 2, Locke does not refer to Paul or Jesus, citing instead a number of passages from the Hebrew Bible, which make it clear that the "supreme judge of all men" is God himself.[138]

Interestingly, when Locke lists the various New Testament passages about a final judgment at the hands of Christ, he uses legal language to portray Christ as the chief magistrate. In the *RC*, it is Jesus who serves as king, sitting on his throne, giving laws to his subjects, and executing punishment for transgressors. Jesus has authority to reward and punish—not simply as a representative in a delegated role but rather as the inherently "righteous judge of all men."[139] Jesus is the "Lord" who declared that those "becoming his subjects" are to "live by his laws"; in this way Christ would "receive them as true denizens of the new Jerusalem." "What he expects from his followers," writes Locke, "he has sufficiently declared as a legislator." Those who are lost—"for what omissions and miscarriages he shall judge and condemn to death"—will, along with the righteous, witness the final judgment with Christ "sitting upon his great and glorious tribunal."[140]

Second, Locke alludes to Christological contexts when defining the nature of God, creation, and humanity in the cardinal passage of his *Second Treatise*. When Locke lays out the foundations of his theory of equality in paragraph six, he chooses his language carefully. He states not only that all humans are the workmanship of God (specified as "one omnipotent, and infinitely wise maker"), but that "all" are "the servants of one sovereign master, sent into the world by his order, and about his business; they are his property, whose workmanship they are."[141] The phrase "by his order" cannot simply appeal to natural instinct; it is a reference to positive law, probably (given his proclivity to quote from Genesis) enshrined in Genesis 1–2. But the phrase may also be related to the last line—"whose workmanship we are." Together, this would form a possible allusion to Ephesians 2:10, where St. Paul[142] states that "we are His workmanship, created in Christ Jesus for good works, which God prepared beforehand, in order that we might walk in them." Paul's language is deeply Christological. But when one considers the middle underlined phrase, "about his business," the Christological relation seems more evident. In Luke's gospel, the twelve-year-old Jesus, once found in the Temple, responds to his parents, "Wist ye not that I must be about my father's business?"[143] In this short section, Locke moves beyond Plato's description of God as the "maker and father of this universe" to establish the notion that God is the one portrayed in scripture as the personal Father proclaimed by Jesus.[144] These two points of interest do not settle Locke's Christological views as they pertain to a theology of the Trinity. What these points do clearly suggest, however, is that Locke's working model for "God" is the one the New Testament describes.

## Locke's moral, political, and legal need for God: Basis, model, and foundation

### God as the basis of moral behavior in view of a just society

Throughout his writings, Locke recognizes that appealing to habit and custom may work for the bulk of humankind, but those with higher rational faculties and a penchant for philosophical reflection will need a greater reason for behaving morally; to such persons Locke only and always offers reasons either grounded in or consistent with the nature and will of God.[145] Locke's emphasis on theological grounds for moral motivation is rooted in a larger theological account of moral behavior. In Book II of the *Essay*, Locke deals with the topic of moral relations, which he defines as conformity to the rule that judges one's voluntary actions.[146] Getting clear on the nature of moral relations is of paramount importance, and tracing both the precise nature of morality and the basis of moral motivation is clearly on Locke's mind.[147]

Locke offers a line that, at first, seems to imply some form of "hedonistic" philosophy: that good and bad are "nothing but" pleasure or pain.[148] But Locke quickly qualifies this statement. What is "Morally Good and evil" is determined by conformity not to one's personal sense of pleasure but "to some law." This conformity (or lack thereof) renders good or evil consequences resulting "from the will," "power," and "decree of the Law-maker," and this is called reward or punishment.[149]

What "law" does Locke have in mind? Moral concerns rise above civil law, so Locke considers two other types. "Divine" Law refers to "that supreme rule" of an "invisible Law-maker" who, by the light of nature or through revelation, "commands or forbids," thus declaring good and evil.[150] This law is foundational for moral behavior, and Locke connects it with God's nature and role as final judge.[151]

Locke also speaks of laws of opinion or reputation, meant to apply to virtues and vices. Locke acknowledges that a catalog of virtues or vices may differ from culture to culture, but when they refer to actions that "in their nature" are right and wrong, they refer to that which is "co-incident with the divine law."[152] Justice and truth are common bonds in society; even thieves acknowledge this in daily life or when they expect a fair hearing before the law.[153] Locke recounts a number of right or wrong actions "and a thousand other such Rules" that all humans seem to recognize.[154] In fact, in most places the accepted virtues and vices correspond with the unchangeable Rule of Right and Wrong, which the law of God hath established—there being nothing that so secures the good of mankind as conforming to God's laws as he set them, and nothing leads to mischief and confusion as the neglect of them.[155]

There is great power in public persuasion, and positive peer pressure can help to form good behavior. Humans seldom reflect on the penalties that result from forsaking the law of God, but they will consider changing their behavior if it will affect their reputation.[156] However, Locke is not interested in what is communally acceptable as much as he is interested in the "Truth in Morality."[157] Locke finds this truth in the prescribed will of God. Locke defines virtue as "actions conformable to God's Will, or to the Rule prescribed by God, which is the true and only measure of Vertue, when Vertue is used to signifie what is in its own nature right and good."[158] For this reason, moral good and evil cannot simply be the resulting effects of pleasure or pain; there exists "true intrinsick good or ill that is in things."[159] But this can only be if things get their intrinsic value from their creator. Thus, "truth in morality" depends upon the existence of God:

> Our own Being furnishes us … with an evident, and incontestable proof of a Deity; And I believe no Body can avoid the Cogency of it … Yet this being so fundamental a Truth, and of that Consequence, that all Religion and genuine Morality depend thereon.[160]

When one reflects on Locke's treatment of moral relations in the *Essay*, along with how he sketches out a portrait of a just society in his political writings, it becomes clear that not just any god will do the work for Locke's political theory. Locke envisions a society in which such virtues as charity, love, bounty, liberality, promise keeping, and goodwill are held as sacrosanct fundamental principles of morality, rooted in the nature and will of the Creator.[161] But this means the very nature of moral behavior meant to define a just society is directly related to the nature of God.

In the *LCT*, Locke recognizes that the Magistrate ought not to punish individuals for private sins that transgress the heart of God (listing such things as "Covetousness, Uncharitableness, and Idleness").[162] But Locke does allow the Magistrate to wrest control from those who are "arrogant, ungovernable, and injurious to their Brethren."[163] Thus, when Locke offers his description of the kind of citizens whose moral behavior expresses the ends of a just society, he is not afraid to enforce executive punishment in order to protect societal interests.[164]

Locke shows throughout the *Second Treatise* that this assumed list of virtues and vices is in accordance with the nature and will of God. Locke adds to the list given in the *LCT*, including "uprightness and wisdom."[165] The truth in morality expresses itself in the body politic through how one treats their neighbor. Locke specifically cites the Golden Rule ("do unto others as you would have them do unto you"), but the basis of true moral behavior is deeper: it is based on love of neighbor. Society must not condone acts of dishonesty or indifference rooted in a man's "love of himself" but promote actions, which "be from a true love of mankind and society, and such charity as we owe all one to another."[166] It is "vain ambition" and "evil concupiscence" that ruins the real meaning of power and honor.[167] In truth, rulers are to act "with affection and love to those under" their control.[168]

In short, Locke traces the outline of a just society through citizens acting rightly, but the moral character of good citizens is defined by the notion of virtue and vice rooted in the nature and will of God. Locke's political philosophy does not operate outside of these parameters. Remove the creator God whose nature is consistent with Christian teaching, and the "truth in morality" will find no leg on which to stand.

## God as the basis of obligation

Throughout Locke's writings, he argues that in order for there to exist an obligation to obey any law, there must necessarily be a lawmaker with the ability to render rewards and punishments. This applies to positive laws within a commonwealth but also the law of nature within the state of nature. For example, in the sixth essay of *Questions*, Locke seeks to provide grounding for human obligation in the light of this law of nature. Locke first establishes that there is, indeed, a law of nature, but Locke makes it clear that the "law of nature" is the express divine will of God (to rule the moral life) made known by the principles of nature:

> For we are bound to something for the very reason that he, under whose rule [*ditione*][169] we are, wills it. That thing binds "terminatively," or by delimitation, which prescribes the manner and measure of an obligation and of our duty and is nothing other than the declaration of that will, and this declaration by another name we call law. We are indeed bound by Almighty God [*a Deo enim optimo maximo obligamur*][170] because He wills, but the declaration of His will delimits the obligation and the ground of our obedience; for we are not bound to anything except what a law-maker in some way has made known and proclaimed as his will.[171]

"The divine will" is binding, and "it can be known by the light of nature, in which case it is that law of nature (*lex naturae*) which we are discussing," or it can be known by positive divine law.[172]

Locke explains whence the obligation to obey natural law arises: (1) we have a liability to pay dutiful obedience to the creator and supreme lawmaker who (a) created us, and (b) gave us his will to follow; in addition, (2) we have a liability to punishment when we fail to pay dutiful obedience in this regard.[173]

This necessary connection of legal and moral obligation to the creator, lawgiver, and final judge is a staple of Locke's philosophy, as one can see in the *Essay*. It is a universal and certain conclusion, writes Locke, that if any one person exists, they are under obligation to fear and obey God.[174] But the reasons given for this moral duty form the basic elements of his entire moral theory. Locke writes, "But what Duty is, cannot be understood without a Law; nor a Law be known, or supposed without a Law-maker, or without Reward and Punishment."[175] Indeed, "without a Notion of a Law-maker, it is impossible to have a Notion of a Law, and an Obligation to observe it."[176] As a simple summary, Locke lists "the Ideas of God, of Law, of Obligation, of Punishment, [and] of a Life after this" as the basic elements of his moral theory.[177]

Locke continues this theme in his political works. Rulers may find exemption from laws within their own territories, "but this I am sure, they owe subjection to the laws of God and nature" for "no body, no power, can exempt them from the obligations of that eternal law."[178] The law of nature retains its obligations whether in the state of nature or in civil society precisely because it is "the will of God."[179] God as creator and lawmaker is marshalled forth as the basis for parental obligation to care for their children and a child's "perpetual obligation" to honor parents.[180] It is precisely because of God's role that "no state … can absolve children" of their eternal duty.[181] In fact the basic drive to enter society (and the concomitant sense of obligation) is related to God as creator: "God having made man such a creature, that in his own judgment, it was not good for him to be alone, put him under strong obligations of necessity, convenience, and inclination to drive him into society."[182] Locke even speaks of the obligation humans have toward one another—to do no harm, to love, and to respect self-preservation—as resulting from God's role as creator and lawmaker.[183]

Locke's religious writings make the same point. The moral law (also known as the law of nature) refers to the dictates of the Creator and lawgiver; thus the law is of "eternal obligation" to everyone, always and everywhere the same.[184] The very nature of God (and via creation, the very nature of humanity in God's image) is central to Locke's case for moral obligation:

It is impossible that he should justify those who had no regard to justice at all whatever they believed. This would have been to encourage iniquity, contrary to the purity of his nature; and to have condemned that eternal law of right, which is holy, just, and good: of which no one precept or rule is abrogated or repealed; nor indeed can be, whilst God is an holy, just, and righteous God and man a rational creature. The duties of that law, arising from the constitution of his very nature, are of eternal obligation; nor can it be taken away or dispensed with, without changing the nature of things, overturning the measures of right and wrong, and thereby introducing and authorizing irregularity, confusion, and disorder in the world ... This is the law of that kingdom, as well as of all mankind; and that law, by which all men shall be judged at the last day.[185]

Locke acknowledges that philosophers have long articulated the need for moral behavior; however, they often spoke of right reason "without making out its obligation from the true principles of the law of nature, and foundations of morality."[186] These "true principles" arising from the "foundations of morality" can only come from a believable authority—which Locke unequivocally claims to be the God who is creator, lawmaker, and final judge who rewards and punishes.[187] It becomes clear that, without the notion of God, Locke is without a moral foundation for insisting that humans "are under Obligations antecedent to all humane Constitutions."[188] God the Creator, lawmaker, and final judge is essential to providing a foundation of authority for moral obligation. Remove God, and Locke's theory has no obligatory force.

## God as the model for legal punishment

When a new edition of the *Two Treatises* appeared shortly after Locke's death, it contained the following epigraph, borrowed from Livy, but chosen by Locke himself: "But if the weak are left no civil rights to protect them from the mighty, nevertheless I will seek protection from the Gods, who punish human pride."[189] For Locke, a truly ethical political system that involves enforcing laws and offering judgment under the threat of punishment must be modeled on the notion of an ultimate court with ultimate punishment for moral wrongdoing— and, in fact, makes no sense without it. Locke speaks often of the final judgment by the "Supreme" or "righteous" "judge of all men" who, at the end of time, will render judgment for the deeds done in this life—eternal reward for some but also eternal punishment for others.[190] These references do not simply appear in soteriological discussions but also with reference to matters of justice in which heaven is portrayed as the highest court and God as the appellate Judge.[191]

Whether a dispute should arise between two persons in the state of nature, or a subject should believe the judgment of the highest magistrate on earth to be unjust, when no "appeal on earth" is available, Locke reminds his readers of their right to "appeal to heaven."[192] In view of the gravity of making one's appeal before the judgment seat of God, Locke adds an unusually strong warning that one should count the cost:

> He that appeals to heaven must be sure he has right on his side; and a right too that is worth the trouble and cost of the appeal, as he will answer at a tribunal that cannot be deceived, and will be sure to retribute to every one according to the mischiefs he hath created to his fellow subjects; that is, any part of mankind.[193]

Locke's constant reference to final judgment—with rewards and punishments—serves a greater role than simply one of motivation with rhetorical flair.[194] For Locke, the entire legal structure of appeals, judgments, and executive punishments is rooted in this larger view. In the *Second Treatise*, Locke begins by recognizing one's natural right to life and liberty to such a degree that one "may not, unless it be to do justice on an offender, take away, or impair the life, or what tends to the preservation of the life, the liberty, health, limb, or goods of another."[195] The execution of punishment deprives a person of these very things. Yet Locke considers it to be "the law of nature" that in seeking to "do justice" "every man hath a right to punish the offender, and to be executioner of the law of nature."[196]

How does one balance these two truths—that human life and liberty are sacrosanct, yet everyone has the right to deprive another of these very things for the sake of "justice"? Locke hints at the answer as he seeks to lay down constraints. Punishment is not to be an act of selfish retribution but rather an action in the interest of justice "so far as calm reason and conscience dictate."[197] Locke appears to think that human liberty is constrained by a higher common rule that makes society possible; this higher principle carries an intuitive sense that justice requires punishment.[198]

Yet Locke must make several moves to establish the legitimacy of political acts of punishment. He declares that the right to punishment must of necessity be a law of nature; otherwise, "I see not how the magistrates of any community can punish an alien of another country" outside their jurisdiction.[199] In addition, this law of nature that gives the right to punish as an act of restraint also allows the right to punish an offender for the sake of reparation with regard to the offended party.[200] This is an appeal to the nature of justice, which, once again, rises above any personal vendetta.[201] The magistrate has the right to punish, if the public good necessitates, and can remit punishment of crime, but he is not allowed to indulge the satisfaction of the injured party.[202] Whether in the state of nature or within the structure of a commonwealth, punishments are only to be in accord with those things, "which are certain by reason," and the "laws of municipal laws of countries are right onlysofar as founded on the law of nature, and by it are to be regulated and interpreted."[203]

In the interest of preserving communal peace, we enter into society and "wholly give up" the power to punish others—deferring to the rule of law.[204] If the judgment of the magistrate seems unlawful, one may make an appeal to the highest court of the land; if such is not available, "there is nothing left but patience" as one awaits the judgment of God.[205] This approach by Locke suggests that the "law of nature" with regard to right punishment in accord with justice requires the larger framework that political society is modeled after the judgment of God. The magistrate is not the highest court available, and his judgment is not the final arbiter; punishment is to be evaluated in the light of justice as will be executed in the final judgment. Locke makes this connection clear in the *LCT*. When there is a dispute between a magistrate and his subjects concerning what constitutes a public good, writes Locke,

> Who shall be Judge between them? I answer, God alone. For there is no Judge upon earth between the Supreme Magistrate and the People. God, I say, is the only Judge in this case, who will retribute unto every one at the last day according to his Deserts; that is, according to his sincerity and uprightness in endeavouring to promote Piety, and the publick Weal and Peace of Mankind.[206]

In fact, it is only within the larger context of God as creator and humans operating under his direction that the idea of humans bringing punishment upon one another can be declared a "law of nature." For Locke, there is "nothing more evident" that a state of equality exists among all people—"without subordination or subjection"—

> unless the lord and master of them all should, by any manifest declaration of his will, set one above another, and confer on him, by an evident and clear appointment, an undoubted right to dominion and sovereignty ... for men being all the workmanship of one, omnipotent, and infinitely wise maker; all the servants of one sovereign master, sent into the world by his order, and about his business; they are his property, whose workmanship they are, made to last during his, not one another's pleasure: and being furnished with like faculties, sharing all in one community of nature ... cannot be supposed ... as if we were made for one another's uses, as the inferior ranks of creatures are for ours.[207]

Though Locke speaks of those "transgressing the law of nature" whereby one "declares himself to live by another rule than that of reason and common equity," his appeal to natural right to deprive an equal party (who is "without subordination or subjection") of life, liberty, or property is hollow without his direct religious appeal. Locke gives a clear grounding and model whereby government may recognize the right to govern, subject, and punish others. Without this model, the argument falls flat. Why does Locke repeatedly speak of an accuser's ultimate right for an appeal to heaven? Because the entire foundation for the justice system operates according to heaven's dictates and is only in accordance with "the law of nature" if the justice meted out on earth is approved in heaven. In this way, Locke's political case for issuing rewards and punishments is modeled after the authority of God. Without an ultimate lawmaker with the power to render rewards and punishment, Locke has nothing to which he can appeal to legitimate the rendering of punishment (against a person's will) by any power structure.

## The eschatological judgment of Christ and the right to revolution

One final area of consideration involves the relationship between the future judgment by Christ and Locke's philosophical basis for any right to revolution. In the final chapters of the *Second Treatise*, Locke discusses the problem of tyrannical rule and the right for citizens to rise up in revolution to dissolve a government in cases where such action would prevent or end tyranny.[208] But Locke does not simply opine that revolution may be a good idea; he asserts a fundamental right—even an obligation—to enact revolution:

> *Whenever the Legislators endeavor to take away, and destroy the Property of the People*, or to reduce them to Slavery under Arbitrary Power, they put themselves into a state of War with the People, who are thereupon absolved from any farther Obedience, and are left to the common Refuge, which God hath provided for all Men, against Force and Violence. Whensoever therefore the *Legislative* shall transgress this fundamental Rule of Society; and either by Ambition, Fear, Folly or Corruption, *endeavor to grasp* themselves, *or put into the hands of any other an Absolute Power* over the Lives, Liberties, and Estates of the People; By this breach of Trust *they forfeit the Power*, the People had put into their hands, for quite contrary ends, and it devolves to the People, who have a Right to resume their original Liberty.[209]

But what gives any community of citizens the right to rebel against tyrants? The answer is not found in anarchy, as if there simply is no judge to adjudicate. Locke argues on precisely the opposite grounds: when arbitrary power and tyrannical rule have so removed a government from its God-given purpose, it falls to the citizenry to act in anticipation of the coming judge, Jesus Christ. This is the import of Locke's "appeal to heaven" language, which appears, interestingly, in this context of revolution.[210] Earlier I argued that this "appeal" to heaven refers to the future judgment of God; I also suggested that the future judge of God is a reference to the eschatological judgment of Christ at his return. Greg Forster made the important connection between Locke's justification for rebellion and God's judgment after death. But here I wish to make an equally important connection: the justification for rebellion is rooted in an expectation of the return of Christ. If there were no judge between people, there could be no non-arbitrary right to rebellion; likewise, if there was a present way to adjudicate ultimate judgment, there could be no right to mass rebellion. In order for the logic of Locke's argument to work, the right to rebellion must include two beliefs: (1) there is a judge of all people, and (2) that judge is not a human magistrate executing judgment on earth at present but rather is the righteous judge of all who will execute judgment when He returns. That future judge, according to Locke, is Jesus Christ. This means Locke's argument is more than theistic and ethical; it is Christocentric and eschatological.[211] Citizens have the right to rebel, precisely because they have the obligation to hold a government or to act in ways against that government that will garner approval by Christ upon his return.

## Summary and conclusion

"God," for Locke, is no simplistic deistic conception of a remote generator; Locke's God is the personal, revealing God of Christian tradition. Though always seeking the broadest and most inclusive representation of God (as found in the classical tradition), Locke is moved—by force or by intent—to outline divine characteristics that cannot admit all candidates. Believing the same God who reveals himself in nature also appears in both testaments, Locke clearly has in mind (throughout his writings) the God Christians worship, described in expressly biblical terms. His writing is not explicitly Trinitarian, and Jesus is presented in terms of a functional Christology (where the main emphasis is on Jesus as the moral exemplar for humanity). However, Jesus's authority is without question, his life serves as the model for what it means to be "about His [God's] business" in the world, everything said about him in scripture is true, and he will serve as the "righteous Judge" at the end of time. Locke is not seeking to provide an essay in the divine nature and only records what he considers necessary to make a general case for a broad audience. Taken as a whole, it is hard to see how any other "god" than the self-revealing God of Christian scripture could be the one Locke has in mind, serving to ground his moral and political theory. Locke works under the assumptions of a Christian narrative, one that includes positive obligations from God, codified in scripture, carried out by humans according to the example of Christ, in the light of a final judgment, and with respect to God's sovereign Lordship. Within this framework, Locke is able to offer a coherent moral foundation for his political theory.

This chapter, then, provides the first plank in Locke's theological platform upon which his political theory rests. Locke establishes the existence of God as the basis for any standard of virtue, sense of obligation, and right for political structure, including laws and punishments. Like others in his Latitudinarian orbit, Locke saw the danger of avowed atheism, but his concern was both practical and political: an explicit denial of God's existence was more than irrational; it would remove any foundation for moral obligation. Locke could find room to tolerate ignorance of God's claims, but there could be no toleration for the willful rejection of God himself. A just society begins with recognition of the image-bearing nature of humanity, and personal morality is rooted in God's claims, aims toward true happiness, and must be connected to a proper teleology. Only a "true" idea of God can adequately account for both a just society and the ground for personal morality. If one removes Locke's conception of God from his moral and political theory, it is difficult to see how that theory can hold together. God serves as the linchpin for Locke's political philosophy.

5

# Natural Law, the Law of Nature, and a Theology of Creation

In the previous chapter, this book argued that Locke posits the existence of God as a foundational and necessary component of his moral and political philosophy. In the cardinal passage of his *Second Treatise*, Locke relies on convictions about God the creator in delineating his anthropology, that is, the nature of humanity, our relationships between one another, and our teleological purpose within a theologically rich view of creation. The basic tenet of Locke's political philosophy is that human beings are "all equal and independent," share in "one community of nature," and have dominion over "the inferior creatures," due to explicitly theological reasons:

> For Men being all the Workmanship of one Omnipotent, and infinitely wise Maker; All the Servants of one Sovereign Master, sent into the World by his order and about his business, they are his Property, whose Workmanship they are, made to last during his, not one anothers Pleasure.[1]

Locke bases his view of human equality not only in the mere formal truth that human beings are born "of the same species and rank" and thus reasonably obligated to one another (in a modern humanitarian sense) but in the claim that humans were created by God, given a particular role in the world, and are morally obligated to Him. Humans, subservient to God's will, are deemed equal "by Nature"—a term referring to the will and action of the creator—not "what is natural" in a modern sense. As a result, human equality is a governing "Law of Nature."[2] This opening theological salvo to a work on political theory intimates that Locke is sketching the bare outline of an approach to natural law, which, in turn, serves as part of a larger theology of creation.

However, this point is often overlooked by those whose interest in Locke is purely political.[3] In an introductory chapter to his influential edition of the *Two Treatises*, Laslett offers an anemic reading of Locke's language. Laslett grants that

Locke was offering what seemed to him to be a "proposition of common sense,"[4] but in the present age one need not take Locke's language seriously to reach the desired effect:

> It is an existentialist proposition, which men have not thought it worth while to question seriously until our own day, and it relies not so much on the proved existence of a Deity as upon the possibility of taking what might be called a synoptic view of the world, more vulgarly a God's-eye view of what happens among men here on earth. If you admit that it is possible to look down on men from above, then you may be said to grant to Locke this initial position.[5]

There are three great problems with Laslett's claim, the first two of which have already been addressed in the previous chapter. First, Locke's position very much does rely on "the proved existence of a Deity" and a particularly Christianized version of one. Second, only a deity (and, possibly, only the kind of deity Locke describes) can provide the kind of explanatory function that grounds moral obligation and sets the agenda for legitimate government on behalf of "the good." But the third great problem with Laslett's revaluation of Locke is that simply taking a "God's-eye view" of human action will not bear out the serious implications of why and how creation is intended to function. Laslett's approach erases teleology, substitutes description for prescription, and fuses two horizons (God's vs. the world's) in a way that only confounds rather than clarifies Locke's central point. By failing to fully appreciate Locke's positing of a deity, Laslett is unable to recognize the development of Locke's theological view of creation, with all its deep implications for Locke's political theory.

## Locke, the Christian natural law theorist

John Locke's natural law teaching has been a major topic of research since Lamprecht offered the first detailed analysis nearly one hundred years ago.[6] However, the watershed moment for this line of inquiry occurred in 1954, when Locke's early *Questions* were published, remarkably, for the first time.[7] This find has allowed scholars to analyze a systematic treatment of some key questions contemplated by the young Locke early in his career and to seek development, diminishment, expansion, or contradiction of his views throughout his published works. Locke references "natural law" and "the law of nature" frequently in diverse contexts—political, philosophical, and religious—yet much remains a matter of contention with regard to the nature and scope of both ontological and epistemological renditions in Locke's works. Whatever consensus has emerged is nuanced, to be sure, with many detractors;[8] however, this chapter will argue that Locke is rightly viewed as a natural law theorist, even if one concludes he is far from traditional in his understanding.[9]

As Locke neared the end of his time as Censor of Moral Philosophy, he prepared the traditional valedictory address, rich with the usual irony and tongue-in-cheek references appropriate for the occasion. Having completed his lectures on the law of nature, Locke made reference to them as somewhat unsuccessful:

> I took part this year in your disputations on such terms that I always went out at once beaten and enriched. Such indeed was the grace of your victory that your arguments, to which I so often yielded, added as much to my knowledge as they detracted from my reputation. That law about which was all our strife had often eluded my fruitless quest, had not your way of life restored that very same law which your tongue had wrested from me. Hence it can be doubted whether your disputations assaulted the law of nature or your behaviour defended it, more keenly.[10]

If this passage is meant to be taken seriously, Locke recognizes that his quest to explain and expound the scope and content of the law of nature left something to be desired—a conclusion echoed by more contemporary readers of Locke.[11] Locke notoriously never set out a demonstration of the science of morals and even spoke of the difficulties of doing so.[12] However, recognizing the difficulty of providing a "complicated proof" relating to the law of nature does not betray his acceptance of, and reliance on, the existence and implications of that law.[13] While this book does not attempt to argue for the validity or success of his natural law theory, it is possible to set out what his theory espouses and recognize how indebted his political theory is to his conception of natural law. A careful reading of the entire corpus of Locke's works reveals that some central tenets laid down in the *Questions* continued to serve as foundational for Locke's thinking, and later additions and substitutions are largely used to support the general framework of his early work. Locke's description of the law of nature—appearing throughout his works—is clearest in those early essays as well as in the *RC*. With these works serving as bookends, it is possible to describe in broad outline Locke's fairly coherent natural law theory as revealed in the corpus of his works.[14]

## The basics

To discover how Locke affirms the basic outline of a natural law theory, it is helpful to consult Aquinas.[15] I wish to use Aquinas as a benchmark advisedly without minimizing the distance between him and Locke. Locke scholars have long disputed which aspects of Locke's thinking can be classified as part of an intellectualist/rationalist theory, voluntarist theory, or if Locke's project involves a confusion of categories. In a helpful article, Francis Oakley notes that the Christian natural law tradition offers a myriad of streams, and Locke freely draws from various wells, including ones less Thomistic—a move that forms part of the problem for assessing Locke as a natural law theorist.[16] On the other hand, his diversity of resources speaks to the wide and general sense in which Locke's project operates as it relates to natural law. "So far as his natural-law thinking is concerned," writes Oakley, "the Locke who emerges is unquestionably and unqualifiedly a voluntarist. But he is a voluntarist of the late-medieval stamp," which includes elements "seemingly intellectualistic in nature" due to the covenantal nature of his approach.[17] Others have suggested, intriguingly, that Locke might have been a combination theorist, allowing a divine command theory to exist alongside a natural law theory, causing him to be a voluntarist about obligation but not about value.[18] Since my purpose in this chapter is simply to identify Locke's natural law theory as one rooted in his theology of creation, exploring Locke's connection with Aquinas will help serve to establish the broad parameters by which Locke's approach may be rightly labeled a natural law approach.

Aquinas affirms the existence of a natural law that emanates from the rational plan ordering all of creation, which he calls the "eternal" law.[19] While every part of creation can be said to "partake" of this eternal law (evidenced by derived teleological inclination), human beings as rational creatures "participate" in the eternal law since they have a share in "Eternal Reason."[20] This participation is what Aquinas refers to as "natural law." The function of the natural law is to provide discernment between good and evil,[21] and thus "the first precept of natural law" is "that *good is to be done and pursued, and evil is to be avoided*."[22]

Throughout his writings, Locke is unequivocal about the existence of a law of nature.[23] In a general sense, everything in creation operates according to "authoritative and fixed laws which are suited to its own nature," and Locke believes it unthinkable that human beings would be exempt from similar "jurisdiction."[24] In terms specific to human beings, the law of nature is not simply a description of contractual agreement within a given society; rather it is the "eternal and established law of right and wrong" that "prescribes what is to be done and what is to be avoided."[25] Locke recognizes this "law" of nature (borrowing language from the Stoics) is equivalent to the "moral good" or "virtue" sought after by philosophers or the practical principles leading to moral character Cicero referred to as "right reason."[26] Locke's general account here echoes a conventional understanding of the natural law tradition.[27]

Similarly for Locke, the law of nature is "knowable by reason," also referred to as "the light of nature."[28] In the *Questions*, Locke declares the law of nature is "sufficiently known to men ... since it is possible to know it by the light of reason alone."[29] For Locke, reasoning must be normative for humanity. "[God] gave [man] reason," writes Locke, "and with it a law: that could not be otherwise than what reason should dictate:[30] unless we should think, that a reasonable creature should have an unreasonable law."[31] The normativity of reason for humanity stands, even in the face of failure to live up to the demands of reason;[32] "if dispensed with in any point, government and order are at an end; and there can be no bounds set to the lawless exorbitancy of unconfined man."[33] In the *Questions*, however, Locke is careful to eschew the idea that the law of nature is a dictate of reason; instead, he ascribes to reason the role of "interpreter" rather than "maker" of the law of nature.[34] When, in the *Second Treatise*, Locke speaks of a "law of nature" to govern mankind, and speaks of "Reason, which is that Law" (or speaks of Reason as "the common Rule and Measure, God hath given to Mankind"), he may simply be using shorthand to conclude that the law of nature is the law of reason (i.e., the law that accords with reason, the reasonable law that reason discovers).[35]

According to Locke, this law that exists, and is knowable, is also normatively binding on all rational creatures, thus all of humanity.[36] This agrees with Aquinas, who declares that natural law (in terms of general principles) "is the same for all."[37] Man is a rational creature, writes Locke; thus the law of nature is "the law of reason," which indicates "what is and what is not consonant with a rational creature, and by that very fact commanding or prohibiting."[38] Not only does this suggest there is a rational basis for morality;[39] it also acknowledges man's voluntary nature with the freedom to act in compliance with or in defiance of the law of nature.[40] Since "tis [God] that commands what reason does," to go against what reason demands is "to disobey God" in an act of "direct rebellion."[41]

It is no surprise from whence comes the source of obligation. For Locke, as for Aquinas, this law is established by God, the creator, in accordance with what is suitable to man's nature.[42] The law of nature "is the command of the divine will," and all creatures respond to the laws of governance "in their obedience to his will."[43] Locke is emphatic that the law of nature cannot be a dictate of reason but rather "is the declaration of a superior will," the will of an "omnipotent lawmaker."[44] In the *Second Treatise*, Locke emphatically equates "the law of nature" with "the will of God."[45] In the sixth essay of *Questions*, Locke connects the binding nature of the law with the established will of God. He writes, "The law of nature (*legem naturae*) is binding on all men" since "God, the author of this law, has willed it to be the rule of our moral life."[46] In this regard, Locke believes that moral obligation is grounded in his understanding of God, and morality is acting in obedience to that superior will.[47]

Interestingly, Aquinas flags up problems that admit variation in the application of natural law. In reply to the question "Whether the Natural Law Is the Same in All Men?," Aquinas draws a distinction between the "general principles" of reason (the "truth" of which is "the same for all, and is equally known by all") and "the proper conclusions of speculative reason" ("the truth" of which "is the same for all, but is not equally known to all").[48] Even self-evident things are not known to be so by everyone.[49] In addition, Aquinas notes that matters of detail and added conditions to a given situation create great variance in how to apply principles of reason.[50] When Aquinas sets out to explain why God would provide revelation ("Divine law"), he references "the uncertainty of human judgment, especially on contingent and particular matters," wherein "different people form different judgments on human acts; whence also different and contrary laws result." These laws can and do err because reason alone is incapable of forming perfect judgments in this regard.[51]

These considerations by Aquinas may help explain why Locke also affirms an "eternal and established" law, which is "every-where the same,"[52] applying to Christians and nonbelievers alike,[53] and yet believes this law may admit of degrees or variation. Locke considers certain allowances. All humans have the same "nature" but possess differing measures of "light." "The light of nature"[54] has not penetrated in its full glory into every mind; humans in history were only required to comply "as far as [God] had revealed it to them."[55] In a number of places in the *RC*, Locke shows sympathy for ignorance in some matters[56] and speaks to the fact that one is only obligated as far as he is made aware,[57] making use of that "light" to which he is acquainted.[58] In fact, Locke is quite pessimistic about the extent to which the world could have knowledge of morality "by mere natural light"[59] and believes a God of mercy can and will respond fairly in this regard.[60] Locke is equally realistic concerning human failure to live up to the moral standards of which he is aware—a fact Locke mentions flatly in the early essays but associates with grace in the *RC*.[61] In addition, there may not be a rule to cover every possible situation (thus a need to develop moral virtues),[62] and the lawgiver, having total prerogative, will include other considerations.[63]

These allowances are important in clarifying the various ways the "law of nature" may be applied. But variation in application and prerogative of the lawgiver neither change the law nor remove obligation for compliance. As a moral standard, the law of nature applies to every rational creature and can be known through one's reasoning faculties.

But what, precisely, is the content of this moral law of nature? The answer must be more than a simple acknowledgment that a law exists; the duties of morality refer to actions, not beliefs, and they are to be carried out in practice, not by simple assent.[64] Locke, as is his custom, roots his discussion of the moral requirements of the law of nature in God's role as moral lawgiver. For Locke, it is "a part of the law of nature, that man ought to obey every positive law of God, whenever he shall please to make any such addition to the law of his nature."[65] This statement suggests "the eternal law of right" can include "additions" to "the law of nature," which, being "suitable to his nature," can justly be called the law of "his" nature. The juxtaposition of "addition" with "eternal" implies that the one, unchanging standard is that God, the lawgiver, is to be obeyed with the particulars being not everywhere fixed but subject to his will. Yet Locke does not believe God's will is arbitrary,[66] nor does his theory allow any form of moral relativism. Instead, this passage reflects Locke's legislative framing of the topic, emphasizing the prerogative of the lawgiver without undermining the laws or their content.[67]

In the *Essay*, Locke claims there are three kinds of law "that Men generally refer their Actions to, to judge of their Rectitude, or Obliquity": opinion, civil, and divine.[68] Locke's delineation of divine law echoes language from the opening of the first essay on the law of nature that even in his discussion of the law of opinion Locke speaks of actions, which "in their nature" are right and wrong, which makes them "co-incident with the divine law."[69] For Locke, "the Law of God" is "that supreme rule," which is "the Rule of Right" by which one differentiates between "Good" and "Evil."[70] "If I have the Will of a supreme, invisible Lawmaker for my Rule," writes Locke, "then, as I supposed the Action commanded, or forbidden by God, I call it Good or Evil, Sin or Duty."[71] How does one know what actions are "commanded or forbidden by God," determining the difference between virtue and vice? Locke says the "Law which God has set to the actions of Men" are "promulgated to them by the light of Nature, or the voice of Revelation."[72] Here Locke acknowledges that the particulars of the moral law—a law that can be known by the light of nature[73]—are also prescribed by revelation. Such a concession sets the groundwork for Locke's discussion of the content of the law of nature in the *RC*.

If one defines the content of the law of nature as the moral stipulations required by God for humanity, Locke appears to find this content written[74] in the New Testament: "Such a law of morality Jesus Christ hath given us in the

New Testament … by revelation. We have from him a full and sufficient rule for our direction, and conformable to that of reason."[75] "There is not, I think," writes Locke, "any of the duties of morality, which [Christ] has not, somewhere or other, by himself and his apostles, inculcated over and over again to his followers in express terms."[76] If one would but open "the inspired books," they will find "all the duties of morality lie there clear, and plain, and easy to be understood."[77] In other words, as Tuckness writes, "a full law of nature would be roughly equivalent to the moral teachings of the New Testament."[78] As a chief example, Locke centers his attention on the Sermon on the Mount, which gives a fuller account of the content of the moral law with proper application—far greater than ever was or could be written:[79]

> There he preached to the people only morality; clearing the precepts of the law from the false glosses which were received in those days, and setting forth the duties of a good life in their full obligation and extent, beyond what the judiciary laws of the Israelites did, or the civil laws of any country could prescribe, or take notice of.[80]

Eschewing any notion of innate ideas, and challenging the irrationality of certain readings of scripture (such as the doctrine of double-predestination), Locke develops a natural law theory that assumes all the commands of God are rational, can be deduced by reason, and can never be contrary to reason.[81]

The basic outline of Locke's natural law theory can be summarized as follows: is there a law of nature? Yes. What is its scope? It is eternal and established, the law of right and wrong. Is it knowable? Yes. How is it established? By God, the creator, in accordance with what is suitable to man's nature. How is it knowable? By reason. Who is amenable to this law? Every creature endowed with reason. How may one identify the content of this law of nature? While any particular moral rule could theoretically be discovered through reflective use of reason, the moral requirements for humanity can be found codified clearly and succinctly in the New Testament, all of which accord with right reason. This short summary is consistent with his teaching elsewhere, establishing him as a Christian natural law theorist.[82]

## Teleology

Locke's teleological perspective on human nature is explicitly theological. Nature is ordered, and God's ordering of human nature is directed toward ultimate happiness in the afterlife.[83] In the *RC*, Locke admits that "mankind … must be allowed to pursue their happiness"; indeed, writes Locke, this "cannot be hindered," for "happiness" is "their chief end."[84] This term is used elsewhere in the *RC* in a way that may help illuminate the trajectory of his thinking.[85] Those who chose to follow Christ not only entered into a system that accords with reason but "got into the way of truth and happiness."[86] After all, the gospel (meaning "good news") provides "happy tidings" of the Messiah's arrival.[87] This provides the framework for assuming one's "happiness or misery" depends on obedience to the will of Christ.[88] This is intimated in John 13:17, where, as Locke notes, Jesus claims "happy are ye if you do" what Christ commands.[89] Thus, in a later section, reflecting on the New Testament's vastly superior code of ethics, Locke advocates "that all would be happy, if all would practise it."[90]

But Locke is interested in much more than "temporal happiness of any people," which is the most natural religion can seek or even attempt to provide.[91] True happiness can only be understood from "consideration of another life" beyond this one.[92] In the original Garden of Eden, Adam existed in a "happy state of immortality."[93] Through the coming of Christ, those who received pardon, such as the thief on the cross, will find themselves "re-instated in an happy immortality."[94] This will occur in the final resurrection of the just, "to enjoy in that 'new world' a happy eternity."[95] Locke grounds the system of morality (which he calls "the law of nature") on "this foundation," namely, the certain view of future reward.[96] But this grounding provides more than satisfaction for one's reasoning faculties: "it has another relish and efficacy to persuade men," writes Locke, "that if they live well here, they shall be happy hereafter."[97]

This theological perspective is not confined to Locke's explicitly theological works. In the *LCT*, Locke is concerned with religious freedom so that an individual may seek the salvation of her soul according to her conscience, since this is a matter of "eternal Happiness or Misery."[98] "No man whatsoever ought therefore to be deprived of his Terrestrial Enjoyments, upon account of his religion," because a person's acceptance or refusal of religious rites are done so "that they shall obtain Happiness by that means."[99] Locke makes a remarkably clear exposition of the end goal for human affairs:

> Every man has an Immortal Soul, capable of Eternal Happiness or Misery; whose Happiness depending upon his believing and doing those things in this Life, which are necessary to the obtaining of Gods Favour, and are prescribed by God to that end; it follows from thence, *1st*, That the observance of these things is the highest Obligation that lies upon Mankind, and that our utmost Care, Application, and Dilligence, ought to be exercised in the Search and Performance of them; Because there is nothing in this World that is of any consideration in comparison with Eternity.[100]

This leads Locke to advocate the pursuit of happiness as a teleological pursuit. Locke affirms that the civil government must deal with issues pertaining to "Temporal lives here upon earth"; yet the same government making laws ensuring "things that contribute to the Comfort and Happiness of this Life" also protect the liberty for "every Man" to attend to "the care of his own Eternal Happiness, the attainment whereof can neither be facilitated by another Mans Industry, nor can the loss of it turn to another Mans Prejudice, nor the hope of it be forced from him by any external Violence."[101] Liberty, then, relates not just to temporal acquiring of property but also to matters of "eternal salvation": "Everyone one should do what he in his Conscience is perswaded to be acceptable to the Almighty, on whose good pleasure and acceptance depends their eternal Happiness. For Obedience is due in the first place to God, and afterwards to the Laws."[102]

Locke shows the same basic regard for happiness in his philosophical work. For Locke, humans have, by nature, a desire to pursue happiness.[103] This inclination is more than a tendency; it is an obligation, given by the creator.[104] "The highest perfection of intellectual nature lies in a careful and constant pursuit of true and solid happiness" writes Locke; therefore "the care of our selves ... is the necessary foundation of our *liberty*."[105] "Care of our selves" includes consideration of the afterlife, and this is because of the teleological aspect of human nature: God "has so plentifully provided us with the means to discover, and know him, so far as is necessary to the end of our Being, and the great concernment of our Happiness."[106] But no temporal joy can compare to "that perfect durable Happiness hereafter," even if some mistakenly disagree.[107] For this reason "Virtue and Religion are necessary to ... Happiness," since "the future State" of "perfect Happiness or Misery" is an issue of ultimate concern, disproportionate to any "Pleasure and Pain in this Life."[108] The final abode of a human soul depends on one's behavior in this life, and "the measures of Good and Evil that govern his choice" differ depending on how one views the prospect of eternity.[109]

The language of "living well" and finding "happiness" (both here and hereafter) which is one's "chief end" incorporates Aristotle's *eudaimonia* within Locke's ethical schema, albeit with explicitly theological overtones.[110] Locke's decision to speak of one's ethical pursuit toward the happy state of immortality as a "substantial good" reinforces his intellectual debt both to Aristotle as well as Aquinas. In fact, Locke views happiness not only in terms of achieving personal joys in eternity but in the participation of God himself. God "scattered" and "blended" various degrees of pleasure and pain throughout all areas of human existence so "that we finding imperfection, dissatisfaction, and want of complete happiness, in all the Enjoyments, which the Creatures can afford us, might be led to seek it in the enjoyment of him, *with whom there is fullness of joy, and at whose right hand are pleasures for evermore.*"[111]

The teleological aspect of man's nature (toward eternal happiness) is just one aspect of his larger theology of Creation. But Locke's recognition that Creation is purposeful can be found throughout his works, including his early *Questions*. "Since on the evidence of the senses it must be concluded that there is some maker of all these things whom it is necessary to recognize as not only powerful but also wise," writes Locke, "it follows from this that he has not created this world for nothing and without purpose."[112] Humanity is directed toward eternal happiness through following the dictates of reason; being fitted with the capacity for reason is part of God's purposes for humanity, and thus acting in accordance with reason is acting in accordance with one's purpose as given by God through creation. Even Locke's discussion of eternal rewards and punishments in the afterlife—and the motivation for ethical action in this life that results—are wedded to the notion that creation is purposeful, and human ethical actions toward God and neighbor, in accordance with reason, are also in accord with what will bring about true pleasure and avoid pain. Thus man is endowed with reason and a desire for pleasure precisely because he is made to act in accordance with the purposes of creation.[113] While Locke rejects the notion of innate ideas, he does not reject innate inclinations.[114]

## Locke's doctrine of creation

### Sparkes: Connecting teleology and Locke's doctrine of creation

In a 1973 article entitled "Trust and Teleology," Sparkes sought to identify Locke's doctrine of creation and explore the ways in which it impacted Locke's political philosophy.[115] Centering on the concept of teleology—"divine and human" that "pervades Locke's political thinking"—Sparkes posited Locke's law of nature as "the foundation of his political theory. It is not a set of discrete principles, but a system based on the doctrine of the creative activity of God."[116] Humans are the workmanship of God, and thus all moral duties are ultimately religious ones.[117] From these starting principles, Sparkes concludes

> that the central doctrines of Locke's politics have a theological basis, a doctrine of Creation similar to the Thomist one. Locke does not elaborate this doctrine; he presupposes it. It is not a hidden, esoteric element in his thought; it is there on the surface, but in a scattered and fragmentary form.[118]

However, Sparkes's evaluation of Locke hits a sour note: according to Sparkes, Locke "extends [his] doctrine of Creation to human productive activity with crippling results for his political theory."[119] Locke fails to draw a critical distinction between God's *ab nihilo* (*bara*/creating) activity and human productive (*asah*/making) activity; thus, according to Sparkes, Locke collapses divine creation and human creation:

> Locke fails to see the limitations on human creation imposed by the fact that men must work on given material. The ethic of the *Treatises* is creation-centred, but Locke regards the products of human creation with as much reverence as the products of divine creation. As a result, his political theory pays no attention to the brute *facticity* of environment, social, biological and physical … The Law of Nature is a system of broad moral principles, and broad moral principles alone are not sufficient to establish the network of rules which is conceptually central to human society. Arriving at this system of rules requires attention to environment, and since environments differ, so do societies. Locke fails to see this … Locke, while extending sacrosanctity to the products of human creation, neglects the important human creative activity of on-going adaptation.[120]

In reality, though, Sparkes fails to appreciate the multidimensional character of Locke's doctrine of creation. As this section will attempt to show, mainstream Christian tradition affirms that *creatio ex nihilo* includes what is sometimes called *creatio continua*—emphasizing the constant and radical dependence of all creation, including humanity, upon God for its very existence. Also, throughout his political writings, Locke pairs his discussion of the teleological character of the human vocation with the developmental nature of societal formation; at the same time, he also emphasizes one's individual freedom to seek the good as one discovers it. In addition, Locke's unwavering acceptance of *creatio ex nihilo* forever draws a distinction between the creator's work and anything produced by the creation; yet he also accepts a participatory role for humanity as part of the vocation for being human. This does not collapse divine and human creation but speaks of a limited partnership arising from Locke's doctrine of creation. What Sparkes did get right, however, is that Locke indeed bases his political philosophy on a teleological doctrine of creation.

## Creatio ex nihilo *and the business of being human*

Locke's acceptance of *creatio ex nihilo*, discussed in the previous chapter with respect to the nature of God, carries profound implications for Locke's doctrine of creation. The twin facts that God alone is Creator and all "materials" used by the creator originate with him cause Locke to speak of all parts of the created order as God's "workmanship." In fact, Locke refers to "the Creation" as "one and the first great piece of [God's] Workmanship."[121] Yet all else in creation represent "the less-excellent pieces of this Universe" when compared to "all ... knowing Beings,"[122] since humans, made in the image of God, represent "so curious and wonderful a piece of workmanship" that they stand at the apex of the created order.[123]

"Image of God" stands as an important identity marker for humanity throughout Locke's writings. In Chapter 4 of the *First Treatise*, Locke seeks to establish humanity's right to dominion of the earth. However, writes Locke, dominion applies to the whole species:

> God in this Donation, gave the World to Mankind in common, and not to *Adam* in particular. The word *Them* in the Text must include the Species of Man, for 'tis certain *Them* can by no means signifie *Adam* alone. In the *26th* Verse, where God declares his intention to give this Dominion, it is plain he meant, that he would make a Species of Creatures, that should have Dominion over the other Species of this Terrestrial Globe: The words are, *And God said, Let us make Man in our Image, after our likeness, and let them have Dominion over the Fish, &c.* They then were to have Dominion. Who? Even those who were to have the *Image* of God, the Individuals of that Species of *Man* that he was going to make ... God makes him *in his own Image after his own Likeness*, makes him an intellectual Creature, and so capable of *Dominion*. For wherein soever else the *Image of God* consisted, the intellectual Nature was certainly a part of it, and belong'd to the whole Species, and enabled them to have *Dominion* over the inferiour Creatures.[124]

In this theologically pregnant passage, Locke declares that to be human is to be "image of God" and that "image of God" refers to that set of rational creatures signified as "man," given the task of (and ability to exercise) dominion over the earth.

For Locke, the blessing pronounced in Genesis 1:28 clearly shows the "setting of Mankind above the other kinds of Creatures, in this habitable Earth of ours" is "nothing but the giving to Man, the whole Species of Man, as the chief Inhabitant, who is the Image of his Maker, the Dominion over the other Creatures."[125] Locke is convinced "this lies so obvious in the plain words" of scripture that "'tis impossible for any sober Reader" to think otherwise.[126]

In the *Second Treatise*, Locke continues to build on this theme of humans, made in the image of God, as the workmanship of God. He suggests that humans are given a vocation as a direct result of their place in the creation.[127] The particular "business" of humanity involves dominion, but when one considers the role that "image of God" plays in Locke's theological anthropology, it becomes clear that the business of humanity is to "image" God on earth by exerting dominion as God would have it and as God exerts dominion over humanity.[128] Locke thus links "image" with "workmanship." When one considers Locke language in the *First Treatise*[129] it becomes apparent that God is "imaged" on earth in that the human species plays the role of God's representative upon the inferior world.

Locke makes this point rather explicitly in the *Essay*. God has given humanity what is needed for "the Business we have to do here," and, while Locke includes "the Conveniences of Living" as part of "our business in this world," he adds that knowledge of God "and knowledge of our Duty" are "our business" as well.[130] Yet "our business" is to be "about His [God's] business," writes Locke in the *Second Treatise*.[131] This translates into a human vocation as God's representative in all areas of life. For example, Adam and Eve—and by extension, all parents after them—were obligated to train, care for, and raise their children "not as their own Workmanship, but the Workmanship of their own Maker, the Almighty, to whom they were to be accountable for them."[132] "Workmanship" points to "dependence and duty," and the human vocation includes the duty to image God on earth.[133]

Also dependent upon the Edenic theme, Locke adds that human "dependence and duty" requires that Adam's race seek to regain paradise, since immortality is part of the divine image. "Adam being the Son of God," writes Locke, "had this part also of the likeness and image of his father, viz. that he was immortal. But Adam, transgressing the command given him by his heavenly Father, incurred the penalty; forfeited that state of immortality, and became mortal."[134] "After this," continues Locke, "Adam begot children: but they were 'in his own likeness, after his own image;' mortal, like their father."[135]

But God "willing to bestow eternal life on mortal men" sent Jesus, who "was properly the Son of God … So that being the Son of God, he was like the Father, immortal."[136] Locke's Adamic Christology connects with his understanding of theological anthropology. Drawing not only from Genesis but also *imago* language in the New Testament,[137] Locke concludes that "immortality is a part of that image, wherein those (who were the immediate sons of God, so as to have no other father) were made like their Father."[138] Jesus, "not having forfeited that sonship by any transgression; was heir of eternal life, as Adam should have been, had he continued in his filial duty."[139] Locke notes that through Christ and in Christ, humans are "conformed" by God "to the image" of Christ[140]: "This image, to which they were conformed, seems to be immortality and eternal life."[141] Thus, Locke concludes,

God has now a son again in the world, the first-born of many brethren, who all now, by the Spirit of adoption, can say, Abba, Father. And we, by adoption, being for his sake made his brethren, and the sons of God, come to share in that inheritance, which was his natural right; he being by birth the Son of God: which inheritance is eternal life.[142]

The storyline, then, for Locke is clear: Adam, as the son of God, possessed immortality as a necessary component of being in the image and likeness of his father. Yet having lost immortality, his children bore his image of mortality. However, in Christ, God "has a son again in the world"[143] who possesses immortality and offers this part of the image of God to all Christians who are now sons of God in Christ, sharing in the inheritance of eternal (immortal) life. Though Adam's race inherited mortality, "men are, by the second Adam, restored to life again."[144] Locke draws on a couple of Pauline passages[145] that teach the *telos* of the business of humanity is to, in the end, "after his image, which is the image of the Father, become immortal."[146] "This may serve a little to explain the immortality of the sons of God," writes Locke, "who are in this like their Father, made after his image and likeness."[147]

## Implications for the present: God's continuing providential sustaining of the world

*Creatio continua* (which is simply a part of *creatio ex nihilo*) refers to the integral role of divine conservation in any doctrine of Creation. The world is not only posited but sustained in being—moment by moment—by the creative power of God. This view stands in direct opposition to Deism in which God sets up a self-sustaining world.[148]

In Book II of the *Essay*, concluding his discussion of duration and expansion, Locke's thoughts turn to the theological. Human beings—indeed, all finite beings—are incomparable with God's infinite duration, knowledge, and power. In pointing out this vast difference, Locke touches upon all creaturely dependence upon God, which leads him to make a statement lending itself to this portion of *creatio ex nihilo*:

> What I say of Man, I say of all finite Beings, who though they may far exceed Man in Knowledge and Power, yet are no more than the meanest Creature, in comparison with God himself. Finite of any Magnitude, holds not any proportion to infinite. God's infinite Duration being accompanied with infinite Knowledge, and infinite Power, he sees all things past and to come; and they are no more distant from his Knowledge, no farther removed from his sight,

than the present: They all lie under the same view: *And there is nothing, which he cannot make exist each moment he pleases. For the Existence of all things, depending upon his good Pleasure; all things exist every moment, that he thinks fit to have them exist.*[149]

The two aspects of *creatio ex nihilo* (discussed in this chapter) appear in Locke's theology of creation pointing to a radical dependence upon God—applied to the entire universe. Yet Locke links "dependence" with "duty" and specifically emphasizes the "business" of being human as using rationality to live in equality with other humans, exert dominion over the "inferior" creatures, and attain immortality in the afterlife. In these ways, the business of being human is to "image" God on earth and to bear this image for all eternity.

## Locke's covenantal theology

The particular aspects of Locke's theology of creation discussed in this chapter dovetail with work by others concerning Locke's covenantal theology. In this light, Locke's natural law doctrine finds its proper home, and Locke's conciliatory use of various traditions makes sense.[150] For example, scholars have recognized elements in Locke's natural law theory that can be associated with both voluntarist and intellectualist positions.[151] However, instead of declaring Locke to waver inconsistently between positions, Oakley notes that Locke may simply be borrowing an open position from the late medieval period, which conceived of God's omnipotence in the context of a covenant theology.[152]

Before Tetlow published the results of her research in 2006, Locke's covenantal theology of law was "the most singular unstudied part of his theology."[153] According to Tetlow,

> Locke adopted the federal covenant theology arising from the Swiss Reformation in which the Adamic Covenant and its law of nature were fundamental. This legal theology of promise, consent, duty, and reward gave Locke a way to reconcile the intractable problem of God's sovereignty and man's free will. God is infinite, just, good, and eternal, yet enters into a relationship of consent with individuals and communities. His Covenant of Grace is a gift offered, but one which can be rejected … The "law of nature" which is central to all of Locke's thinking is that same "law of reason" God gave to Adam at the beginning and still remains in effect after Christian redemption.[154]

Speaking of "the law of nature at creation,"[155] Tetlow's emphasis on Locke's covenantal theology (drawn primarily from revelation) opens a window for a fresh analysis of Locke's political schema in the light of his doctrine of creation. According to Tetlow, Locke's "Latitudinarianism and covenantalism set a framework for a common understanding of how political society ought to be structured and governed."[156] The results of this chapter fit well within the larger structure outlined by Tetlow, reinforcing the claim that Locke's doctrine of creation is pivotal for understanding the grounds of his moral and political philosophy.

## Locke's theology manifested through political application

Locke's theological reflection on the law of nature as it relates to his theology of creation yields fruit for his political theory. The political results of his theological analysis can especially be seen with respect to the issues of freedom and human equality. These two areas will now be explored.

### Human equality

Locke's category of distinctly "human" rights relates to a distinctly human equality. Yet qualifying rights and equality belonging to humans as a species simply because they are human continues to be a tall order in nonreligious philosophical and political ethics.[157] Locke admits the difficulty. With respect to rights, duties, and equality, Locke speaks of "mankind" (those "of the same species and rank ... sharing all in one Community of Nature") as a moral community of equals, distinct from "the inferior creatures,"[158] yet species classification is a human creation, and some animals do not fit neatly into those categories.[159] Locke's understanding of who is a "man subject to law" is quite simply "a corporeal rational being."[160] But the rationality test could apply beyond the arbitrary confines of species:

> For were there a Monkey, or any other Creature to be found, that had the use of Reason, to such a degree, as to be able to understand general Signs, and to deduce Consequences about general *Ideas*, he would no doubt be subject to Law, and in that Sense, be a *Man*, how much soever he differ'd in Shape from others of that Name.[161]

Locke spends several pages of the *Essay* dealing with the issue of changelings—"something between a Man and a Beast."[162] Locke responds to those who find "Religion threatened" by the existence of changelings by resting afterlife concerns "in the hands of a faithful Creator and a bountiful Father."[163] Locke rejects as equally unfounded the notions that (1) anything with the "outward Shape and Appearance of a Man, must necessarily be designed to an immortal Being" and (2) that "whatsoever is of humane Birth, must be so."[164] It would seem that, for Locke, one cannot make a moral distinction simply on the basis of species distinction.

At first blush, it would appear that moral distinction relates to a rational faculty. However, Locke notes that the variation on rationality both within and without the human species only exacerbates the problem. Nonhuman animals "have some Reason," writes Locke, while a significant number of humans exhibit signs of diminished reasoning capacity, especially at the beginning and final stages of life.[165] In fact, it is "evident," writes Locke,

> that there is a difference of degrees in Men's Understandings, Apprehensions, and Reasonings, to so great a latitude, that one may, without doing injury to Mankind, affirm, that there is a greater distance between some Men, and others, in this respect, than between some Men and some Beasts.[166]

How, then, does Locke settle on a moral "state of equality" inclusive of "all mankind" "by nature," separating them from "the inferior creatures?"[167] The answer, for Locke, is theological as well as teleological. It is true that Locke's definition of "person" emphasizes autonomous rational agency, something that in and of itself may not require a theological account.[168] However, this language does not sit alone in Locke's anthropology; instead, human capacity gives way to human obligation. As this chapter earlier addressed, it is the teleological aspect of the human vocation that plays a central role in the definition of humanity as that being made "in the image of God" and created to be "about His business" in the world. Thus a self-regulating capacity must somehow be married to a particular vocation in order for Locke's emphasis on human equality to make moral sense.

Locke finds this vocation in the acknowledgment of, praise to, and voluntary service on behalf of the Creator. In the introduction to the *Essay*, Locke writes that "we ... have Cause enough to magnify the bountiful Author of our Being" since God has given to humanity "Whatsoever is necessary for the Conveniences of Life, and Information of Vertue; and has put within the reach of their discovery the comfortable Provision for this Life and the Way that leads to a better."[169] In short, human cognition is coupled with human obligation in that "they have Light enough to lead them to the Knowledge of their Maker, and the sight of their own Duties."[170] Locke's doctrine of human equality, then, is rooted in his *theological* anthropology.

In his book *God, Locke, and Equality*, Jeremy Waldron sets out his own analysis of how Locke arrives at human equality on the basis of theology.[171] According to Locke, perception may be found in various animals, but the capacity for abstraction separates humans from the "inferior creatures." This capacity for abstraction leads one to the knowledge of God's existence. The awareness of God leads to an awareness of God's demands, as one reflects upon the law of nature. This reflection has an existential result in which the human thinks of herself as a person existing moment to moment. This ability proves one to be in a specific moral relation to God. As a result of ascertaining this knowledge, the human is motivated to discover God's positive commandments and obey him. Thus, it is the capacity for this series of conclusions resulting from abstraction that defines one as a "man" in a moral sense; all such beings are to be treated as "[God's] Property ... made to last during his ... Pleasure."[172] From this conclusion, Locke derives the prohibition against destroying, harming, or exploiting any member of the same class.

In Waldron's representation, Locke's approach bears striking resemblance to that of Benjamin Whichcote, who rejected any Platonic definition of a human being on the grounds that "a very near representation" of human rationality is found "in the sagacity of inferiour Creatures." What distinguishes human beings is that their superior rationality brings them to "take cognizance of God."[173] But something is left wanting from this conclusion as a total representation of Locke's approach to human equality. How does Locke make application to human beings without cognizance of God or to those individuals lacking such abilities due to age or intelligence? Concerning infants, Waldron posits a range of property, which applies to normal human reason, and then suggests that, for Locke, a "*special relation*" exists between the infant and that range.[174] Just as Locke says that children are born "to"—not "in"—the basic equality shared by all mankind, Waldron insists that parental responsibility is to treat infants as potential sharers of equality.[175] If Waldron is correct in suggesting this is Locke's proper claim, it would reinforce the teleological character of Locke's overall schema. Children are to be nurtured, trained, and led toward a share in basic equality; thus the parental role is "governed by the equality that is grounded on God's vision for their offspring."[176]

However, if Waldron's ingenious assessment is not correct, it may prove unnecessary. In paragraph six of the *Second Treatise*, Locke writes the following:

> For Men being all the Workmanship of one Omnipotent, and infinitely wise Maker; All the Servants of one Sovereign Master, sent into the World by his order and about his business, they are his Property, whose Workmanship they are, made to last during his, not one anothers Pleasure.[177]

In his reply to Waldron, Tate correctly notes that this signal passage—not only for Locke's *Second Treatise* but for Waldron's analysis—emphasizes the moral nature of mankind as an objective status from God's perspective, rather than a subjective accomplishment due to human achievement:

> Read in terms of its literal meaning, what Locke is describing in this passage is an *objective* status—our status as *God's* creatures. And taken in and of itself, what the passage indicates is that this status as "creatures" is determined not by us but by He who created us, thereby making us *His* property. In other words, our status as God's creatures is not determined subjectively, by anything we think or do on our own account—either in terms of our own beliefs or actions or our views about God Himself. None of these, after all, determined that we be created and given the status of "creatures." Rather, it seems, our status as God's creatures is determined entirely by God, in terms of *His* progenitive capacity in creating us, and *His* prerogative in doing so.[178]

Tate's analysis of this passage is persuasive, yet his further derision of Waldron's larger perspective (discussed in Chapter 2) does not follow from this insight. On the contrary, Tate's exegesis grounds Locke's argument for human equality in a doctrine of natural law, which proceeds from a particular doctrine of creation: that human beings exist, serve, and find status at the pleasure of God in view of a divine perspective. It may not be within the scope of human intelligence to ferret out just who exists among the moral community of equals other than by respecting the words of revelation that distinguish "mankind" from the other animals as those made "in the image of God" and given the vocation of dominion. Humans are given the command to acknowledge God and appropriately serve him, yet each person is individually responsible, and freedom requires that each person be given room and opportunity to do so.

Thus, while Locke may very well have supported expanding the moral community of equals *in a political sense* to include an animal outside the species of *homo sapien sapien* who shows the capacity for abstraction (and thus the capacity to respond to the creator's invitation), he offers a pragmatic political circle that includes all human beings due to inherent right and/or special responsibility (in the case of infants or the mentally deficient). This political choice seems based on a moral imperative to allow individuals to respond to their peculiar calling and vocation as God's creatures bearing His image, as God wills. If Tate is correct, Waldron's larger project in support of the religious turn in Locke scholarship remains intact, and the teleological aspect of Locke's doctrine of creation is only further enhanced.

# Freedom

## *An analysis of three crucial texts*

In the *Essay*, Locke offers a philosophical account of freedom. It might be surprising to discover that Locke considers "Whether Man's Will be free, or no" to be an "unreasonable, because unintelligible, Question."[179] Locke considers the notion of a "free will" to make as much sense as "swift" sleep or a "square" virtue—"Liberty being as little applicable to the Will" as these. Liberty applies to an agent: a person can be free, her will cannot.[180] Freedom is a power—the power to do or avoid an action according to one's preferences.[181] Freedom can only exist where there is volition, so freedom relates to the active power of choice.[182] Humans share passive power with the lower animals, but the active power of volition, whereby they willingly order their lives, is something they share with God.[183] Freedom, then, is a power relating to the life of the mind. Through making judgments—"the acquiescing of the mind"—the human freely chooses, exercising freedom by use of, consistent with or in opposition to the will.[184] Troubles in life relate to an "uneasiness" that seeks to determine the will away from the good, yet humans have the power to "suspend" satisfying the desires of the will, determine the right course of action, and then act appropriately; in this way humans can refuse the desires of the will and choose the good, which leads to happiness.[185] For Locke, "this is the source of all liberty."[186]

In the *Two Treatises*, Locke also provides a political account of human freedom that arises first in the state of nature. Humans are naturally (and equally) free "to order their actions and dispose of their possessions and persons as they think fit."[187] By "possessions and persons" Locke means property, over which a person has sovereign power, save for the creator's prerogative.[188] Yet humans do not wield an arbitrary power in this regard but one that accords with right reason.[189] Laws—whether positive law or the law of nature—provide protection for humans to pursue reasonable ends in the acquisition and expenditures regarding possessions.[190] A person can use their political freedom according to individual interests but cannot give up freedom itself.[191] Yet an individual can transfer her own right to adjudicate justice (through her own perception of the law of nature) to the commonwealth through consent to belong to a governed society.[192] In this way, the free acts of a public authority or the commonwealth as a whole on behalf of the individual are considered the free acts *of* the individual.[193] For a person to be under another's power, consent is paramount in ensuring the natural exercise of freedom.[194] An implicit consent may be assumed if a person's possessions happen to lie within societal jurisdiction, but only a tacit consent may make a naturally free person a citizen with necessary political obligation.[195] Once a person makes such a commitment, the political obligation lasts forever.[196] The body politic may also be thought of as a united or corporate entity, given the right to protection and self-preservation according to its members in the state of nature. The freedom of the people, like the freedom of the individual, is not arbitrary, but reasonable.[197] When a decision is unreasonable, or when there is a breach of trust, the individual may make an appeal, yet even the appeal is to the community, even when manifested in the sovereign under whose jurisdiction she belongs.[198]

In the *RC*, Locke offers a religious account of freedom. From the initial page of the work, Locke berates a particular "extreme" reading of scripture that "shook the foundations of all religion."[199] By this Locke is referring to a particular interpretation of Calvinism in which human beings bear the guilt of Adam's sin and thus, according to Locke's reading, are "doomed to eternal, infinite punishment, for the transgression of Adam."[200] Such a view, writes Locke, is "little consistent with the justice and goodness of the great and infinite God."[201] For Locke, each person stands or falls on the merit of their own actions or omissions, and God will render fair and appropriate judgment according to "the deeds done in the body" (not by virtue of another's deeds). He makes the same point in the *Essay* by arguing against transferring personhood on the basis of the goodness of God; "person" must apply to the same individual on both sides of the resurrection if reward or punishment in the afterlife is to accord with the character of God.[202] Locke's strong insistence on personal responsibility as a necessary human duty coincides with his understanding of God's standard for final judgment: while Christians are accepted by grace, all people are accountable to the moral law of nature. Simple assent to the proposition that Jesus is the Messiah is essential to salvation and justification but not sufficient; judgment includes consideration of a freely chosen ethical life, lived in obedience to the law of nature and the positive teachings of scripture.[203] Denying freedom to mankind would make them "bare Machins," incapable of virtue.[204] As a result, freedom is an essential religious value; without it, God's judgment is rendered meaningless and human *telos* is unintelligible.

### *Polin's promising proposal*

Writing in 1969, Raymond Polin convincingly showed that Locke's philosophical treatment of freedom weaves together his moral and political theories in a coherent philosophical system rooted in a theological concept of divine order.[205] Far from articulating the kind of absolute anarchic freedom Popple and his heirs have read eisegetically into Locke's works, Locke himself offered a nuanced appreciation of freedom within a larger sense of order that restricts and restrains moral and political practice in addition to promoting independence. Polin writes that, for Locke,

> freedom … is nothing but the means given by God to human creatures capable of intelligence, reason and society to incorporate themselves into the order of this world, when they grow mature enough to discover and understand its meaning. Freedom as such is always to be understood as correlative with order. The human being, Locke discovers, as a being capable of freedom and reason, is bound to the divine order of the world through an obligation, the obligation to make himself actually free and reasonable, either in the order of the relations he establishes with other men, or in his relations with the reasonable order of the world. For Locke, freedom exists and is meaningful only if it is bound to the obligation to achieve a reasonable order and a moral one.[206]

Polin first reaches this conclusion with respect to Locke's account of philosophical freedom. Freedom accords with judgment, and judgment is intended to function in accordance with right reason. Freedom is a negative reality for humanity in that humans exchange the desire for the good in favor of the passions. In this sense, writes Polin, freedom represents a freedom for evil.[207] Yet human sharing in the active powers is part of what it means to be made in the image of God. It can even be said that God himself, in a sense, is bound by the good, if one thinks of this in terms of God's self-limiting nature.[208] This means that, for humans, fulfilling the desires of the will can be a volitional act, but choosing to suspend those desires is the end to which freedom points. In this sense, human "freedom" is, in its intended sense, the freedom to choose the good, as reason dictates.[209] Locke makes the same point in his political writings, linking freedom with the ability to move beyond "caprice" and to follow the dictates of reason to seek the good.[210] The result, writes Polin, is that "freedom acquires meaning only when it is related to an order, to the order of the world itself, which is the order of reason."[211]

But this relationship between freedom and reason suggests that "liberty has no meaning outside the right use of the understanding," and "the very existence of the understanding … finds its end, its final cause, in the right use of liberty."[212] What is the right use of both liberty and understanding? Locke is quite clear on this matter: it is to seek ultimate happiness by attending to God's will in this world and attaining eternal salvation for the next. Thus "freedom … finds its meaning in the very end of the existence of men in this world … The metaphysical and even theological dogma of eternal salvation constitutes indeed the foundation and the right justification for the existence of freedom."[213]

For Locke, the human inclination to pursue happiness is more than a tendency; it is an obligation.[214] Freedom, then, is an "essential function" of obligation, constituting "a decisive moral power," accomplishing "a moral function" in guiding the human toward eternal salvation.[215] The theological dimension also provides the most assured motivation for suspending the determination of the will, since it is in view of eternal bliss that fulfilling some desires of the will is deemed unworthy of our consideration.[216] Theology, then, explains the meaning and function of the human power of freedom, directly relating to questions of justification, obligation, and motivation.[217] Polin summarizes his case in the following way:

> Our freedom is ... a freedom of beings capable of reason, in a world organized in such a way that, with the power of reason and freedom given to us by God, we are capable of accomplishing a meaningful duty, that obligation for eternal happiness which happens to be the motive of our creation and the principle of our temporal existence.[218]

Polin also reaches a similar conclusion regarding Locke's account of political freedom. Polin claims the ground of political obligation is that of moral obligation: "the reasonable use of freedom according to the law of nature."[219] This immediately limits freedom, provides its meaning, and guides its use. Man's sovereignty over his actions and his body does not allow suicide or murder—precisely because man is God's property, and a person's life is to last as long as the Creator, not the individual, decides.[220] Locke points to obligation, and, in view of one's ultimate obligation to seek eternal salvation in the pursuit of happiness, Polin notes that suicide and murder would equally interrupt that pursuit.[221] The social relations between individuals are essentially moral, and only political when transferred to the body politic.[222] Yet, as Polin notes, it retains its moral quality: "A political obligation is developed from the publication of civil laws and takes it meaning from the law of nature and the reasonable order which it teaches in the form of a moral obligation."[223]

What is true for the individual is also true for the people as a commonwealth: the binding of moral commitments constitutes trust in view of a common good.[224] Polin adds that "all the powers transferred through the trust are ordered towards a certain end in conformity with a teleological reckoning. According to the trust, the rulers' freedom is bound by the obligation of acting towards its end."[225]

It is not a piece of added rhetoric for Locke to claim that a person's final appeal is "to heaven"; it reinforces the just and reasonable basis upon which a community may make judgments, and it reminds readers that political communities may only carry out temporal justice.[226] There is a necessary connection between this conclusion and the limits placed upon "free and voluntary societies" such as religious ones; one cannot use temporal means to coerce judgments of eternal consequence.[227] Toleration on matters that can only "appeal to heaven" is thus required for political freedom. In this light, Locke's clear statements against atheists and his arguably intolerant stance toward Catholics would imply a serious contradiction for Locke were it not for his theological and teleological conception of freedom. Freedom for Locke "is fundamentally a moral freedom," since man is a moral man, and a liberal political system ordered by the law of nature must be a "reasonable" liberalism, concomitant with a "true" freedom that is "a limited, obliged and meaningful freedom."[228]

In addition to Polin's penetrating insights concerning Locke's philosophical and political accounts of freedom, consider how Locke's religious account evidences a consistent approach. In addition to his reservations on how certain Calvinistic readings of scripture reject the justice and goodness of God, Locke also appeals to the nature of consent. Adam cannot serve as a stand-in for all of humanity for the same reason that a commonwealth cannot represent an unwilling participant: "millions had never heard of" Adam, "and no one had authorised to transact for him, or be his representative."[229] The law of nature imposes moral duties, which are included among the requirements of Christianity, and even the call to obey positive laws recorded in scripture is rooted in the law of nature: "it being a part of the law of nature, that man ought to obey every positive law of God, whenever he shall please to make any such addition to the law of his nature."[230] Thus, the law of works refers to the moral obligation to use one's freedom to follow the reasonable dictates of the law of nature, and this same law of nature provides the grounding obligation to seek revelation, whereby one encounters the law of faith. The fate of one's eternal soul must be attained through consent in accordance with the moral duties of the law of nature.

To conclude, humans possess a natural freedom, which, distinguished from license, has an essentially moral character rooted in duty. To speak in terms made famous by Isaiah Berlin, Locke moves beyond the defense of negative liberty, which characterizes the position of Hobbes, and instead conceives of freedom as the positive conformity of one's actions to the reasonable dictates of the law of nature.[231] Humans possess a certain nature, which includes moral obligation to freely pursue the good that ensures true happiness, manifested ultimately in the salvation of one's soul. Theology, then, serves as the grounding principle of freedom, as well as serving as the principle motivator for pursuing the natural ends for which the human is fitted.[232]

## Summary and conclusion

This chapter has argued that Locke is a Christian natural law theorist whose views concerning the law of nature are part of a larger theology of creation. The human *telos* is to pursue the business of bearing the image of God on earth, and this telos is seen politically in Locke's treatment of equality and human freedom. This Christian theology of creation is fundamental to Locke's argumentation and provides the second plank in support of Locke's political philosophy.

That humans are born in freedom or liberty to pursue goodness, justice, and happiness is, for Locke, the fundamental law of nature. Since we are called to be "about [God's] business," liberty, for Locke, is teleologically oriented, not absolute. However, Locke championed voluntary consent and liberty of conscience as opposed to state coercion. Human beings were created not simply to live free but to live well. Since God enjoyed freedom and goodness, humans made in God's image ought to use freedom to pursue the good. This included living a life in search of future heavenly reward and avoiding everlasting punishment.

Locke recognized a theological threat to his political philosophy in the doctrine of double predestination. In this sort of hyper-Calvinism, God appears as nothing more than arbitrary power, and moral goodness must be found in something other than God's essential character. Locke sees the nature of a just society rooted in the nature of God, and the results of this chapter reveal a particularly Latitudinarian account of creation that leads Locke to reject predestination as theologically odious and philosophically dangerous. Locke's political philosophy takes freedom and consent seriously as a Christian principle. Locke's Latitudinarian theology of creation is one rooted in freedom and participation, and his political theory assumes that when free people in free societies participate in government, they emulate the very character of God.

# 6

# Revelation, Reason, and Scripture

Locke describes God and the human vocation to obey the law of nature in language consistent with (and often drawn from) Christian scripture. The question arises how dependent Locke might be for his conception of God on scripture and what would constitute "His (God's) business" in the social and political realms. Locke's high regard for reason and heavy emphasis in the *Essay* on deductive logic and empirical tests in matters relating to God and morality have led some to question Locke's understanding of revelation in general and of scripture as revelation in particular.[1] With careful attention paid to Locke's argumentation in the *RC*, this chapter will show that, for Locke, revelation is not in competition with reason; instead, revelation largely clarifies, enhances, and adds grounds for obligation and motivation toward the good to which reason points. In addition, the revelation of God in scripture provides assurance that Locke's political aims do, in fact, form a Christian political philosophy. Whether or not Locke is conscious of his dependence on scripture,[2] it is clear that he relies on his conviction that God has provided revelation of Himself in scripture and this revelation—detailing a "true idea" of God—provides essential elements of Locke's political theory.

## The constitution: A model for appreciating Locke's approach to scripture

Raymond Polin's article on Locke's conception of freedom summarizes the essential role of a constitution for setting boundaries and enshrining communal trust within Locke's vision of polity. According to Polin, "one could gather the whole" of Locke's key terms "in a single formula: the trust must be expressed under the form of a constitution, of fundamental laws, which determine the nature of the common good and the ways through which it is to be achieved."[3] Jeremy Waldron echoes these sentiments. For Locke, when a group of legislators attempts to arrive at just and fair conclusions drawn from right principles, a written constitution is far superior to applying "the light of reason" to the laws of nature.[4]

In this chapter, I will show that the political dynamic at work in a legislature's reliance on a written constitution parallels in important ways the theological dynamic at work in Locke's own commitment to the truths he believes are given in the text of scripture. Locke does not advocate any religious litmus test for a person to be admitted to the body politic; they need not assent to the witness of Christ and the apostles concerning salvation from sin through the cross. Equally, Locke is clear that scripture does not provide a blueprint for political constructions. However, as Locke lays out his political theory, he is himself bound by truths revealed in scripture and builds a theory consonant with revelation. In fact, as will be explained later, some of Locke's central political claims result from reflection on truths revealed in scripture.

For example, Locke advocates religious toleration by the body politic precisely because it is not only "agreeable to the Gospel of Jesus Christ" to be peaceful but the fulfillment of the revealed Christian duty to show charity, rather than seeking to "exercise Lordship over" others.[5] Locke further declares that toleration is necessary in order to allow every person to make a voluntary assent of faith—making his case for the necessity of faith on the basis of scripture itself. Locke's theory of property includes a requirement to act out of *agape* love for one's neighbor—a proposition drawn directly from scripture and likely unsupported without appeal to the authority of scripture or of Christ himself. His case for human equality requires a theology of creation that is rooted in biblical terminology of humans as God's "workmanship," created in his "image" to be "about His business," and commanded to have "dominion." And, for Locke, these are not mere pious phrases.

Finally, Locke's skepticism concerning humanity's ability to glean all necessary truths from reflection on the law of nature leads him to advocate lives of faith, surrendering to truths revealed in scripture, as the proper end for one pursuing a life of reason. Revelation, then, plays not only a substantial but necessary role in Locke's formation of his moral and political philosophy—so much so that it proves difficult to articulate a secular defense of key aspects of Locke's political theory without regard to revelation.

## The particular agenda of Locke's political works

Locke is explicit about his particular agenda in the *Essay*: to provide deductive rational argument (called "reason") as far as can be provided "as contradistinguished to *faith*," which "is the assent to any proposition, not thus made out by the deductions of reason, but upon the credit of the proposer, as coming from God, in some extraordinary way of communication" (which he calls "revelation"). Yet Locke considers both of these as "way[s] of discovering truths to men." The distinction is not to place one over the other in terms of validity or truthfulness but in terms of appropriateness to "argue with anyone, or ever convince a gainsayer."[6]

Locke is interested in finding common ground and appealing to that which one party in a dispute does not consider an authority (i.e., scripture) is a far less commendable approach than to deal with that which both parties acknowledge (i.e., reason). This view does not take away from Locke's estimation of the importance of scripture. In some ways, it enhances it. Locke believes many of the truths of scripture are evident as plain truths of reason and echoes of the same voice. Religion is well grounded in reason, since God "has so plentifully provided us with the means to discover and know him, so far as is necessary to the end of our being, and the great concernment of our happiness."[7] Locke's more elaborate (and possibly unfortunate) talk of "mathematical certainty" and "being certain that there is a God" should not detract from the fact that this section of the *Essay* is simply reasserting what Christian scriptures themselves testify, that humanity is "without excuse" for not acknowledging Him whose existence "lies plain before them, for God has shown it to them."[8] In this respect, Locke does not stray far from a long Christian tradition concerning the implications of God's perfection.[9]

This understanding may provide a clue for how to approach the *Second Treatise* as well.[10] Locke's relative lack of direct citations to scripture (not as "lacking" as some assert)[11] is tactical, part of a general notion that truths of revelation, consistent with reason, may be presented in terms of reason alone. This is not to belittle revelation;[12] on the contrary, reason was to be seen as an emanation from the same origin as revelation itself. In the light of this contention, it is all the more important to note scriptural references throughout his works. Locke views Christian scripture as authoritative, though he is hesitant to use too many direct references for fear that one might assume them to be self-evident interpretations. Locke is doubtful that all will agree on interpretations of scripture.[13] Since this is so, one may legitimately ask why he references scripture at all. For Locke, the principles of reason and the foundations of moral law support and point to the generally agreed basic truths of historic Christianity, fully in accord with the language and cadence of scripture.

## Locke's theology of scripture

### Locke's high view of scripture

Locke considered Bible study to be a Christian imperative, one he took seriously.[14] Even the cadence of scripture affected Locke's own writing; Damaris Cudworth once remarked that she could not understand some of Locke's letters without consulting the New Testament.[15] Since some scholars reject the strong biblical foundation of Locke's political theory, and since Locke shares affinities with a wide variety of theorists—including Jean Le Clerc, whose writings seem to question the inspiration of scripture—it is important to recognize Locke's high view of scripture.[16]

Locke's rhetoric concerning the authority and veracity of the Bible is high and clear. Even in the *Essay*, Locke says directly that "every thing said in the text [is] infallibly true."[17] In the *Second Treatise*, Locke refers to both the Old and New Testaments as "the positive law of God," cites scripture to establish "divine authority," and approvingly references a quote by Hooker, which declares any human law of jurisprudence must be made and enforced "without contradiction to any positive law of scripture."[18]

His clearest expressions can be found in the *RC*. Locke claims "the inspired books" (including the New Testament) provide "a full and sufficient rule for our direction," expressing every duty of morality, which "lie there clear, and plain, and easy to be understood."[19] This is fortunate, since "man ought to obey every positive law of God," and "all divine revelation requires the obedience of faith."[20] In terms of a moral code, the New Testament has no equal. Speaking of the ethical teachings offered by "our Saviour and his apostles," Locke writes: "It is all pure, all sincere; nothing too much, nothing wanting; but such a complete rule of life, as the wisest men must acknowledge, tends entirely to the good of mankind, and that all would be happy, if all would practise it."[21]

But holy writ offers more than kernels of truth by way of morality. Scripture records many teachings of Jesus of which Locke asserts: "It is sure all our Saviour's discourses were wise and pertinent"[22] and that "what he delivered cannot but be received as the oracles of God, and unquestionable verity."[23] What scripture records concerning the teachings of Christ is considered to have historical veracity. The New Testament provides "his [Jesus'] history … the history of our Saviour, writ by the evangelists … [and the] history of the apostles, writ in the Acts."[24] What of the general epistles? "These holy writers, inspired from above, writ nothing but truth; and in most places, very weighty truths to us now."[25] There are central truths, articles of faith, within scripture, but any divine revelation must be regarded as truth.[26] This is why Locke proposes one interpret the Bible in ways consistent with "the plain direct meaning of the words and phrases."[27] The text is "the written Word of God … a collection of writings, designed by God, for the instruction of … mankind."[28]

## High view is not fideism

If on one end of the spectrum some disregard Locke's regard for scripture, there are those on the other end who ascribe to Locke a simple fideism—one that regards faith as superior to, independent of, and even antagonistic to reason.[29] But this view does not do justice to Locke's thinking. First, such a view requires a monumental epistemological break with his life-long regard for the faculty of reason and empirical enquiry in matters of truth. Second, it is offered to explain Locke's rejection of a natural law discoverable by reason, yet Locke's writings late in life testify that he continued to believe both reason and revelation were means whereby one could access the moral law.[30] Third, it disregards the grounds for such a high view of scripture, which Locke provides in the *RC*. Locke embedded his high claims within the context of historical testimony concerning the miracles of Jesus, and the failure to find any denial of Jesus's mighty works among his own contemporaries.[31]

Locke recounts the preaching of Jesus in Samaria, where, before large and diverse crowds, Jesus performed miracles as a testimony to the veracity of his message; the retelling of these miracles reached even "the mighty and accomplished emperor … Julian himself" who could not raise an objection to the veracity of Jesus's miracles.[32] In similar fashion, Locke claims such testimony continues to show itself to "the ordinariest apprehension" as evidence of Jesus's reliable message.[33] Being convinced by the miracles of Jesus, the "bulk of mankind" is able to be "enlightened" to accept "all his commands" as "principles" and thus to "read the inspired books, to be instructed" as to the "duties of morality."[34] Locke is careful to disabuse the minds of some who might contend this is a case of class distinction (a view that might have been suggested by Locke's earlier reference to the "the greatest part" of humanity who "cannot know, and therefore they must believe"[35]). He claims the veracity of miracle-backed testimony not only is "the surest, the safest, and most effectual way of teaching" but appeals to everyone, including those with the greatest faculties of reason.[36]

Locke makes a similar case in his *Discourse of Miracles*.[37] Locke appears to follow the kind of procedural thinking present in some modern evangelical-leaning theologians.[38] Jesus made certain claims; his miracles (and preeminently his resurrection) vindicated his claims, but it also, in turn, vindicated the scriptures, which (previously) prophesied his resurrection, and (later) spoke from the Spirit, which Jesus claimed would be sent subsequent to his resurrection. Thus, the vindication of Jesus is seen as vindication of the scriptures as a reliable witness. In the words of Parker, "Locke was no mere fideist when it came to matters of biblical interpretation"; yet the full picture of Locke reveals "an inquisitive and rational mind in tension with one equally committed to biblical revelation."[39]

## Reason as "judge and guide in everything?" Providing a context against enthusiasm

In truth, there is a constant interplay in Locke's works between reason and revelation to such an extent that one can only see them as complementary and interdependent.[40] Locke is convinced that the "full and sufficient rule for our direction" in moral issues—given by revelation in the New Testament—is "conformable to that of reason."[41] In fact, this is the proper context in which to understand Locke's claims about the role of reason as the final arbiter. In the *Essay*, Locke famously identifies reason as "our judge and guide in everything."[42] Locke begins *Of the Conduct of the Understanding* with similar praise for the faculty of reason:

> The last resort a Man has recourse to in the Conduct of himself, is his Understanding ... whatsoever Faculties he employs, the Understanding, with such Light as it has, well or ill informed, constantly leads, and by that Light, true or false, all his operative Powers are directed ... The Faculty of Reasoning seldom or never deceives those who trust to it; its Consequences from what it builds on are evident and certain.[43]

Some commentators point to these passages as evidence for Locke's esteeming reason above revelation and thus constraining the power and role of revelation as given in Christian scriptures.[44] This is a mistaken interpretation. In Locke's most famous passage in this regard—which falls within a chapter discussing how to adjudicate contemporary and extra-biblical enthusiastic utterances (which some claim to be given by the Holy Spirit)—Locke explains himself along the lines expressed above:

> Reason must be our last judge and guide in everything. I do not mean that we must consult reason, and examine whether a proposition revealed from God can be made out by natural principles, and if it cannot, that then we may reject it: but consult it we must, and by it examine, whether it be a *revelation* from God or no.[45]

Locke is concerned with those who use proof texting (citing a passage, individually interpreted, as an argument against what is deduced by reason) as a means of argument.[46] But such a position further solidifies the notion that Locke maintains fundamental agreement between the "truths" of scripture and what "truths" may be derived from reason.

But it is clear the bulk of Locke's ire seems to be directed toward the grave dangers of superstition, enthusiasm, and peculiar private interpretations—the very things Bishop Burnet described as central vices in the estimation of the Latitudinarians.[47] Instead of broad, general principles given in scripture, which all rational people can rationally accept upon reading, or equally discover on their own (through the light of reason), Locke is concerned with stilted readings (or revelations) belonging to particular groups, codified into oppressive laws and intolerant prescriptions. This is evident by Locke's speaking in the present tense of that which passes for revelation—"inspirations and delusions"[48]—as well as his explicit claims in *A Second Vindication of the Reasonableness of Christianity* of 1697:

> I was flatter'd to think it might be of some use in the World; especially to those who thought either that there was no need of Revelation at all, or that the Revelation of our Saviour required the Belief of such Articles for Salvation, which the settled Notions and their way of reasoning in some, and the want of Understanding in others, made impossible to them. Upon these two Topiks the Objections seemed to turn, which were with most Assurance, made by *Deists* against *Christianity*; but against *Christianity* misunderstood. It seem'd to me, that there needed no more to shew them the Weakness of their Exceptions, but to lay plainly before them the Doctrine of our Saviour and his Apostles, as delivered in the Scriptures, and not as taught by the several Sects of Christians.[49]

Locke acknowledges the interpreter's proneness to err (and, on the best of occasions, to only give probable conjectures concerning the true meaning of scripture) in contradistinction to the author of revelation "who cannot err and will not deceive." In this case, "the mind ... is bound to give up its assent to such a testimony, which, it is satisfied, comes from" this errorless source. It is only up to the interpreter to decide, by use of reason, whether something is indeed a revelation from God; once that decision is established, veracity is established.[50] Rather than being radical, the general claim "scripture is inerrant, my interpretation is not" is standard fare in later Protestant reform movements.

But if stilted, peculiar readings of scripture were considered a challenge to mutual toleration and peaceful coexistence by people required to follow the dictates of reason, religious enthusiasm (whereby one receives a personal message from the Lord, which cannot be verified by scripture and may be contrary to scripture) was an even graver threat. As was shown in Chapter 3, Locke shared with Whichcote, More, and other Latitudinarians this deep aversion to religious enthusiasm. It would have been easy for Locke to show the profound problem with religious enthusiasm by declaring no need for revelation (since the law of nature may be discovered by reason, the judge and guide in everything). But Locke writes at length admitting the need for revelation (as this chapter will show), indicating that the grave threat of religious enthusiasm is the possibility of a rival standard to which all are accountable. Instead, Locke declared that reason is the sole judge and guide in everything in order to counter the claims of those who would offer counterclaims to the rational truths given in scripture, and the moral obligations enjoined therein. When one considers the deep sense in which Locke believes in a need for revelation, the threat posed by religious enthusiasm becomes clear.

## The need for revelation and the coming of the Messiah

Locke moves beyond expressing a high regard for revelation in scripture by establishing an epistemological need. In the *Essay*, Locke fully assures his readers of the indispensable role of revelation (in accord with reason) to provide "truths to men," which are not capable of being deduced from reason alone.[51] Revelation, in fact, conveys *"the proper matter of faith,"* which not only is in accord with reason but which includes truths that are *"above reason"*:

> There being many things wherein we have very imperfect notions, or none at all, and other things, of whose past, present, or future existence, by the natural use of our faculties, we can have no knowledge at all; these, as being beyond the discovery of our natural faculties, and *above reason*, are, when revealed, *the proper matter of faith*.[52]

Locke extends this point in the *RC*. The vast majority of humanity could not deduce God's moral requirements without revelation, and even the wisest among us could not produce the full range or entire catalog of nature's law through unassisted reason.[53] Locke makes many concessions for unusual cases—noting certain people with higher rational capacities, and the mercy of God in condescending in the light of our insufficiency, but the logic of his argument is that revelation did more than codify and clarify that which was available in the world. Some truths are beyond our grasp, and the vast majority of mankind would never have identified and retained knowledge of God's moral laws without the advent of revelation. Humanity often slips into the error of failing to recognize our debt to revelation, opting instead (due to being "favourable enough to our own faculties") to claim that all great truths within our intellectual grasp have arrived by "the strength and native light of our own minds."[54] But this is patently false, for "many are beholden to revelation, who do not acknowledge it."[55]

This is especially true in establishing a moral law upon which to build a fair and just society. The dictates of philosophers lack true authority and, thus, provide no ultimate grounds for motivating others to follow their lead. The philosophers were incapable of "making out its obligation from the true principles of the law of nature, and foundations of morality."[56] This is because any standard, to be "universally useful," must "have its authority, either from reason or revelation."[57] Yet Locke has already shown that the former approach—that of reason—has not sufficiently produced the desired effects. Locke believes the latter approach—that of revelation—provides that which unassisted reason could not provide: a "sure standard."[58]

Locke, then, makes two basic points. First, human reason, unassisted by revelation, has not and cannot provide the complete picture of man's moral duty, that is, the law of nature, nor offer a ground for obligation to keep the law of nature.[59] Second, the revelation brought by Christ provides this total picture, is in accord with reason, and offers both true authority and persuasive motivation.[60] In making this claim, Locke portrays Christ as the authoritative revealer, expounder, clarifier, interpreter, and codifier of God's will concerning man's moral duties.

It is on account of these considerations that Locke emphasizes "nature reason no-where had cured" not only the failing of moral codes but the differing approaches to them throughout the world, "*nor was like to cure* the defects and errours in them."[61] The reason is clear:

> Those just measures of right and wrong, which necessity had anywhere introduced, the civil laws prescribed, or philosophy recommended, stood on their

true foundations. They were looked on as bonds of society, and conveniences of common life, and laudable practices. But where was it that their obligation was thoroughly known and allowed, and they received as precepts of a law; of the highest law, the law of nature? *That could not be, without a clear knowledge and acknowledgement of the law-maker, and the great rewards and punishments*, for those that would, or would not obey him.[62]

The explicit emphasis on the afterlife is necessary; pursuit of the ethical for its own sake will not carry the burden of authority or persuasive motivation to create a just society. "The philosophers, indeed, showed the beauty of virtue," writes Locke, "but leaving her unendowed, very few were willing to espouse her."[63] The term "unendowed" is quite telling. Locke had earlier endorsed the view that "the duties of that law" of morality for man arise "from the constitution of his very nature."[64] The problem, Locke claims, is myopia: those who taught that one can harness the grounds for virtue in human nature alone offered "airy commendations" that "satisfied not many,"[65] with good reason. Obligation and persuasive appeal are much better to be found in the Christian story, which provides a secure pledge (by the resurrection of Christ) for the hope of immortality, clear teaching concerning the threat of punishment, and the obligation to seek virtue in accord with the Savior's commands.[66] Thus the Christian hope unites reason and self-interest in accord with virtue.[67]

But Locke wishes to make one more move, which appears to be a necessary one. A scheme that includes "consideration of another life," with rewards and punishments, provides the one and only basis for morality. "Upon this foundation," writes Locke, "*and upon this only*, morality stands firm, and may defy all competition. This makes it more than a name; a substantial good, worth all our aims and endeavors; and thus the gospel of Jesus Christ has delivered it to us."[68] The link between future reward and punishment with the basis of morality cannot be clearer, yet Locke intends his language to be inclusive of a larger portrait. Earlier in the *Essay*, Locke declared "that all Religion and genuine Morality depend" upon God's existence;[69] though Locke here adds the significance of God's ultimate judgment, one should not miss the fact that Locke's basis for morality extends beyond mere pleasure or pain. Morality matters because God matters; morality derives its definition from the nature of God, not simply how compliance with or failure to achieve morality may affect an individual. Locke was always concerned with "Truth in Morality," since there exists "true intrinsick good or ill … in things."[70] The doctrine of Creation—enveloping God's nature, human telos, and human judgment—provides the fitting framework in which to understand the basis of morality for Locke. One must not only believe in rewards and punishments, but that God is the one providing such ends, and that such ends will be based on the law of works (or, through pardon, also through the law of faith). Thus, "morality stands firm" and serves as "a substantial good" in light of the larger scheme of God's existence and will, ultimately "delivered … to us" in "the gospel of Jesus Christ."[71]

## An exception that proves the rule: The case of the justified heathen[72]

To be fair, however, when one consults the wider corpus, it is apparent that Locke does not believe moral certainty is the sole possession of those who have access to divine revelation.[73] Even in the *RC*, Locke claims one can know that there is a law of nature and can obediently comply with its regulations in such a manner and to such an extent as to find one's chief end—including the rewards of the afterlife.[74] Yet these assertions are based on God's prerogative (as lawgiver), and his merciful character, in adjudicating cases in which a person has complied with God's law only insofar as he has become aware of it or is capable of obeying it.[75] As such, they serve as exceptions to the general rule: that the "bulk of mankind" shall not live (eternally) by reason alone. Revelation confirms the theistic basis of his theory, fills in what is obscure, and teaches truths, which (though theoretically epistemologically available independent of revelation and amenable to the law of reason) can only (practically speaking) be understood by the light of revelation.[76]

In this light, consider a provocative section of the *RC* where Locke makes two cases for justifying the "heathen."[77] Locke's first case involves those living before the coming of Christ who had only the promises of Christ recorded in the Old Testament.[78] Locke acknowledges that biblical "faith" involves responding to whatever revelation is available; one is not required to know more than that to which he has access. Instead, biblical "faith" involves relying on the "goodness" of God and trusting whatever promises "the light of nature" or revelation (to which one has access) may declare.[79] In the Old Testament, God grants clemency to those who "rest assured of his rewarding those who rely on him, for whatever, either by the light of nature, or particular promises, he has revealed to them of his tender mercies, and taught them to expect from his bounty."[80] The mention of "the light of nature" as equally valid to God's revelatory promises in providing grounds for hope in God's gracious bounty is striking. But this is keeping with Locke's dependence on the character of God as the basic foundation of his moral theory. God is just (which implies fairness) and good (which carries the notion of mercy, sympathy, and understanding). "Those therefore, who pleased

God," writes Locke, "and were accepted by him before the coming of Christ, did it only by believing the promises, and relying on the goodness of God, as far as he had revealed it to them."[81]

This sets the stage for Locke's second case, namely, what of those who (whether past or present) hear nothing of the Messiah?[82] In a pregnant passage, Locke moves beyond epistemological humility and reflections on God's mercy,[83] opting instead to offer the possibility of full acceptance on the basis of God-honoring (and perhaps even specifically *Christian*) ethics gleaned by the use of reason alone:

> God had, by the light of reason, revealed to all mankind, who would make use of that light, that he was good and merciful. The same spark of the divine nature and knowledge in man, which ... showed him the law he was under ... showed him also the way of atoning the merciful, kind, compassionate Author and Father of him and his being, when he had transgressed that law. He that made use of this candle of the Lord, so far as to find what was his duty, could not miss to find also the way to reconciliation and forgiveness, when he had failed of his duty.[84]

Locke then reveals some surprising soteriological implications of this view:

> The law is the eternal, immutable standard of right. And a part of that law is, that a man should forgive, not only his children, but his enemies, upon their repentance, asking pardon, and amendment. And therefore he could not doubt that the author of this law, and God of patience and consolation, who is rich in mercy, would forgive his frail offspring, if they acknowledged their faults, disapproved the iniquity of their transgressions, begged his pardon, and resolved in earnest, for the future, to conform their actions to this rule, which they owned to be just and right. This way of reconciliation, this hope of atonement, the light of nature revealed to them: and the revelation of the gospel, having said nothing to the contrary, leaves them to stand and fall to their own Father and Master, whose goodness and mercy is over all his works.[85]

Where Locke derives certain portions of this remarkable passage are easy to discover: God's merciful nature, especially with regard to "frail" humans, has already been established; the requirements of "faith" and "repentance" (renouncing wrong and choosing to live ethical lives) were described at length in the first half of the *RC*, and the specific case of God forgiving people who forgive their neighbors is taken from the Sermon on the Mount, which Locke endorses as describing truths of the moral law of nature.[86] It is also clear that Locke is applying his understanding of Romans 2:14, where "gentiles which have not the law, do (i.e., find it reasonable to do) by nature the things contained in the law" actually "show the work of the law written in their hearts."[87] Contrary to an oft-repeated claim in Locke scholarship, Locke does not believe that the only thing required for salvation or justification is to believe that Jesus is the Messiah.[88] Instead, Locke goes to great lengths to show the ethical imperative in the covenant of grace, which, importantly, *already existed* in the covenant of works, that is, the law of nature. Christians are assured the promise that their faith will count for righteousness, covering the defect in any disobedience to the moral law. His reading of Romans 2, coupled with clear examples where belief *minus* ethical behavior led to divine rejection,[89] apparently leads Locke to consider cases where ethical behavior *minus* belief in the Messiah can lead to divine acceptance, their behavior counting as "faith" in the bounty of God's grace, derived from meditation on the works of nature, by the light of reason.

But this "exceptional case" in fact proves the rule. What the "heathen" discovers is not simply some general notion of goodness but a specifically Christian teaching found in the Sermon on the Mount, fitting a biblical description of the character of God. In addition, the claim that faults can be defined as such, and forgiveness granted, makes proper sense within a revelatory context. It is doubtful such a bundle of beliefs can be found inherently in virtually any other system. That is, the substantive good, perceived by the "heathen," is the character of God and way to forgiveness that is taught in Christian doctrine, yet is fully in accord with reason, such that the light of reason could point to it. Defending this situation, however, depends on accepting that biblical portrait of God, as well as the promise of forgiveness as delivered in the scriptures.

## Revelation's mandate and Locke's politics

### "Thou shalt love thy neighbour as thyself": Locke's doctrine of charity

One way in which Locke's reliance on revelation directly affects his political aims can be found in Locke's theory of property. In a section of the *Second Treatise* entitled "Of Property,"[90] Locke sets out to explain and defend how one may have a right to private property, given that God has given the earth to mankind in common. Locke suggests a right to take what is necessary for subsistence is included in the right to life, and when a person mixes their own labor with the common ground, that which is produced may rightfully be his. However, Locke offers several limiting conditions, such as taking only an amount that will not lead to wasted spoilage and leaving "enough and as good" for others.[91] Locke discusses justified modifications to these conditions due to the invention of money and the possibility of leaving less land in exchange for more produce.

The purpose of this section is not to defend Locke's theory of property but to explore his argumentation as it relates to his theological assumptions derived from scripture. As this section will show, Locke's theory of property provides an excellent example of his reliance on and incorporation of revelation into his political theory. It also serves as a test case of sorts, since his theory of property has recently been used as a model for precisely the opposite conclusion.[92] According to Stanley Brubaker, Locke's theory of property—as expressed in the *Two Treatises*—"is nothing less than a story of man's Enlightenment," offering "a case against Revelation as an independent source of authority," opting instead for a story of man "coming into his own mind, freed from the irrational claims of Revelation."[93] According to Brubaker, Locke begins a chapter of the *Second Treatise* dealing with property "with feet planted in both reason and revelation, or so it might seem, but he will pivot and push forward on mature reason alone … [as] man works his way from being the 'servant of God,' his 'Workmanship,' to one who is fully 'Master of himself.'"[94] According to Brubaker (following Strauss), Locke uses Filmer's misuse of scripture as a foil so that Locke himself could "[train] his sights on scripture itself."[95] Focusing exclusively on the *Two Treatises*, Brubaker uncovers a "[severe] … critique of Christianity" in which Locke, who is "inclined toward a deism of sorts," utilizes the theological-sounding "workmanship thesis" as a heuristic and pedagogical tool to say that "man must work to own his own mind."[96]

Brubaker's argument is flawed for a number of reasons. First, his method misleads him. Brubaker outlines his method in the following manner:

> I follow closely the sequence in which Locke presents his points in *Two Treatises* … I make little reference to Locke's other works: Locke wrote the *Two Treatises* anonymously, without referring to his other works and he wrote his other works without referring to the *Two Treatises*. Accordingly, we may safely believe Locke thought the *Two Treatises* fully accessible on its own.[97]

Locke may very well have intended the *Two Treatises* to be "fully accessible on its own" in terms of laying out the practical aspects of a political construction, but (as this book has argued) one is not able to fully access the grounds for Locke's political theory through reading the *Two Treatises* alone. Locke's *LCT* fails to reference his other works and makes a stand-alone argument, yet, read in isolation, the *LCT* represents a political agenda born out of Christian commitments, penned by an author with serious religious scruples. One can hardly read the fourth book of the *Essay* without recognizing a certain *reliance* on faith (resulting from the acceptance of revelation as an independent source), which does not fit any deistic portrait. Finally, of course, Locke's distinctly religious works—which are at once deeply philosophical and political as well—appear as stand-alone writings and, read by themselves, present a diametrically opposite picture of Locke than that suggested by Brubaker.

In addition, Brubaker fails to appreciate Locke's intentional and strategic desire to avoid appeals to scripture when appeals to reason will suffice. Brubaker makes a great deal of noise about Locke citing but not "explicating" scripture, as well as referencing "anatomists and philosophers" as authorities, and notes that Locke derives human duties toward the creator "not from scripture" but rather "as an inference from natural reason, informed by empirical evidence."[98] From this flimsy case, Brubaker concludes "this interpretation of Locke as a sort of deist contrasts … with the common portrayal of Locke as a Christian."[99] Yet we learn from Locke's other writings that he is profoundly influenced by a particular method of persuasion reminiscent of the Apostle Paul's rhetorical strategy in Athens, namely, to appeal to common authorities that do not need controversial explication as scripture so often does.

In fact, as Waldron has noted, Locke's theory of property included a necessary link to theology drawn from the dictates of revelation; the command to love one's neighbor is transposed into a "doctrine of charity."[100] In the opening pages of the *Second Treatise*, Locke sandwiches a reference to Hooker between his two pillar passages advocating human equality:

> This *equality* of Men by Nature, the Judicious *Hooker* looks upon as so evident in it self, and beyond all question, that he makes it the Foundation of that Obligation to mutual Love amongst Men, on which he Builds the Duties they owe one another, and from whence he derives the great Maxims of *Justice* and *Charity*.[101]

Hooker, it appears, is not the only one being judicious, since Locke astutely observes that "mutual love," as codified in the golden rule or Christ's second greatest commandment, serves as the basis of Hooker's entire Theo-political treatise. This is, in part, because it serves as the basis of Jesus's own teachings. In the *RC*, Locke reminds his readers that Jesus "closes all his particular injunctions, with this general golden rule," citing Matthew 7:12.[102] It is not a coincidence that this general notion of a golden rule plays a significant role in all aspects of Locke's theory as well. In his *Of the Conduct of the Understanding*, Locke states, "Our Savior's great Rule, that *we should love our Neighbor as our selves*, is such a Fundamental Truth for the regulating human Society; that I think, by that alone, one might without difficulty, determine all the Cases and Doubts in Social Morality."[103] In the *Essay*, Locke claims that the slogan "*That one should do as he would be done unto*" is, in fact, "that most unshaken Rule of Morality, and Foundation of all social Virtue."[104] Yet knowledge of this rule is not innate, for Locke. Instead, one becomes aware of this rule by the light of reason and reflection on the law of nature.

But scripture pushes deeper than simple "care" or "concern" for another being, and Locke appears to draw moral imperatives from this fact. This can be seen in how Locke views responsibility toward the self, the creation, and one's neighbor. Locke views self-preservation as not only a right but also a duty to which one is "bound" in the light of the fact that humans are the property of their Maker, God.[105] His theory of labor implies a "teleology of natural resources"[106] and uses the language of "must" and "necessity" in contexts where the commands given at Creation suggest the use of resources in the fulfillment of our (and their) intended purpose.[107] This implies a "teleology of appropriation," which can be discerned by reasonable reflection within a system that embraces and endorses a biblical theology of creation.[108] This is found in the fact that human beings cannot simply do as they please toward the created order without restriction, and the positing of any moral restrictions implies some sense of responsibility and accountability that relates directly to teleology.[109]

What is interesting, as Locke points out, is that beyond the "spoliation" and "sufficiency" provisos (which offer restrictions resulting from Locke's theological teleology), there is a principle of charity toward one's neighbor that has all the earmarks of a political position dependent on teachings that result directly from revelation.[110] In the *First Treatise*, Locke lays out this principle of charity as a moral requirement within his political schema, claiming that "*Charity* gives every Man a Title to so much out of another's Plenty, as will keep him from extream want, where he has no means to subsist otherwise" on the basis that "God requires" every man "to afford to the wants of his Brother."[111] Waldron notes that here Locke "says it is *always* wrong for the rich to withhold goods from the poor, and that 'Charity gives every man a title' to the surplus goods of another when he is desperately in need of them."[112] Thus charity, "regarded as a specifically Christian virtue is for Locke no reason for thinking that it is unenforceable, or anything less than a duty."[113]

Waldron makes the claim that this principle of charity may be applied to Locke's theory of property in the *Second Treatise* as an extension of his natural law teaching; a person is obligated not only to preserve himself but also "as much as he can, to preserve the rest of mankind."[114] Yet other considerations lead to a far more concrete explanation. In the *RC*, Locke declares that charity, described as a "moral precept of the gospel," is a moral imperative for all mankind, affecting issues of righteousness and judgment.[115] He then adds that while philosophers may divine this moral precept from reflection on the law of nature, they cannot make it obligatory, or, if they do, it would have no binding force.[116] Only by linking a moral precept to the authority of Christ the lawgiver can one establish binding authority.[117] It could be argued that the gospel simply codified a principle in nature that has its own inherent obligatory force, being not a peculiar command of Jesus connected to belief but a general law of nature concerning moral action. But Locke does not appeal to the law of nature when laying down the principle of charity in the *First Treatise*, and Laslett wisely provides a suggestive footnote: "Locke may here have in mind the injunction in Luke xi. 41."[118] Locke claims that "we know" the principle of charity to refer not only to a duty but a right, and thus "we know" its binding nature upon all men.[119] Locke's appeals to Jesus's words in scripture make this connection obvious and evident; without it, it is hard to see how the principle of charity is necessitated by the law of nature.

## Voluntary faith: The basis for toleration

Scripture also plays a crucial role in grounding Locke's argument for religious toleration. This should not be surprising, since the *LCT* is a letter originally addressed to Philip van Limborch, "the chief theologian of the Remonstrants" who, according to Loconte, "offered Locke perhaps the most Biblically rooted humanism he had yet encountered."[120] Locke and Limborch held in common a number of intellectual commitments;[121] as Woolhouse notes, both men shared "a belief in the importance for Christianity of tolerance and a virtuous life, and of studying the New Testament as a guide to faith."[122] The similarities between Limborch's *Theologia Christiana* and Locke's *LCT* further suggest that the two men shared (and perhaps informed one another of) an appreciation for the biblical rootedness of the relationship between faith and toleration.[123]

Locke's explication in the *RC* concerning the nature of faith provides a helpful supplement to his rendition of the same in the *LCT*. The impetus for Locke's earlier letter came from an inquiry concerning his "thoughts about the mutual toleration of Christians in their different Professions of Religion," including "Presbyterians, Independents, Anabaptists, Arminians, Quakers, and others."[124] Yet the work expands his interest to include advocacy for the toleration of Jews,

Muslims, and praying pagans.[125] There are clearly limits to Locke's tolerance, however; Locke holds Catholics in deep suspicion, and atheists are not to be tolerated at all.[126]

The ultimate reason for Locke's perspective is religious in nature.[127] Locke believes "there [is] but one Truth," one "true religion," one "narrow way which leads to Heaven."[128] There is no greater search than the search for this one true way, since, for the sake of one's soul, obedience to God comes before obedience to any civic laws or concern for the public peace.[129] Locke acknowledges in the *LCT* that the one true religion is the way of "the church of Christ," those who practice "the Worship of the True God," recognizing "Christ" as "our Legislator."[130] The Christian faith not only provides a way to heaven but promotes peace and the general welfare here on earth: Christianity, writes Locke, is "that Religion, which carries the greatest opposition to Covetousness, Ambition, Discord, Contention, and all manner of inordinate Desires; and it is the most modest and peaceable Religion that ever was."[131] For this reason, Locke's separation of church and state is designed, at least in part, to protect the church.[132]

Two questions arise from these concessions by Locke. First, if Christianity is the "most peaceable Religion that ever was," why not require all people in society (or, at least, all religiously minded people) to belong to the Christian faith? Second, can one remove Locke's Christian connection with religious toleration and still retain a viable argument? These questions will be answered in turn.

Locke does not simply believe his views on toleration are consistent with scripture; he appeals to scripture as the very source for the basis and limits of his view. The gospel of Christ is a gospel of peace, promoting toleration. This is in keeping with the behavior of Christ but also what is necessitated by two crucial theological truths: (1) the nature of faith requires voluntary consent, and (2) final judgment—even for those expressing faith in Christ—will, in some sense, be according to works. If faith cannot be coerced, but only accepted willingly, then the Christian religion must not be required of any person in civil society, lest the very requirement deprive a person of the faith requested. If discovering the proper way to worship God and to obey His laws plays an important role in one's future reward or punishment, then a wide toleration for different opinions must be set in place, lest the government actively involve itself in depriving its members of eternal reward. "The end of all Religion is to please" God, writes Locke, and "Liberty is essentially necessary to that end."[133] For Locke, the Christian scriptures require religious toleration—not only as a good model for governance but also as sound theology. Atheists have no part or interest in the search for eternal matters, and Catholics pose the possible threat of allegiance to another source of revelation outside of scripture and thus a divided loyalty. In essence, then, Locke believes the scriptures provide the basis for supporting a religiously tolerant society precisely for religious reasons, which has positive effects for all of society.[134]

According to Loconte, the *LCT* "brought together a sophisticated secular approach to political authority with a profoundly Biblical view of Christian discipleship."[135] But remove Locke's appeal to the Christian faith as expressed in scripture, and one is at a loss to explain the ground and limits for his appeal to religious tolerance. Religion, historically, has proved to be a seedbed of conflict, and one could easily pardon Locke were he to advocate banishing all religious people for the sake of peace. But tolerating religion is absolutely necessary precisely because finding the true religion is the telos of faith and essential for eternal reward. The biblical description of faith, then, is central to Locke's case for religious tolerance; without this element, one is at a loss to explain the ground and limits of Locke's case.

## Summary and conclusion

Locke's appeal to revelation alongside reason ought to give one pause before ascribing deistic tendencies to Locke. Some have erred in limiting Locke's essential category (for knowledge of God) to reason alone, thus (1) isolating his particular arguments for the existence of God, (2) evaluating the validity of such arguments in the light of a particular philosophical method, then (3) positing what little remains as the only semblance of God inherent in his theory, devoid of revelation. Such a caricature of Locke puts him at odds with his expressed determination against "the vain philosophy, and foolish metaphysics of some men" who minimize the importance of revelation.[136] Locke is clear in opposing those who make "Jesus Christ nothing but the restorer and preacher of pure natural religion; thereby doing violence to the whole tenor of the New Testament."[137] Scripture, for Locke, fills out essential details concerning the nature, existence, and will of God. Revelation is portrayed as an equally valid avenue for knowing God and his will and is even a greater avenue for knowing particular obligations and how to flesh them out.

It appears, then, that Locke's third theological plank for his political philosophy is the recognition of scripture as God's divine and final revelation. Locke believed scripture provides a complete description of God's will concerning how to live a moral life, as well as a description of grace found in Jesus Christ. Locke saw no conflict between the truths of scripture and the truths of reason. Reason operates as a "primary intellectual virtue" in matters of religion, but reason clarifies truths in accordance with the law of nature and the dictates of heaven as revealed in scripture.[138] For Locke, some truths in scripture were "above reason" but never "against" reason.

The great theological danger to Locke's association between reason and scripture was religious enthusiasm. If one rooted their moral and religious claims in unverified personal revelation from God, there could be no shared standard of truth, such as can be gleaned by reasoned reflection on the law of nature and the teachings of scripture. Locke's concern with religious enthusiasm stems from his belief that God has already revealed himself in ways that lead to shared knowledge without the need for improvement. Locke envisions a society that seeks out moral truths by reasoned reflection on a body of shared knowledge. Seeking direct, personal revelation implies the need to improve on that body of shared knowledge and undermines the finality of God's revelation in scripture.

# Conclusion

Placing Locke within the religious contexts of his own day, this book has sought to establish Locke as a Latitudinarian political philosopher whose moral and political theory rests on a theological platform composed of three planks: God, the law of nature, and revelation. A careful examination of Locke's understanding of each plank shows that Locke's mature political thought is driven by Christian (rather than religiously generic) theological convictions in ways deeper and richer than often assumed. Locke's moral and political philosophy requires "a true idea" of God—one consistent with the description of God given in scripture, associated with Christian tradition, and proclaimed from Anglican pulpits. Locke's treatment of the law of nature reveals his indebtedness to a larger theology of creation from which such political aims as human freedom and human equality find their source. Finally, Locke's political theory is born out of reflection on divine revelation and assumes the Christian scriptures to offer a true and definitive understanding of God's will—leading to political injunctions rooted in biblical commands and affirmations. Locke believes that scripture mandates a wide religious toleration and the generous love of neighbor essential to a harmonious and peaceful society. In short, Locke's three points of emphasis are far from peripheral considerations or generic descriptions; they form the heart of a Latitudinarian political philosophy intended for broad appeal.

In common with other Latitudinarians, Locke was deeply concerned with some practical dangers that could damage that state, and this feeds into his advocacy of the three planks. His first plank involves establishing the existence of God as the basis for any standard of virtue, sense of obligation, and right for political structure, including laws and punishments. The great danger to this was avowed atheism. Locke's second plank is establishing the fundamental law of nature: that humans are born in freedom or liberty to pursue goodness, justice, and happiness. The great danger to this was hyper-Calvinism. Locke's third plank is establishing the role of scripture as God's final divine revelation that clarifies truths in accordance with reason and the law of nature. The great danger to this was the "false zeal" of religious enthusiasm. In each case, Locke offered a political philosophy rooted in theological principles, and he argued vehemently against theological dangers that threatened his political project.

Locke modeled his writing after the broad and generous reach of the Latitudinarians. Much of the reason why Locke may sound "secular" or "generic" in the presentation of his political theory is for theological purposes. Taking an "Areopagus" approach, Locke seeks the broadest and most inclusive form of dialogue in order to allow his deeply theological project to garner wide acceptance by a populace beset with religious differences. In a number of respects, Locke can be styled a Pauline political philosopher. Borrowing language from what were considered in his times to be Pauline writings, Locke affirms that humans are the "workmanship" of God, with a created *telos*, which includes cultivating a life of "good works" (Eph. 2:10). A God whose existence is known by all (Rom. 1:18–22), a law of nature, which applies to all (Rom 2:15), and a judgment according to works that awaits all (Rom. 2:6)—complete with punishment or reward—are just some of the Pauline claims that are central to Locke's theological (and political) project.

Locke's biblical emphasis, coupled with his Latitudinarian concerns, helps solidify the central claims of this book: namely, that Locke should be read as a Christian political philosopher, whose arguments not only self-consciously depend upon Christian assumptions but also offer a decidedly Latitudinarian political philosophy. Locke's three theological planks, lashed tightly together in his thought, form the platform on which his political theory rests. By rooting Locke's political philosophy in the more specified theological constructions outlined above, this book seeks to offer a substantial contribution in making the recent theological turn in Locke scholarship.

# Notes

## Introduction

1   For this approach, see Leo Strauss, *Natural Right and History* (Chicago: University of Chicago Press, 1953), 203-04, 212, 249-51; Richard H. Cox, *Locke on War and Peace* (1960; repr., Washington, DC: University Press of America, 1982); C. B. MacPherson, *The Political Theory of Possessive Individualism: Hobbes to Locke* (Oxford: Oxford University Press, 1962); William T. Bluhm, Neil Wintfeld, and Stuart H. Teger, "Locke's Idea of God: Rational Truth or Political Myth?" *Journal of Politics* 42, no. 2 (1980): 415-16; Patrick Coby, "The Law of Nature in Locke's Second Treatise: Is Locke a Hobbesian?" *The Review of Politics* 49, no. 1 (1987): 3-28; Thomas L. Pangle, *The Spirit of Modern Republicanism: The Moral Vision of the American Founders and the Philosophy of Locke* (Chicago: University of Chicago Press, 1988), esp. 145, 176, 186; Robert Horwitz, "Introduction," in *Questions Concerning the Law of Nature*, by John Locke, trans. Robert Horwitz, Jenny Strauss Clay, and Diskin Clay (Ithaca, NY: Cornell University Press, 1990), 1-62; Michael S. Rabieh, "The Reasonableness of Locke, or the Questionableness of Christianity," *The Journal of Politics* 53, no. 4 (November 1991): 933-57; Ulrich Im Hof, *The Enlightenment*, trans. William E. Yuill (Oxford: Oxford University Press, 1994), 169; Michael P. Zuckert, *Natural Rights and the New Republicanism* (Princeton, NJ: Princeton University Press, 1994), 207; Peter C. Myers, *Our Only Star and Compass: Locke and the Struggle for Political Rationality* (Lanham, MD: Rowman & Littlefield, 1998); Jacques Barzun, *From Dawn to Decadence: 500 Years of Cultural Life, 1500 to the Present* (New York: HarperCollins, 2000), 362-63; Michael P. Zuckert, *Launching Liberalism: On Lockean Political Philosophy* (Lawrence: University Press of Kansas, 2002); John Donald Conrad, "Locke's Use of the Bible in 'The Two Treatises,' 'The Reasonableness of Christianity,' and 'A Letter Concerning Toleration'" (PhD diss., Northern Illinois University, DeKalb, IL, 2004).
2   Jeremy Waldron, *God, Locke, and Equality: Christian Foundations of Locke's Political Thought* (Cambridge: Cambridge University Press, 2002). For the phrase "the religious turn," see Paul E. Sigmund, "Jeremy Waldron and the Religious Turn in Locke Scholarship," *The Review of Politics* 67, no. 3 (Summer 2005): 407.
3   See Kim Ian Parker, *The Biblical Politics of John Locke*, Editions SR 29 (Waterloo, ON: Wilfrid Laurier University Press, 2004); Greg Forster, *John Locke's Politics of Moral Consensus* (Cambridge: Cambridge University Press, 2005); Joanne

E. Tetlow, "The Theological Context of John Locke's Political Thought" (PhD diss., The Catholic University of America, Washington, DC, 2006); Victor Nuovo, *Christianity, Antiquity, and Enlightenment: Interpretations of Locke*, Archives Internationales D'Histoire Des Idées 203 (Dordrecht: Springer, 2011); Joseph Loconte, *God, Locke, and Liberty: The Struggle for Religious Freedom in the West* (Plymouth: Lexington Books, 2014).

4   John Locke, "Sic Cogitavit de Intellectu humano [Draft A]," in *Drafts for the Essay Concerning Human Understanding, and Other Philosophical Writings, Vol. 1: Drafts A and B*, by John Locke, ed. Peter H. Nidditch and G. A. J. Rogers (1671; Oxford: Clarendon Press, 1990), 41. In this book, Locke's spelling and grammar are reproduced as found in the sources cited.

5   John Locke, *An Essay Concerning Human Understanding*, ed. Peter H. Nidditch (1689; 1975; rev. repr., Oxford: Clarendon Press, 1979) (*E* or *Essay*).

6   *E*: 2.28.4: 351.

7   *E*: 2.28.8: 352.

8   Peter H. Nidditch, "Forward," in *Essay*, xix–xx. The first quote was penned by James Tyrrell in a margin note of his own copy of the *Essay*. See H. R. Fox Bourne, *The Life of John Locke* (London: Henry S. King & Co., 1876), Vol. 1, 248–49. In Locke's "Epistle to the Reader" (attached to the 1689 published edition of the *Essay*), he explains the origin of the work began with "five or six Friends meeting at my Chamber, and discoursing on a Subject very remote from this" (*Essay*, 7). Tyrrell noted this meeting was when Locke "first raised the issue of human understanding." Nidditch notes Tyrrell "was present at the original meeting."

9   John Locke, "Second Treatise of Government," in *Two Treatises of Government: A Critical Edition with an Introduction and Apparatus Criticus*, ed. Peter Laslett, 2nd ed. (1690; 1967; repr., Cambridge: Cambridge University Press, 1988) (*2nd T*), 265–428.

10  *2nd T*: 6. See also *2nd T*: 4.

11  See John Tulloch, *Rational Theology and Christian Philosophy in England in the Seventeenth Century*, 2 vols. (London: William Blackwood and Sons, 1872).

12  Francis Oakley, "Locke, Natural Law, and God—Again," *History of Political Thought* 18, no. 4 (Winter 1997): 624–25.

13  John W. Lenz, "Locke's Essays on the Law of Nature," *Philosophy and Phenomenological Research* 17, no. 1 (September 1956): 105–13; Alex Scott Tuckness, "The Coherence of a Mind: John Locke and the Law of Nature," *Journal of the History of Philosophy* 37, no. 1 (January 1999): 73–90; see Coby, "The Law of Nature," 3–28, for options. John William Tate, "Dividing Locke from God: The Limits of Theology in Locke's Political Philosophy," *Philosophy and Social Criticism* 39, no. 2 (2013): 161n.92, agrees with Laslett that Locke had no "conscious design to integrate" his political and philosophical writings but denies incoherence between the two. Contra Michael P. Zuckert, "Locke-Religion-Equality," *The Review of Politics* 67, no. 3 (Summer 2005): 419.

14 Tate, "Dividing Locke from God," 133–34: "Few scholars have ever doubted the sincerity" of Locke's "deep religious faith and the importance that he placed upon it in his own life and in the lives of others."

15 See, e.g., Daniel E. Flage, "Locke and Natural Law," *Dialogue* 39, no. 3 (June 2000): 435: "virtually no one denies" Locke was a proponent of a natural law theory of ethics and politics. Cf. Steven Forde, "Natural Law, Theology, and Morality in Locke," *American Journal of Political Science* 45, no. 2 (April 2001): 398: even those who espouse that "there is no natural law teaching according to Locke" usually mean that Locke fails to adequately address the scope and content of it. For this latter claim, see Rabieh, "The Reasonableness of Locke," 951; cf. Strauss, *Natural Right and History*, 204, 220.

16 Cf. notes 2 and 3 above. This applies to Locke's notion of natural "rights" as well. For an attempt to reconstruct Locke's theory of rights without theological premises, see A. John Simmons, *The Lockean Theory of Rights* (Princeton, NJ: Princeton University Press, 1992), esp. 11. For a recent account showing that Locke's theory of rights is thoroughly dependent on its theological premises, see Eleanor Curran, "An Immodest Proposal: Hobbes Rather than Locke Provides a Forerunner for Modern Right Theory," *Law and Philosophy* 32 (2013): 520–27.

17 This is a summary of the view proposed by Max L. Stackhouse. See Kevin J. Vanhoozer and Owen Strachan, *The Pastor as Public Theologian: Reclaiming a Lost Vision* (Grand Rapids, MI: Baker Academic, 2015), 18–19. For more on Stackhouse's approach, see the essays in *Public Theology for a Global Society: Essays in Honor of Max L. Stackhouse*, ed. Deirdre King Hainsworth and Scott R. Paeth (Grand Rapids, MI: Eerdmans, 2010).

18 John Locke, "The Reasonableness of Christianity as Delivered in the Scriptures," in *The Works of John Locke in Nine Volumes*, by John Locke, 12th ed. (London: C. Baldwin, 1824), Vol. 6, 1–158 (*RC*), which reprints Locke's second edition of 1696. Reference to the critical Clarendon edition (John Locke, *The Reasonableness of Christianity as Deliver'd in the Scriptures*, ed. John C. Higgins-Biddle [Oxford: Clarendon Press, 1999]), which "represents a late (if not necessarily final) revision of the text" (cxxiv), will be cited as needed.

19 John Locke, *A Letter Concerning Toleration*, ed. James H. Tully (1689; Indianapolis: Hackett, 1983) (*LCT*). In 1695, Locke penned the *LCT* as a Latin text, addressed to Philip van Limborch. It was published in Holland as the *Epistola de Tolerantia* in April 1689. However, six months later, William Popple published an English translation in London. As James Tully, "Note on the Text," in *LCT*, 19, notes, "it is this edition which Locke defended against the attack by Jonas Proast throughout the three further letters and never once questioned the accuracy of the translation." Popple later offered a second corrected edition. Citations to *LCT* refer to Tully's 1983 publication, which reproduces William Popple's original 1689 translation, incorporating corrections in spelling and typography from Popple's second edition.

20  This sympathetic description of Volf's approach is provided in Vanhoozer and Strachan, *The Pastor as Public Theologian*, 20.
21  Leslie Newbigin, *The Gospel in a Pluralist Society* (Grand Rapids, MI: Eerdmans, 1989), esp. 224–35; Leslie Newbigin, "The Trinity as Public Truth," in *The Trinity in a Pluralistic Age: Theological Essays on Culture and Religion*, ed. Kevin J. Vanhoozer (Grand Rapids, MI: Eerdmans, 1997), 1–8.
22  Oliver O'Donovan, *The Desire of the Nations: Rediscovering the Roots of Political Theology* (Cambridge: Cambridge University Press, 1996), 2.
23  O'Donovan, *The Desire of the Nations*, 2.
24  O'Donovan, *The Desire of the Nations*, 2.
25  O'Donovan, *The Desire of the Nations*, 3.
26  O'Donovan, *The Desire of the Nations*, 2–3, 279.
27  See Tetlow, "The Theological Context of John Locke's Political Thought," 444.
28  John Perry, *The Pretenses of Loyalty: Locke, Liberal Theory, and American Political Theology* (Oxford: Oxford University Press, 2011), 68, 101.
29  I am grateful to Greg Forster for making just this point in private correspondence.
30  Greg Forster, private correspondence.
31  I refer here to the Latitudinarian Christianity of his own day. However, although certain aspects of his theory would not favorably translate into contemporary debates (such as his exclusion of avowed atheists from public political life), and some of his distinctions are naive (such as thinking of religious devotion as private, while concern for civic goods is public), there is a core philosophical claim that resonates profoundly with some contemporary theological impulses.
32  John Locke, *Essays on the Law of Nature: The Latin Text with a Translation, Introduction, and Notes, Together with Transcripts of Locke's Shorthand in His Journal for 1676*, ed. and trans. W. von Leyden (1664; 1954; reissue, Oxford: Clarendon Press, 1988) (*LN*). The Horwitz edition (John Locke, *Questions Concerning the Law of Nature: With an Introduction, Text, and Translation*, trans. Robert Horwitz, Jenny Strauss Clay, and Diskin Clay [1664; Ithaca, NY: Cornell University Press, 1990] [*QLN*], from which the title *Questions* finds its origin) will be consulted as needed.
33  John Dunn, *The Political Thought of John Locke: An Historical Account of the Argument of the "Two Treatises of Government"* (Cambridge: Cambridge University Press, 1969), 198; Forde, "Natural Law," 406.

# Chapter 1

1  For example, see Im Hof, *The Enlightenment*, 169, 206; A. C. Grayling, *The Age of Genius: The Seventeenth Century and the Birth of the Modern Mind* (London: Bloomsbury, 2016), 3–4, 25, 290, 300, 302. Cf. note 1 of this book's Introduction.

2   For Locke as a proponent of "atomistic" individualism over and above social obligations, see Charles Taylor, *Sources of the Self: The Making of Modern Identity* (Cambridge, MA: Harvard University Press, 1989). For Lockean man as a "lone rights-bearer," see Mary Ann Glendon, *Rights Talk: The Impoverishment of Political Discourse* (New York: Free Press, 1991), 71. Describing Locke's theory as "completely secular," see Barzun, *From Dawn to Decadence*, 362–63. For Locke as "a decidedly modern philosopher" who affirms "an ahistorical, asocial atomistic individualism" and reinterprets Christianity "so as to use it to overcome the attitudes characteristic of the biblical orientation," see Zuckert, *Launching Liberalism*, 1, 7, and 164.

3   For example, Strauss, *Natural Right and History*; Zuckert, *Launching Liberalism*. Cf. note 1 in this book's Introduction.

4   *LCT*: 47.

5   *2nd T*: 6.

6   Henning Graf Reventlow, *The Authority of the Bible and the Rise of the Modern World* (1984; Philadelphia, PA: Fortress Press, 1985), 244.

7   Reventlow, *The Authority of the Bible*, 244.

8   Some of his peers noted that in the corpus of his work, Locke is suspect on the doctrine of the Trinity, leaves the immortality of the soul uncertain, and grants the possibility at least of thinking matter. See Jonathan I. Israel, *Radical Enlightenment: Philosophy and the Making of Modernity 1650–1750* (Oxford: Oxford University Press, 2001), 524. Thomas Beconsall, *The Ground and Foundation of Natural Religion, Discover'd, in the Principal Branches of It, in Opposition to the Prevailing Notions of the Modern Scepticks and Latitudinarians, with an Introduction Concerning the Necessity of Revealed Religion* (London: n. p., 1698), iv–vii claimed that Locke belonged among the Deists, while John Edwards, *Some Thoughts Concerning the Several Causes and Occasions of Atheism, especially in the Present Age, with some Breif Reflections on Socinianism: And on a late book entitled The Reasonableness of Christianity as Delivered in the Scriptures* (London: Printed for J. Robinson at the Golden Lyon, and J. Wyat at the Rose in S. Paul's Churchyard, 1695), charged Locke with Socinianism and thus (by assumed linkage) intentionally sowing the seeds of atheism. See William M. Spellman, *John Locke and the Problem of Human Depravity* (Oxford: Oxford University Press, 1988), 28, 83.

9   *LCT*: 21. Cf. Maurice Cranston, *John Locke: A Biography* (London: Longmans, Green, & Co., 1957), 260.

10  John Toland, *Christianity Not Mysterious: Or, a Treatise Shewing, That There Is Nothing in the Gospel Contrary to Reason, Nor Above It: And That No Christian Doctrine Can Be Properly Call'd a Mystery*, 2nd ed., enlarged (London: Printed for Sam Buckley at the Dolphin over against St. Dunstans Church in Fleetstreet, 1696). Cf. William M. Spellman, *John Locke* (London: Macmillan, 1997), 30, who points out that Toland's use of Locke's epistemology "unfortunately linked the philosopher

with one of the more vocal protagonists in the Deist controversy." See also John C. Biddle, "Locke's Critique of Innate Principles and Toland's Deism," *Journal of the History of Ideas* 37, no. 3 (July–September 1976): 411–22.

11  Hans Aarsleff, "Locke's Influence," in *The Cambridge Companion to Locke*, ed. Vere Chappell (Cambridge: Cambridge University Press, 1994), 252.

12  Israel, *Radical Enlightenment*, 523. Israel notes that Locke "did enjoy a vast triumph, but only from the 1730s onwards and only within one branch" of the Enlightenment (527). Note Israel's concluding postscript: "Locke was simply not very important in the Early Enlightenment until the 1730s" (527).

13  Israel, *Radical Enlightenment*, 524; John Dunn, "The Politics of Locke in England and America in the Eighteenth Century," in *John Locke: Problems and Perspectives, A Collection of Essays*, ed. John W. Yolton (Cambridge: Cambridge University Press, 1969), 79.

14  Israel, *Radical Enlightenment*, 524. I borrow the term "Lochisti" from Israel, who claims the term is not original with him.

15  Dunn, *The Political Thought of John Locke*, 7–8, esp. n.3. See also Dunn, "The Politics of Locke," 45–80.

16  Dunn, "The Politics of Locke," 79–80. For more on the influence of the *Two Treatises* on the American Revolution, see James Tully, "Rediscovering America: The Two Treatises and Aboriginal Rights," in *An Approach to Political Philosophy: Locke in Contexts*, ed. James Tully (Cambridge: Cambridge University Press, 1993); David Armitage, "John Locke, Carolina and the Two Treatises of Government," *Political Theory* 32 (2004): 602–26; Stephen M. Dworetz, *The Unvarnished Doctrine: Locke, Liberalism and the American Revolution* (Durham, NC: Duke University Press, 1990); Pangle, *The Spirit of Modern Republicanism*.

17  Dunn, *The Political Thought of John Locke*, 8.

18  Spellman, *John Locke*, 3.

19  Spellman, *John Locke*, 123, 142.

20  For the wonderful phrase "God intoxicated," see John Redwood, *Reason, Ridicule and Religions: The Age of Enlightenment in England, 1660–1750* (Cambridge, MA: Harvard University Press, 1976), 9.

21  Spellman, *John Locke*, 142.

22  Nicholas Wolterstorff, "Locke's Philosophy of Religion," in *The Cambridge Companion to Locke*, ed. Vere Chappell (Cambridge: Cambridge University Press, 1994), 174: "Our common practice of treating seventeenth- and eighteenth-century European philosophers as if they were secular philosophers does most of them a very ill turn."

23  Jonathan Scott, "England's Troubles: Exhuming the Popish Plot," in *The Politics of Religion in Restoration England*, ed. Tim Harris, Paul Seaward, and Mark Goldie (Oxford: Blackwell, 1990), 108–11; Cf. Jonathan Scott, *England's Troubles: Seventeenth-Century English Political Instability in European Context* (Cambridge:

Cambridge University Press, 2000), 89. Challenging the claim that after 1660 religion became a minor issue compared to financial and political matters, see Tim Harris, "Introduction: Revising the Restoration," in *The Politics of Religion in Restoration England*, ed. Tim Harris, Paul Seaward, and Mark Goldie (Oxford: Blackwell, 1990), esp. 3–4.

24. In a chapter entitled "The False Face of the Natural Law," Michael Bertram Crowe, *The Changing Profile of the Natural Law* (The Hague: Nijhoff, 1977), 224–32, follows Otto Gierke, *Natural Law and the Theory of Society: 1500–1800*, trans. Earnest Barker (1934; repr., Cambridge: Cambridge University Press, 1950), 99, 289n.11, in linking Locke with Rousseau as advocates of a natural law rooted in human reason—one that had no need to "introduce the name of God," and which could easily be detached from any idea of God. The origins for such a move are traced from Grotius through Pufendorf, the latter of whom was a popularizer of Grotius and a great influence on Locke (See Richard Tuck, *The Rights of War and Peace* [Oxford: Oxford University Press, 1999], chap. 6). Crowe, *The Changing Profile of the Natural Law*, 230, also claims the rise of mathematical models for morality led to a calculative science of morality—of interest to Locke but also foundational for Hume and other nontheological thinkers who recognized that "mathematics ... does not in any readily available sense depend upon the will of God" (see also 231n30). Matthew L. Lamb, "Inculturation and Western Culture: The Dialogical Experience between Gospel and Culture," *Communio* 21 (1994): 141, parallels Locke with Hobbes as rejecting a theocentric and teleological conception of human nature in favor of the "instrumentalization of nature, life, and society," resulting in "no substantive norms ... for what is good." Thus Locke advocates an anthropocentric morality, complete with the "value-neutral" freedom to "pursue one's own individual self-interest." See also Louis Dupré, *Passage to Modernity: An Essay in the Hermeneutics of Nature and Culture* (New Haven, CT: Yale University Press, 1993), 143. Matthew Levering, *Biblical Natural Law: A Theocentric and Teleological Approach* (Oxford: Oxford University Press, 2008), 2, 6, 86, 99, 100, 103, includes Kant, Hegel, and Nietzsche as Locke's compatriots in offering an anthropocentric and individualist alternative to any theocentric and teleological account of natural law. For a response, see Paul Kelly, *Locke's Second Treatise of Government: A Reader's Guide* (London: Continuum, 2007), 48–50 and Chapter 4 of this book.

25. Leo Strauss is famously connected to the "American school," which, finding its origin in Karl Schmidt, sees Locke as part of the shaping of (a problematic) liberal modernity. However, there is a split among the Straussian school of thought, and not all members of the American school follow Strauss's extreme skepticism. Strauss's views have been extended and redacted. See Cox, *Locke on War and Peace*; Zuckert, *Natural Rights and the New Republicanism*; Myers, *Our Only Star and Compass*; Zuckert, *Launching Liberalism*.

26  Strauss, *Natural Right and History*, 212–14, 227–29; Leo Strauss, *What Is Political Philosophy? And Other Studies* (Glencoe, IL: The Free Press, 1959), 201–06. See also Robert Goldwin, "John Locke," in *History of Political Philosophy*, ed. Leo Strauss and Joseph Cropsey, 2nd ed. (Chicago: Rand McNally, 1972), 451–86; Coby, "The Law of Nature," 3–28; Rabieh, "The Reasonableness of Locke," 933–57; Zuckert, *Natural Rights and the New Republicanism*, 237–40, 274.
27  Leo Strauss, *Persecution and the Art of Writing* (Glencoe, IL: The Free Press, 1952), 23.
28  Strauss, *Persecution and the Art of Writing*, 24–25.
29  Strauss, *Persecution and the Art of Writing*, 30.
30  Strauss, *Persecution and the Art of Writing*, 31.
31  John Locke, *The Works of John Locke in Nine Volumes*, 12th ed. (London: Rivington, 1824), Vol. 4, 477.
32  Strauss, *Natural Right and History*, 288.
33  Strauss, *What Is Political Philosophy?* 49.
34  Cox, *Locke on War and Peace*, 1–45.
35  Cox, *Locke on War and Peace*, 58.
36  For example, Cox claims Locke lists several laws of nature but actually believes in only one: the right of self-preservation (Cox, *Locke on War and Peace*, 130, 146, 152). According to Cox, Locke may claim the laws of nature are rational and divine and can be violated (in the style of the Scholastics), but his actual belief is that these laws of nature are constructed by humans for self-protection (in the style of Machiavelli). For an excellent response, see John W. Yolton, review of *Locke on War and Peace*, by Richard H. Cox, *The Philosophical Review* 71, no. 2 (April 1962): 269–71.
37  See, for example, Martin Seliger, *The Liberal Politics of John Locke* (1968; New York: Praeger, 1969), esp. 40–41.
38  MacPherson, *The Political Theory of Possessive Individualism*, 8.
39  MacPherson, *The Political Theory of Possessive Individualism*, 250.
40  Straussians have been severely critiqued as recasting Locke in their own image. Cf. Myles F. Burnyeat, "Sphinx without a Secret," *New York Times Review of Books* (May 30, 1985): 30–36; Stephen Holmes, *The Anatomy of Antiliberalism*, rev. ed. (Cambridge, MA: Harvard University Press, 1996), esp. 86–87, 263–64. Against a "Hobbesian" reading of Locke concerning morality, justice, and self-interest, see Coby, "The Law of Nature," 4; Forde, "Natural Law," 398, 402, 404; Cf. John Locke, *Some Thoughts Concerning Education*, ed. John W. Yolton and Jean S. Yolton (1693; Oxford: Clarendon Press, 1989) (*STCE*), 110. Against MacPherson, see James Tully, *A Discourse on Property: John Locke and His Adversaries* (Cambridge: Cambridge University Press, 1980); James Tully, "Note on the Text," 19. While Ian Harris, *The Mind of John Locke: A Study of Political Theory in Its Intellectual Setting* (Cambridge: Cambridge University Press, 1994), also lists reasons to reject MacPherson's interpretation, Richard Ashcraft, review of *The Mind of John Locke*, by Ian Harris,

*The American Historical Review* 100, no. 4 (October 1995): 1247, views such a reply to be unnecessary, since the readings of both Strauss and MacPherson "have long since been abandoned by modern scholars."

41  On approaching Locke textually (dealing with perennial problems), see Jonathan Bennett, *Locke, Berkeley, Hume* (Oxford: Oxford University Press, 1971), 1–30; Jonathan Bennett, *Learning from Six Philosophers: Descartes, Spinoza, Leibniz, Locke, Berkeley, Hume* (Oxford: Oxford University Press, 2001), Vol. 2; John Mackie, *Problems for Locke* (Oxford: Oxford University Press, 1976). On approaching Locke contextually (within his own historical background), see John W. Yolton, *John Locke and the Way of Ideas* (London: Oxford University Press, 1956); Dunn, *The Political Thought of John Locke*; John Dunn, "What Is Living and What Is Dead in the Political Theory of John Locke?" in John Dunn, *Interpreting Political Responsibility: Essays 1981–1989* (Cambridge: Polity Press, 1990), 9–25.

42  Sigmund, "Jeremy Waldron and the Religious Turn," 407. Though Sigmund notes earlier contributions (as early as 1969), he dates the origins of the "religious turn" to the 1980s. This may reflect a judgment concerning impact in academic circles.

43  Tommaso Vincenzio Moniglia, *Dissertazione contro I Fatalisti* (2 vols; Lucca, 1744).

44  Tommaso Vincenzio Moniglia, *Dissertazione contra I materialisti e altri increduli* (2 vols; Padua, 1750).

45  Nuovo, *Christianity, Antiquity, and Enlightenment*, 98.

46  Mattoon Monroe Curtis, *An Outline of Locke's Ethical Philosophy* (Leipzig: Gustav Fock, 1890). W. F. Willcox, review of *An Outline of Locke's Ethical Philosophy*, by Mattoon Monroe Curtis, *The Philosophical Review* 1, no. 2 (March 1892): 200, quotes Professor Friedrich Jodl, who, writing in the 1880s remarked, "I am not acquainted with any monograph upon the ethics of Locke."

47  Sterling Power Lamprecht, *The Moral and Political Philosophy of John Locke* (1918; repr., New York: Russell and Russell, 1962). James Bisset Pratt, review of *The Moral and Political Philosophy of John Locke*, by Sterling Power Lamprecht, *The American Political Science Review* 13, no. 2 (May 1919): 319, commented that "surprisingly little attention has been given by previous writers to this part of his work."

48  Lamprecht, *The Moral and Political Philosophy of John Locke*, 6.

49  *LN*. These Latin essays, composed between 1660 and 1664, were discovered among Locke's papers housed in Oxford's Bodleian Library.

50  W. Von Leyden, "John Locke and Natural Law," *Philosophy* 31, no. 116 (January 1956): 26.

51  Leo Strauss, "Critical Note: Locke's Doctrine of Natural Law," *The American Political Science Review* 52, no. 2 (June 1958): 490–501. Among those who continued to offer a Straussian reading, see James O. Hancey, "John Locke and the Law of Nature," *Political Theory* 4, no. 4 (November 1976): 439–54, esp. 450.

52  In response to von Leyden and Strauss, and offering a more sympathetic reading of Locke's theological grounding in the *LN*, see John W. Lenz, "Locke's Essays on the

Law of Nature," 105–13, esp. 108; John W. Yolton, "Locke on the Law of Nature," *The Philosophical Review* 67, no. 4 (October 1958): 477–98.
53 Yolton, *John Locke and the Way of Ideas*, ix, 167.
54 Raymond Polin, *La politique morale de John Locke* (Paris: Presses universitaires de France, 1960).
55 Polin is criticized for assuming greater coherence in Locke's works than is warranted. See Dunn, *The Political Thought of John Locke*, xii n.2.
56 Raymond Polin, "Justice in Locke's Philosophy," in *Nomos VI: Justice*, ed. Carl J. Friedrich and J. W. Chapman (New York: Atherton Press, 1963), 262–83; Raymond Polin, "John Locke's Conception of Freedom," in *John Locke: Problems and Perspectives, A Collection of New Essays*, ed. John W. Yolton (Cambridge: Cambridge University Press, 1969), 1–18. See also Richard Ashcraft, "Faith and Knowledge in Locke's Philosophy," in *John Locke: Problems and Perspectives: A Collection of New Essays*, ed. John W. Yolton (Cambridge: Cambridge University Press, 1969), 194–223, who recognizes the significance of Locke's personal theological commitments, though remaining skeptical concerning Locke's consistency.
57 Dunn, *The Political Thought of John Locke*, xi–xii.
58 Dunn, *The Political Thought of John Locke*, x–xi.
59 Roger Woolhouse and Timothy Stanton, "Contemporary Locke Scholarship," in *The Continuum Companion to Locke*, ed. S.-J. Savonius-Wroth, Paul Schuurman, and Jonathan Walmsley (London: Continuum, 2010), 315.
60 Dunn, *The Political Thought of John Locke*, 245–61.
61 In fact, as Spellman, *John Locke and the Problem of Human Depravity*, 89, points out, the anti-Calvinism of the Cambridge Platonists and the Latitudinarians deeply influenced Locke.
62 Dunn, *The Political Thought of John Locke*, 187–99.
63 Dunn, *The Political Thought of John Locke*, 266–67. For others who share this conclusion, see Tully, *A Discourse on Property*; Seliger, *The Liberal Politics of John Locke*, 1969.
64 A. W. Sparkes, "Trust and Teleology: Locke's Politics and His Doctrine of Creation," *Canadian Journal of Philosophy* 3, no. 2 (1973): 263–73, esp. 263.
65 For example, see Samuel Pearson, "The Religion of John Locke and the Character of His Thought," *Journal of Religion* 58 (1978): 244–62; George Alan Windstrup, "Politic Christianity: Locke's Theology of Liberalism" (PhD diss., Princeton University, Princeton, NJ, 1978); Reventlow, *The Authority of the Bible*, 243–85. For the claim that a Christian worldview lay at the center of Locke's intellectual life, see Ricardo Quintana, *Two Augustans: Locke and Swift* (Madison: University of Wisconsin Press), 34; John W. Yolton, *Locke: An Introduction* (Oxford: Basil Blackwell, 1985), 2. Among those who recognize the foundational nature of Locke's theological presuppositions but advocate the radical nature of his political theory, see Tully, *A Discourse on Property*; Tully, "Note on the Text," 19; Richard Ashcraft,

*Revolutionary Politics and Locke's "Two Treatises of Government"* (Princeton, NJ: Princeton University Press, 1986); Richard Ashcraft, *Locke's "Two Treatises of Government"* (London: Unwin Hyman, 1987).

66  Eldon J. Eisenach, "Religion and Locke's *Two Treatises*," in *John Locke's "Two Treatises": New Interpretations*, ed. Edward J. Harpham (Lawrence, KS: University Press of Kansas, 1992), 73, 75.

67  John Colman, *John Locke's Moral Philosophy* (Edinburgh: Edinburgh University Press, 1983).

68  Colman, *John Locke's Moral Philosophy*, 235.

69  Colman, *John Locke's Moral Philosophy*, 8, 235.

70  Colman, *John Locke's Moral Philosophy*, 243.

71  Colman, *John Locke's Moral Philosophy*, 5–8.

72  John Locke, *A Paraphrase and Notes on the Epistles of St. Paul to the Galatians, 1 and 2 Corinthians, Romans, Ephesians*, ed. Arthur W. Wainwright (1705–1707; Oxford: Clarendon Press, 1987), 2 vols. This was posthumously published.

73  See Spellman, *John Locke and the Problem of Human Depravity*, esp. 214, where Spellman notes that Locke, like most Latitudinarians, sought a middle ground between Augustine and Pelagius.

74  Michael Ayers, *Locke, Vol. 1: Epistemology* (London: Routledge, 1991), 113, recognizes religious faith and authority to be a main concern for Locke; Eisenach, "Religion and Locke's *Two Treatises*," 53, 73, claims the *Essay* "can be read as a handbook for Protestant Salvation."

75  John Marshall, *John Locke: Resistance, Religion, and Responsibility* (Cambridge: Cambridge University Press, 1994). I agree with Julian H. Franklin, review of *John Locke: Resistance, Religion, and Responsibility*, by John Marshall, *The American Historical Review* 101, no. 2 (April 1996): 480: "The elaborate and extended account of Locke's positions on ecclesiology and theology is essentially the first complete study of Locke's thought in that domain and is unrivaled in the literature."

76  The charge of Socinianism was made by Edwards (*Some Thoughts Concerning the Several Causes and Occasions of Atheism*) and denied by Locke. See John Locke, "A Vindication of the Reasonableness of Christianity," in John Locke, *Vindications of the Reasonableness of Christianity*, ed. Victor Nuovo (Oxford: Clarendon Press, 2012). For discussion, see Marshall, *John Locke: Resistance*, 205–383. Hugh Trevor-Roper, *Catholics, Anglicans, and Puritans: Seventeenth Century Essays* (1987; Chicago: University of Chicago Press, 1988), 188, speaks of Socinianism in the "narrow" sense of following Faustus Socinus in adopting an Arian perspective on the doctrine of the Trinity but also a "wide sense" of using "human reason generally in matters of faith." Nuovo, *Christianity, Antiquity, and Enlightenment*, 47, claims the "wide sense" could only be construed as an "odious label intended to inculpate and to spread suspicion" if interpreted as "someone who puts reason above tradition and dogma when interpreting Scripture, and who secretly

adopted a Socinian agenda." Against the charge of Socinianism on both counts, see Tetlow, "The Theological Context of John Locke's Political Thought"; Nuovo, *Christianity, Antiquity, and Enlightenment*, 23, 27–29, 37, 47; to an extent, Arthur W. Wainwright, "Introduction," in Locke, *A Paraphrase and Notes on the Epistles of St. Paul to the Galatians, 1 and 2 Corinthians, Romans, Ephesians*, Vol. 1, 37–38. "Still it may be justifiable to call Locke a Socinian," acknowledges Nuovo, "although with a less sinister intent" (*Christianity, Antiquity, and Enlightenment*, 47). Nuovo finds within Trevor-Roper (*Catholics, Anglicans, and Puritans*, 186–99) a third sense in which the term "Socinian" refers to "a Christian Renaissance tradition" exemplified by Erasmus, Hooker, and those of the Oxford Tew Circle. This tradition is defined by "political conservatism, an aversion to radicalism and enthusiasm, an advocacy of toleration, skepticism with respect to abstruse metaphysical and theological issues, acceptance of the freedom of the will and of the possibility of universal salvation, and a view of Christianity as a moral religion" (Nuovo, *Christianity, Antiquity, and Enlightenment*, 48).

77 Harris, *The Mind of John Locke*.
78 Harris, *The Mind of John Locke*, 324.
79 Spellman, *John Locke*.
80 Spellman, *John Locke*, 3.
81 Spellman, *John Locke*, 4.
82 Spellman, *John Locke*, 7.
83 Jeremy Waldron, *God, Locke and Equality: Christian Foundations of Locke's Political Thought* (Cambridge: Cambridge University Press, 2002).
84 RC; John Locke, *Writings on Religion*, ed. Victor Nuovo (Oxford: Clarendon Press, 2002).
85 Nuovo, *Christianity, Antiquity, and Enlightenment*.
86 Victor Nuovo, *John Locke: The Philosopher as Christian Virtuoso* (Oxford: Clarendon Press, 2017). I only became aware of this work in the penultimate stages of editing this book for publication. In the concluding chapter of Nuovo's incisive work (214–46), he alludes to and anticipates some of the theological planks I offer in this book.
87 Nuovo, *Christianity, Antiquity, and Enlightenment*, xvi.
88 Nuovo, *Christianity, Antiquity, and Enlightenment*, 98. In fact, as Curran ("An Immodest Proposal") has argued, modern secular liberalism owes its legacy to Hobbes more than Locke.
89 Nuovo, *Christianity, Antiquity, and Enlightenment*, 125.
90 Nuovo, *Christianity, Antiquity, and Enlightenment*, 126.
91 See, for example, the following: "The Tertiary Conference on John Locke" (Brisbane, Australia); "Locke Tercentenary Conference" (St. Anne's College, Oxford, April 2–4); and "John Locke through the Centuries: Assessing the Lockean Legacy, 1704–2004" (Yale University).

92  Parker, *The Biblical Politics of John Locke*; see also Kim Ian Parker, "A Critical Analysis of Filmer's and Locke's Use of Genesis in the Development of Their Political Philosophies" (MA thesis, McMaster University, Hamilton, Ontario, 1982). In the same year, Conrad ("Locke's Use of the Bible") extended research on Locke's use of scripture in the *Two Treatises* but also in the *RC* as well as the *LCT*. However, Conrad confusingly claims his work supports a Straussian skepticism concerning Locke's true beliefs but also leaves open the possibility that "understanding Locke's theological views may help one understand his political views, and vice versa" (215–16). This may be due, in part, to Conrad's disapproval of Locke's particular hermeneutical moves in dealing with scripture (214–15), as well as his insistence that Locke engages in revisionism concerning Christianity to support his political agenda (214).
93  Tetlow, "The Theological Context of John Locke's Political Thought."
94  Timothy Stanton, "Authority and Freedom in the Interpretation of Locke's Political Theory," *Political Theory* 39, no. 1 (2011): 6–30; Timothy Stanton, "On (Mis)interpreting Locke: A Reply to Tate," *Political Theory* 40, no. 1 (2012): 229–36.
95  John Marshall, *John Locke, Toleration and Early Enlightenment Culture: Religious Intolerance and Arguments for Religious Toleration in Early Modern and "Early Enlightenment" Europe* (2006; Cambridge: Cambridge University Press; repr., 2008); Loconte, *God, Locke, and Liberty*.
96  Forster, *John Locke's Politics of Moral Consensus*; Perry, *The Pretenses of Loyalty*.
97  In addition to Marshall, Harris, and Coleman, see James Tully, *An Approach to Political Philosophy: Locke in Contexts* (Cambridge: Cambridge University Press, 1993), 179–241, and Tuckness, "The Coherence of a Mind," 86. Locke can be said to have hedonistic tendencies in the sense that he recognizes pleasure and pain (in the afterlife) as key motivators for ethical obedience. However, see W. Randall Ward, "Divine Will, Natural Law, and the Voluntarism/Intellectualism Debate in Locke," *History of Political Thought* 16, no. 2 (Summer 1995): 213–16, who also shows that hedonism of this sort is not inconsistent with theological voluntarism.

# Chapter 2

1  Waldron, *God, Locke, and Equality*, 240.
2  Waldron, *God, Locke, and Equality*, 237, emphasis added.
3  Tate, "Dividing Locke from God," 153.
4  Tate, "Dividing Locke from God," 156. Cf. Tate, "Dividing Locke from God," 135; John William Tate, "Locke, God, and Civil Society: Response to Stanton," *Political Theory* 40, no. 2 (2012): 223.
5  Tate, "Locke, God, and Civil Society," 223.

6   Tate, "Dividing Locke from God," 151–52.
7   Tate, "Dividing Locke from God," 137.
8   *LCT*: 26, 33, 35. Locke uses the terms "church" and "state" to distinguish the two realms (55) but elsewhere speaks of "religion" and "civil interests" (55), or "the church" and "the Commonwealth" (26).
9   *LCT*: 47. On the role of the church, see *LCT*: 26, 40, 48, 56. On the role of the state, see *LCT*: 26, 39, 47–49, 55.
10  *LCT*: 55.
11  *LCT*: 32.
12  *LCT*: 33.
13  *LCT*: 28.
14  *LCT*: 26.
15  *LCT*: 33.
16  *LCT*: 32: "Every Church is orthodox to itself; to other, erroneous and heretical."
17  *LCT*: 54.
18  John Locke, "First Tract on Government," in *John Locke: Two Tracts on Government*, ed. and trans. Philip Abrams (1660; Cambridge: Cambridge University Press, 1967), 121.
19  *LCT*: 33.
20  On "consent," see *2nd T*: 22 and 95. Locke acknowledges that agreement on what constitutes the one "true religion" is inadequate as well. See John Locke, *A Second Letter Concerning Toleration*, in *The Works of John Locke in Ten Volumes*, Vol. 6, new ed., cor. (1690; London: Tegg, 1823), 65, 100, 102, 111, 118. Locke even acknowledges some problem with uniting on the concept of "God." See *E*: 1.4.14: 92–93. See also *E*: 1.1.5: 45.
21  *2nd T*: 95–99, 123–24, 131, 138, 171, 222.
22  *LCT*: 26, 28, 32, 33, 39, 40, 47, 48, 49, 55, 56.
23  John Locke, "A Third Letter for Toleration: To the Author of the Third Letter Concerning Toleration," in *The Works of John Locke in Ten Volumes*, Vol. 6, new ed., cor. (1692; London: Thomas Tegg, 1823), 224.
24  *LCT*: 26, 35, 28, 47, 48.
25  Locke, *A Second Letter Concerning Toleration*, 121, emphasis added.
26  *LCT*: 39, 49. Locke uses the phrase "some Peculiar Prerogative" (49). See also *LCT*: 40–42. Against enforcing the religious views of any particular sect as civil law, see *LCT*: 57–58; Locke, *A Second Letter Concerning Toleration*, 65, 89, 90.
27  The Straussian model is addressed in Chapter 1. For those who "divide" the early Locke and the late Locke, suggesting his views migrated from a strict rationalist position toward fideism, see Hancey, "John Locke and the Law of Nature," 451. For a "compartmental" reading of Locke in which Locke self-consciously intended for his political works to remain untouched by his philosophical claims, see Tate, "Dividing Locke from God," 143. For a critique of this approach, see Forde,

"Natural Law," 406; Jeremy Waldron, "Response to Critics," *The Review of Politics* 67, no. 3 (Summer 2005): 497. For those who "distance" Locke from contemporary political debates due to his religious claims, see Dunn, *The Political Thought of John Locke*; Seliger, *The Liberal Politics of John Locke*; Tully, *A Discourse on Property*.

28  Tate, "Dividing Locke from God," 152. For "divide Locke from God," see 137.
29  *LCT*: 52.
30  *LCT*: 23.
31  *LCT*: 25, 32.
32  *LCT*: 27, 26.
33  *LCT*: 35.
34  *LCT*: 45.
35  *LCT*: 43.
36  *LCT*: 43.
37  *LCT*: 33.
38  *LCT*: 50.
39  *LCT*: 52, 23.
40  *LCT*: 23.
41  *LCT*: 55.
42  *LCT*: 24, 32, 34.
43  *LCT*: 55.
44  *LCT*: 55.
45  Tate, "Dividing Locke from God," 153, 156.
46  *LCT*: 33.
47  *LCT*: 34.
48  *LCT*: 35.
49  *LCT*: 35.
50  *LCT*: 27.
51  *LCT*: 47.
52  *LCT*: 26.
53  *LCT*: 27.
54  *LCT*: 27.
55  *LCT*: 27.
56  *LCT*: 28.
57  *LCT*: 38.
58  *LCT*: 38.
59  *LCT*: 38.
60  *2nd T*: 4 and 6. I am not entirely convinced that the erroneous position is justifiably ascribed to Waldron. However, Tate's exegetical solution (whether or not in contradistinction to Waldron) seems to me correct.
61  See Tate, "Dividing Locke from God," 146.

62 Yolton, "Locke on the Law of Nature," 477–98; Raghuveer Singh, "John Locke and the Theory of Natural Law," Political Studies 9 (1961): 105–18. For more on God as clearly involved in obligation, see Sparkes, "Trust and Teleology," 263–73.
63 Forde, "Natural Law," 399, 402, 404.
64 S. B. Drury, "John Locke, Natural Law and Innate Ideas," *Dialogue* 19, no. 4 (December 1980): 531–45.
65 Tate, "Dividing Locke from God," 156.
66 Locke, "First Tract on Government," 121.
67 *LN*: 111; *E*: 1.3.17: 78; 2.28.11: 354–56.
68 *RC*: 143, 149.
69 Forde, "Natural Law," 405, 408.
70 *LCT*: 23.
71 *LCT*: 23.
72 *LCT*: 23.
73 *LCT*: 24.
74 Locke, "First Tract on Government," 121.
75 *LCT*: 25, 23.
76 *LCT*: 23.
77 *LCT*: 52, 23. See also *LCT*: 25.
78 *LCT*: 23.
79 Forde, "Natural Law," 405.
80 For a particularly well-articulated defense of the Christian basis for Locke's account of religious toleration, see Joseph Loconte, *God, Locke, and Liberty: The Struggle for Religious Freedom in the West* (Plymouth: Lexington Books, 2014), esp. 3, 182–86. Locke's argument for toleration includes "conspicuously Christian concerns, ideals, and objectives" (3). In fact, Loconte argues, "Locke embraced an earlier reform movement within Christianity, the Christian humanist tradition, and enlisted its doctrines and ideals to advance a revolutionary defense of religious toleration" (3).
81 *RC*: 134.
82 *RC*: 129, 133, 157.
83 *RC*: 151.
84 *LCT*: 47, 40.
85 *RC*: 157–58.
86 *RC*: 130–32.
87 *RC*: 73, 77.
88 *RC*: 89.
89 *LCT*: 23.
90 As does Flage, "Locke and Natural Law," 435–60.
91 Thomas G. West, "The Ground of Locke's Law of Nature," *Social Science and Philosophy* 29, no. 2 (2012): 1–50.
92 *LN*: 127–31.

93   Roger Woolhouse, *Locke: A Biography* (Cambridge: Cambridge University Press, 2007), 55–56.
94   *LCT*: 27.
95   *E*: 1.4.17: 95.
96   *LCT*: 51.
97   *LN*: 129; *E*: 1.4.8: 88; 1.4.9: 89; 1.4.17: 95.
98   *LCT*: 55.
99   Locke is optimistic in this regard (see, e.g., *RC*: 132–34).
100  Parker, *The Biblical Politics of John Locke*, 3, notes that Locke's conception of liberalism is rooted in a biblical world view and thus his "political platform... does not necessarily lend itself to a modern secular vision but, on the contrary, to a religious one." For an argument suggesting contemporary secular liberalism (described as "a godless doctrine" that "does not appeal to theological premises") still shares similarities (and strengths) with seventeenth-century religiously grounded liberalism, see Paul Kelly, "Liberalism, Secularism and the Challenge of Religion—Is There a Crisis?" in *Cultural Politics in a Global Age: Uncertainty, Solidarity, and Innovation*, ed. Henrietta Moore and David Held (London: OneWorld, 2008), 124–31, esp. 131.
101  Forde, "Natural Law," 78.
102  Forde, "Natural Law," 399. For more on following habit and custom, see *E*: 1.3.24–25: 82–83; 2.28.12: 356–57; 4.16.4: 659–61; cf. *LN*: 127–34.
103  *STCE*: 110.
104  *STCE*: 158–59.
105  One example of this is where Locke describes the "justified heathen" as one who recognizes by the light of nature not simply some general notion of goodness but a specifically Christian teaching (found ultimately in the Sermon on the Mount) whereby he is granted forgiveness and offered eternal life. See *RC*: 128–34.
106  *LCT*: 54.
107  *LCT*: 54. Note, however, that Locke imagines a worshipping pagan. See Locke, *A Second Letter Concerning Toleration*, 62–64.
108  *LCT*: 51.
109  *LCT*: 56.
110  *LCT*: 47.
111  *LCT*: 51.
112  *LCT*: 54.
113  See Tate, "Dividing Locke from God," 163n.124–28.
114  Tate, "Dividing Locke from God," 155.
115  Locke, "A Vindication of the Reasonableness of Christianity."
116  Locke, "A Vindication of the Reasonableness of Christianity," 7, 8. In the critical notes (7n.3), Nuovo claims that atheism had not been a capital crime in England since 1677. Since atheism undermines the "Fundamental Article of all Religion

and Morality," Locke may be speaking of atheism as a crime against Him on whom salvation depends, thus worthy of eternal death at the hands of the ultimate Judge.

117  *LCT*: 23.
118  *LCT*: 54, 56.
119  *LCT*: 47.
120  *LCT*: 54.
121  *LCT*: 38.
122  *LCT*: 38.
123  By way of assessment, it is not clear to me that the exclusion of atheists in contemporary society is required if one adopts the logical structure of Locke's political theory. However, his strong aversion to avowed atheists shows that any interpretation of Locke's theory of civil society that wishes to push religion *out* must explain how to bring atheists *in*.
124  Locke is not alone in this assessment. For the larger context involving fear of atheism in the promotion of religious toleration, see John Marshall, *John Locke, Toleration, and Early Enlightenment Culture: Religious Intolerance and Arguments for Religious Toleration in Early Modern and "Early Enlightenment" Europe* (2006; rep., Cambridge: Cambridge University Press, 2008), 12–13, 694–706.
125  Forde, "Natural Law," 396–409. Forde's own suggestion—that Locke's "philosophical" works are inextricably tied to theological foundations, while his "practical" works are effectively shorn of any religious underpinnings—is highly implausible. Ironically, Forde places the *RC* alongside the *2nd T* and *STCE* in the "practical" category, while identifying the inextricably theological ground of argument in Locke's philosophical works, primarily the *Essay*. This odd move simply reinforces the difficulty of determining a strict self-conscious "bifurcation" in Locke's works.
126  In the *RC*, Locke relies on the narrative of Paul's speech in Athens as a critical text for explicating his own views. Forde, "Natural Law," 407, rightly notes that Locke saw similarities between Paul's context and his own.
127  *E*: 1.3.3: 67.
128  *RC*: 11.
129  In addition to these passages, see Psalm 19:1–4.
130  Forde, "Natural Law," 403. Tuckness, "The Coherence of a Mind," 90, notes that were Locke to have been more overtly religious or made theological appeals in ways less amenable to a wide audience, than his work "would have alienated more readers than it persuaded… [T]here was no need to further alienate people… such a strategy would have been rhetorically and polemically foolish."
131  For example, see Rowan Williams, *Faith in the Public Square* (London: Bloomsbury Continuum, 2012). Williams's distinction between "procedural" and "programmatic" secularism is in harmony with Locke's own views, as well as his

call for "interactive pluralism" (4–5) within an "argumentative democracy," and his high regard for "the irreducible core of human rights" located in the "mutual recognition between human beings" that we are made in the image of God (155, 161). Compare Locke's teaching with Williams's appreciation for the role of habit in forming one's moral life (313), an appreciation for "humanity" as a collective "we" (13), and the necessity of the Church to keep the state from becoming morally an "empty public square."

132  Perry, *The Pretenses of Loyalty*; Forster, *John Locke's Politics of Moral Consensus*.
133  Christopher J. Insole, *The Politics of Human Frailty: A Theological Defence of Political Liberalism* (Notre Dame: University of Notre Dame Press, 2004). Though Insole never credits Locke, he does credit Hooker (whom Locke echoes) and Burke (who echoes Locke). On the latter, see Frederick Dreyer, "Edmund Burke and John Wesley: The Legacy of Locke," in *Religion, Secularization and Political Thought: Thomas Hobbes to J. S. Mill*, ed. James E. Crimmins (London: Routledge, 1990), 111–29.

# Chapter 3

1  For an excellent and sympathetic analysis of these groups, defending their contribution to the rise of Latitudinarianism, see Tulloch, *Rational Theology*; Martin I. J. Griffin, Jr., *Latitudinarianism in the Seventeenth Century Church of England* (Leiden: E. J. Brill, 1992), esp. 15.
2  See Spellman, *John Locke*, 19, who argues Locke's works show a thorough familiarity with these authors.
3  For Tew Circle authors represented in Locke's library, see John Hales (*LL*, 150), William Chillingworth (*LL*, 106), Jeremy Taylor (*LL*, 244), and Henry Hammond (*LL*, 150; cf. 111, 134). For Cambridge Platonists, see Benjamin Whichcote (*LL*, 263), Ralph Cudworth (*LL*, 119), Henry More (*LL*, 192), and John Smith (*LL*, 235). For later Latitudinarians, see Edward Stillingfleet (*LL*, 240), John Tillotson (*LL*, 248–49), Edward Fowler (*LL*, 137–38), Simon Patrick (*LL*, 205), Isaac Barrow (*LL*, 80) and Gilbert Burnet (*LL*, 96).
4  In preparing this chapter, I am especially indebted to Tetlow, "The Theological Context of John Locke's Political Thought," 18–40, who stresses this very point in her excellent work exploring the theological context of Locke's political thought.
5  See, for example, Spellman, *John Locke*, esp. 77; Pearson, "The Religion of John Locke," 248: "On the one hand Locke was deeply committed to the Christian faith which he understood in moral and experiential more than in dogmatic terms but which he believed rested on historic revelation. Yet on the other hand he was troubled both by the claims of enthusiasts to direct revelation and by what he

regarded as indefensible arguments of contemporary churchmen seeking to defend the faith."

6 Tate, "Dividing Locke from God," 133, 157n.1, points out that even Strauss, *What Is Political Philosophy*, 202, 207, 208, made such an acknowledgment. Cranston, *John Locke*, 124: "Even so Locke was always and essentially a deeply religious man, a fact that is sometimes not appreciated ... His religion was that of the Latitudinarian wing of the Church of England. His creed was short, but he held to it with the utmost assurance."

7 Cranston, *John Locke*, 1, 6; Richard I. Aaron, *John Locke*, 3rd ed. (Oxford: Oxford University Press, 1971), 2; Woolhouse, *Locke*, 9.

8 Cranston, *John Locke*, 3; Aaron, *John Locke*, 3. For Locke's reference to being born into this "storm," see Locke, "First Tract on Government," 119.

9 Woolhouse, *Locke*, 12–13; Cranston, *John Locke*, 19–20: "For a boy like Locke, going to Westminster from a zealously Puritan home at an impressionable age, the political atmosphere of the school was both disturbing and compelling. It did not make him a conventional Royalist ... but Westminster did purge Locke of the unquestioning Puritan faith in which he had grown up; and thus, however ironically, Dr. Busby, the great conservative pedagogue, must be given the credit for having first set Locke on the road to liberalism." Based on what may be gleaned from Dr. Crook, Cranston may overstate the case concerning the "unquestioning" atmosphere in Locke's home.

10 Cranston, *John Locke*, 31. This training continued with his MA degree, which involved yet another three years of training in Hebrew, Greek, natural philosophy, and metaphysics. For more on the pervasive scholasticism in the curriculum at both Oxford and Cambridge, see William T. Costello, *The Scholastic Curriculum in Early Seventeenth-Century Cambridge* (Cambridge, MA: Harvard University Press, 1958).

11 Woolhouse, *Locke*, 18.

12 Cranston, *John Locke*, 31.

13 Cranston, *John Locke*, 32.

14 Woolhouse, *Locke*, 19.

15 Cranston, *John Locke*, 32, 34; Woolhouse, *Locke*, 19.

16 Cranston, *John Locke*, 41: "John Owen was almost daily propounding a political philosophy which strikes the modern reader as being in many ways 'Lockean.' Owen was one of the first men to advocate toleration in a disinterested way ... He based his case, in the approved Calvinist way, on the Bible, and he claimed that there was no authority in its pages for the belief, which Calvinists shared with Catholics and Anglicans, that heretics should be repressed. Owen maintained that all men should be free to think and worship as they pleased so long as their faith did not lead them to disturb peace and order. The duty of the Government, he said, was to maintain order and not to impose religion." See also Fox Bourne, *The Life of John Locke*, Vol. 1, 72–79.

17 Woolhouse, *Locke*, 20.
18 See Letter (L) 200 in John Locke, *The Correspondence of John Locke*, ed. E. S. de Beer (Oxford: Clarendon Press, 1976–1989) (*COR*), Vol. 1, 280.
19 Woolhouse, *Locke*, 4.
20 L59 (*COR*, Vol. 1, 83).
21 Marshall, *John Locke: Resistance*, 10.
22 Locke, "First Tract on Government," 117–81. For this assessment, see Woolhouse, *Locke*, 41.
23 L115 (*COR*, Vol. 1, 167).
24 John Locke, "Second Tract on Government," in *John Locke: Two Tracts on Government*, ed. and trans. Philip Abrams (1662; Cambridge: Cambridge University Press, 1967), 185–241. For this assessment, see Cranston, *John Locke*, 63.
25 Woolhouse, *Locke*, 51.
26 *LN*.
27 Cranston, *John Locke*, 79.
28 David L. Wardle, "Reason to Ratify: The Influence of John Locke's Religious Beliefs on the Creation and Adoption of the United States Constitution," *Seattle University Law Review* 26 (2002): 293.
29 Cranston, *John Locke*, 76–77: "He encouraged the fashion among the Oxford virtuosi of combining theological with scientific studies. Boyle knew his Bible well, and would have made an excellent clergyman."
30 L177, L180, L182 (*COR*, Vol. 1: 233–39, 244–50, 253–55). Locke describes these services (of Lutherans, Catholics, and Calvinists) with dismissive humor, though he admits the lives and conduct of the Catholics he met defied his ill-conception of them (246).
31 L175 (*COR*, Vol. 1, 227). Perhaps it was here at Cleves, notes De Beer, Locke first saw a workable form of toleration. See E. S. De Beer, "Introduction," in *COR*, Vol. 1, xix. "What scholars usually fail to note," writes Loconte, *God, Locke, and Liberty*, 43, "is that Cleves could boast a long reforming tradition in the pious and sincere spirit of the *Devotio moderna* of Erasmus."
32 Cranston, *John Locke*, 107, 111.
33 John Locke, "An Essay Concerning Toleration," in John Locke, *An Essay Concerning Toleration and Other Writings on Law and Politics, 1667–1683*, ed. J. R. Milton and Philip Milton (1667; Oxford: Clarendon Press, 2006).
34 Four drafts of this work still exist. See J. R. Milton and Philip Milton, "Textual Introduction," in Locke, *An Essay Concerning Toleration*, 162.
35 See Woolhouse, *Locke*, 86, but also 83–85.
36 John Locke, "The Fundamental Constitutions of Carolina," in John Locke, *Political Essays*, ed. Mark Goldie (1669; 1997; repr., Cambridge: Cambridge University Press, 2006), 160–81. Locke certainly had a hand in it, though his exact involvement is not clear. See De Beer in *COR*, Vol. 1, 279n.2; L279 (*COR*, Vol. 1, 395); John Locke, *The*

*Works of John Locke: A New Edition, Corrected, in Ten Volumes* (London: Thomas Tegg, 1823), Vol. 10, 150.

37 Locke, "The Fundamental Constitutions of Carolina," 177.
38 Locke, "The Fundamental Constitutions of Carolina," 178.
39 This is according to James Tyrrell. Fox Bourne, *The Life of John Locke*, Vol. 1, 248–49; Nidditch, "Forward," xix–xx. Tyrrell noted this meeting was when Locke "first raised the issue of human understanding." However, he mistakenly recalled the date as "winter 1673."
40 E: 7.
41 Locke, "Sic Cogitavit de intellectu humano [Draft A]." Dated July 10, 1671. See G. A. J. Rogers, "Introduction," in Locke, *Drafts for the Essay Concerning Human Understanding*, esp. xiii.
42 Locke, "Sic Cogitavit de intellectu humano [Draft A]," 41.
43 Locke, "Sic Cogitavit de intellectu humano [Draft A]," 41.
44 John Locke, "An Essay Concerning the Understanding, Knowledge, Opinion & Assent [Draft B]," in *Drafts for the Essay Concerning Human Understanding*, 87–270.
45 Locke, "An Essay Concerning the Understanding, Knowledge, Opinion & Ascent [Draft B]," 269. Though Locke removes reference to revelation in *B*'s version of the paragraph, he adds that God's rule for our actions "is conversant about & ultimately terminates in … simple Ideas" such as "Thou shalt love thy neigbour as thy self. & c."
46 Locke, "An Essay Concerning the Understanding, Knowledge, Opinion & Ascent [Draft B]," 214; Cf. 121; Locke, "Sic Cogitavit de Intellectu humano [Draft A]," 82.
47 Cranston, *John Locke*, 172–74. Locke owned copies of several works by Toinard, including *Evangeliorum Harmonia Graeco-Latina* (LL, 249–50), which Locke described as "very useful" (according to Cranston, *John Locke*, 174).
48 L508 (*COR*, Vol. 2, 113): "il y avoit plusieurs de nos meilleurs livres Anglois, quand vous avez la phantasie d'aprandre la langue Angloise vous n'avez qu'a suivre ma methode en lisant touts les jours un chapitre du nouveau testament et en un mois du temps vous deviendrais maistre[.]" The English translation is that of Cranston, *John Locke*, 189.
49 L426 (*COR*, Vol. 1, 648–49).
50 John Locke, *An Early Draft of Locke's Essay, Together with Excerpts from his Journals*, ed. Richard I. Aaron and Jocelyn Gibb (Oxford: Clarendon Press, 1936), 116–18.
51 Forty letters survive from "Philoclea" (Lady Masham) to Locke, dated from January 1682 to April 1688. See *COR*, Vol. 2, 470; Cranston, *John Locke*, 215.
52 I am indebted to Cranston, *John Locke*, 233–34, for a number of insights in this paragraph.
53 For more on the influence of van Limborch on Locke's Theo-political theory, see Loconte, *God, Locke, and Liberty*, 135–48.

54 Cranston, *John Locke*, 234. Tetlow, "The Theological Context of Locke's Political Thought," 40, notes that the subtitle given to Limborch's English translation of his *Theologia Christiana* "shows his desire for a strategic partnership" with liberal Anglicans; the subtitle reads "With Improvements from Bishop Wilkins, Archbishop Tillotson, Doctor Scott, and several other Divines of the Church of England." See Philip van Limborch, *A Compleat System, or Body of Divinity, Both Speculative and Practical, Founded on Scripture and Reason, Written Originally in Latin, by Philip Limborch, with Improvements, from Bishop Wilkins, Arch-Bishop Tillotson, Doctor Scott, and Several Other Divines of the Church of England*, trans. William Jones (London: Printed for J. Taylor and A. Bell, 1702), Vol. 1, title page.

55 Limborch, *A Compleat System*, acknowledges that all things necessary to salvation are found in scripture, but not everything in scripture is necessary to be known or believed in order to attain salvation (Vol. 1, 11); he also affirms the right for humans to exercise individual conscience (Vol. 2, esp. 454–62).

56 Fox Bourne, *The Life of John Locke*, Vol. 2, 6.

57 See Marshall, *John Locke: Resistance*, 332. Locke bought and read books by Episcopius (LL, 130–31) and Velthusius (LL, 257–58) at this time.

58 Marshall, *John Locke: Resistance*, 332.

59 Wardle, "Reason to Ratify," 293.

60 John Locke, "Pacific Christians," in Locke, *Political Essays*, 304–06. Also printed in Fox Bourne, *The Life of John Locke*, Vol. 2: 185–86; Luisa Simonutti, "Circles of Virtuosi and 'Charity under Different Opinion:' The Crucible of Locke's Last Writings," in *Studies on Locke: Sources, Contemporaries, and Legacy, in Honour of G. A. J. Rogers*, ed. Sarah Hutton and Paul Schuurman (Dordrecht, The Netherlands: Springer, 2008), 171–73.

61 Cranston, *John Locke*, 209–10, after citing *2nd T*: 6, writes the following: "I have quoted this paragraph partly in order to emphasise a fact which is often neglected in discussions of Locke's politics, namely that his political theory was based, as Filmer's was, on his religious convictions. It is often said that Locke took an optimistic view of mankind; but he did so only because he believed that men were God's workmanship. He thought a law of nature existed only because God proclaimed it. He believed that men had natural rights, not simply on the traditional Stoic grounds that the very possession of reason entitled men to such rights, but because he believed that God had given men such rights. Nature and Reason were not for Locke, as for so many other theorists, peculiar metaphysical entities with law-giving and privilege-bestowing powers of their own, even though he did sometimes write as if he thought they were; behind Nature and Reason Locke always discerned the person and voice of God."

62 *LCT*: 47.

63 *E*: 4.10.6: 621; 4.3.18: 549; 4.3.20: 552.

64  *E*: 4.18.2: 689. On the neglect of Book IV in Locke scholarship, see Nicholas Wolterstorff, *John Locke and the Ethics of Belief* (Cambridge: Cambridge University Press, 1996), xx.
65  *E*: 3.9.23: 489.
66  *E*: 3.9.23: 490.
67  *E*: 4.18.7: 694; see also 4.7.11: 598–603; 4.18.2: 689; 4.18.4: 690–91.
68  Ruth W. Grant and Nathan Tarcov, "Introduction," in John Locke, *Some Thoughts Concerning Education and of the Conduct of the Understanding*, ed. Ruth W. Grant and Nathan Tarcov (Indianapolis: Hackett, 1996), xix. However, this work was published posthumously in 1706. See John Locke, *Of the Conduct of the Understanding*, repr. from *Posthumous Works of Mr. John Locke*, 2nd impr., Key Texts: Classic Studies in the History of Ideas (1706; Bristol: Thoemmes Press, 1996).
69  Grant and Tarcov, "Introduction," xix.
70  Locke, *Of the Conduct of the Understanding*, par. 22. See also par. 8: "Everyone has a concern in a future Life, which he is bound to look after. This engages his Thoughts in *Religion*; and here it mightily lies him upon to understand and reason right. Men therefore cannot be excused from understanding the Words, and framing the general Notions, relating to *Religion* right."
71  L3328 (*COR*, Vol. 8, 56), italics removed.
72  L3328 (*COR*, Vol. 8, 56).
73  John Locke, "Some Thoughts Concerning Reading and Study for a Gentleman," in *Political Essays*, by John Locke, ed. Mark Goldie (1703; 1997; repr., Cambridge: Cambridge University Press, 2006), 351.
74  "Morum exemplum si quaeras in Evangelio habes." Cited and translated in Cranston, *John Locke*, 481–82.
75  For a similar summary, see Parker, *The Biblical Politics of John Locke*, 35–36.
76  For the large collection of Boyle's works in Locke's library, see *LL*, 91–93. I am indebted to Laurence Carlin, "The Importance of Teleology to Boyle's Natural Philosophy," *British Journal for the History of Philosophy* 19, no. 4 (2011): 665–82, for many Boyle references. For more on Boyle and the connection between his ideas and Locke's own, see Nuovo, *John Locke: The Philosopher as Christian Virtuoso*, 35–58.
77  Robert Boyle, *A Disquisition about the Final Causes of Natural Things: wherein it is inquir'd, whether and (if at all) with what cautions, a naturalist should admit them?, to which are subjoyn'd, by way of appendix some uncommon observations about vitiated sight by the same author* (London: Printed by H. C. for John Taylor, at the Ship in St. Paul's Church-Yard, 1688), A2 (Preface). Carlin, "The Importance of Teleology," 669–72, show that, for Boyle, teleology relating to humanity includes corporeal ends as well as mental ends. Concerning universal ends, writes Carlin, Boyle is emphatic that the creation declares the power of God, as well as communicates His beneficial goodness toward creatures (672).

78  Carlin, "The Importance of Teleology," 672. Reflection on teleology leads directly to positing a powerful, good, and intelligent Creator (Boyle, *A Disquisition about the Final Causes*, 166; cf. Carlin, "The Importance of Teleology," 672), and recognizing a participatory sense in which "the sensible Representations of Gods Attributes" are found "with in ... Creatures" (Robert Boyle, *The Works of the Honourable Robert Boyle in Six Volumes, to Which Is Prefixed the Life of the Author, a New Edition* [London: Printed for J. and F. Rivington, L. Davis, W. Johnston, S. Crowder, T. Payne, G. Kearsley, J. Robson, B. White, T. Becket and P. A. De Hont, T. Davies, T. Cadell, Robinson and Roberts, Richardson and Richardson, J. Knox, W. Woodfall, J. Johnson, and T. Evans, 1772], Vol. 2, 62); thus God's handiwork is portrayed as "participating and disclosing so much of the inexhausted Perfections of their Author" (Boyle, *The Works*, Vol. 2, 26).

79  Boyle, *The Works*, Vol. 2, 31. Carlin, "The Importance of Teleology," 674–75, claims that, for Boyle, "the natural philosopher who possesses a deep teleological understanding of nature, yet is not 'sprung' to devotion is a natural impossibility."

80  Robert Boyle, *The Excellency of Theology, Compar'd with Natural Philosophy, (as Both Are Objects of Men's Study), Discours'd of in a Letter to a Friend, by T. H. R. B. E., Fellow of the Royal Society, to Which Are Annex'd Some Occasional Thoughts about the Excellency and Grounds of the Mechanical Hypothesis by the Same Author* (London: Printed by T.N. for Henry Herringman, 1674), 75. Cf. Carlin, "The Importance of Teleology," 677, 682.

81  Boyle, *The Works*, Vol. 2, 63.

82  Boyle, *The Excellency of Theology*, 123.

83  Boyle, *The Works*, 19.

84  Robert Boyle, *The Philosophical Works of the Honourable Robert Boyle, Esq; Abridged, Methodized, and Disposed under the General Heads of Physics, Statics, Pneumatics, Natural-History, Chymistry, and Medicine, The Whole Illustrated with Notes, Containing the Improvements Made in the Several Parts of Natural and Experimental Knowledge, since His time*, ed. Peter Shaw (London: Printed for W. and J. Innys, at the West-End of St. Paul's; and J. Osborn, and T. Longman, in Pater-Noster-Row, 1725), Vol. 2, 246. Like Locke, Boyle mentions that neither "plant" nor "brute animal" is capable of discerning or offering the worship God desires of rational creatures, that "goodness" is an essential characteristic of God, and that man can believe "upon the historical and other proofs which cristianity offers" that God offers positive law, leading to rewards for the righteous and punishment for transgressors.

85  Carlin, "The Importance of Teleology," 680.

86  Boyle, *The Philosophical Works of the Honourable Robert Boyle*, 247; Boyle, *The Excellency of Theology*, 84–85.

87  Boyle, *The Excellency of Theology*, 84–85.

88  This is also true for Aquinas. See, e.g., *Summa Theologiae* (hereafter *ST*) IIaIIae 1.2; 2.9 ad 2; 4.2.

89 Boyle's influence can be felt in Locke's works beyond issues involving teleology. Loconte, *God, Locke, and Liberty*, 39, notes that Boyle also encouraged the Latitudinarian Peter Pett to pen a pragmatic tract in favor of religious toleration—which suggests Boyle's sympathy for yet another hallmark of Lockean political philosophy.

90 Cranston, *John Locke*, 125.

91 Gilbert Burnet, *Bishop Burnet's History of His Own Time: With the Suppressed Passages of the First Volume, and Notes by the Earls of Dartmouth and Hardwicke, and Speaker Onslow, Hitherto Unpublished. To Which Are Added the Cursory Remarks of Swift, and Other Observations*, ed. Martin J. Routh (1724; Oxford: Clarendon Press, 1823), Vol. 1, 323–24. See also Rosalie L. Colie, *Light and Enlightenment: A Study of the Cambridge Platonists and the Dutch Arminians* (Cambridge: Cambridge University Press, 1957), 22.

92 Gilbert Burnet, *Bishop Burnet's History of His Own Time*, 324.

93 Gilbert Burnet, *Bishop Burnet's History of His Own Time*, 324. Latitudinarians were not monolithic, and some descriptors (such as Socinian) may have accurately described some of the members, especially in later years.

94 Cranston, *John Locke*, 126.

95 Consider the moderating influences of Thomas Cranmer (1489–1556), Sebastian Castellio (1515–1563), and Heinrich Bullinger (1504–1575), each of whom contributed to a wide, tolerant ecclesiology. An open door for those with sensibilities across a wide theological range can be seen in the Thirty-Nine Articles of 1571. For more, see Tetlow, "The Theological Context of Locke's Political Thought," 19–23; cf. Corneilius H. Lettinga, "Covenant Theology and the Transformation of Anglicanism" (PhD diss., The Johns Hopkins University, Baltimore, MD, 1987), 13–85. Locke's library includes six works by Castellio (*LL*, 102) and one compiled by Cranmer (*LL*, 128). Cf. Tulloch, *Rational Theology*, Vol. 1, 43.

96 Tetlow, "The Theological Context of Locke's Political Thought," 20.

97 Cranston, *John Locke*, 126; Tetlow, "The Theological Context of Locke's Political Thought," 19. Contra Marshall, *John Locke: Resistance*, 239–40n.48; Stuart Brown, "The Sovereignty of the People," in *Studies on Locke: Sources, Contemporaries, and Legacy, in Honour of G.A.J. Rogers*, ed. Sarah Hutton and Paul Schuurman (Dordrecht, The Netherlands: Springer, 2008), 54.

98 Locke's library (*LL*, 157) contained not only the sixth edition of Hooker's *Laws of Ecclesiastical Polity* of 1632 but also an eight-volume collection of Hooker's *Works* (both the 1666 and 1676 editions). Locke took detailed notes while reading Hooker in the early summer of 1681 (July 12 and August 31) and also in 1682 (while preparing his *Two Treatises*). See Marshall, *John Locke: Resistance*, 239n.48. His notes show an interest not only in Hooker's legal policies but also epistemological considerations (Locke, *An Early Draft of Locke's Essay*, 116–18; John Locke, "Ecclesia," in *Writings on Religion*, by John Locke, ed. Victor Nuovo

[1682; Oxford: Clarendon Press, 2002], 80). See also Victor Nuovo, "Introduction," in *John Locke: Writings on Religion*, ed. Victor Nuovo (Oxford: Clarendon Press, 2002), xlii–xliii and xlvi–xlvii for more suggestions of Locke's debt to and dependence on Hooker for political perspectives arising from theological (including Christological) considerations. According to Marshall, *John Locke: Resistance*, 11 and 26, Locke's notes from the period between 1659 and 1662 suggest that Locke already "began, at the very least" to read Hooker's works.

99  Robert K. Faulkner, *Richard Hooker and the Politics of a Christian England* (Berkeley: University of California Press, 1981), 2, claims some scholars portray Hooker "as a sort of scout for the liberal general John Locke." While this is an overstatement, Faulkner's distancing of Locke from Hooker is equally overstated (3). It is not a coincidence that Locke cites Hooker as an authority in perhaps the most important (and theologically pregnant) passage of his political writing: *2nd T*: 5, which connects paragraphs 4 and 6, justifying the theological basis for his political thought. Cf. Dunn, *The Political Thought of John Locke*, 169n.4. There are a total of sixteen references to Hooker in the *2nd T*.

100 For this section on Hooker, I am especially indebted to Insole, *The Politics of Human Frailty*, 52–63, 72–80. See also Peter Lake, *Anglicans and Puritans? Presbyterianism and English Conformist Thought from Whitgift to Hooker* (London: Unwin Hyman, 1988), 31 and 145–238, esp. 160–62, 196. Cf. Lee W. Gibbs, "Richard Hooker: Prophet of Anglicanism or English Magisterial Reformer?" *Anglican Theological Review* 84, no. 4 (Fall 2002): 943–60, for a defense of Hooker's mediating position.

101 Insole, *The Politics of Human Frailty*, 54.

102 Richard Hooker, *Of the Laws of Ecclesiastical Polity: Preface, Book I, Book VIII*, ed. Arthur Stephen McGrade (1989, rcpr., Cambridge: Cambridge University Press, 1997). Hereafter, *Laws*.

103 Gibbs, "Richard Hooker: Prophet of Anglicanism or English Magisterial Reformer?" esp. 953. Gibbs describes Hooker as "both Catholic and Protestant, both Thomist and Augustinian/Calvinist, both Aristotelian and (neo) Platonist, both medieval and modern, both conservative and liberal, both refined systematic theologian and ardent polemicist defending and established church" (958–59).

104 *Laws*: pref.8.6: 41.

105 Insole, *The Politics of Human Frailty*, 63. *Laws*: pref.3.7: 15, speaks of "stains and blemishes" in any state, which arise "from the root of human frailty and corruption" that is endemic in humanity and "will be till the world's end complained of."

106 Richard Hooker, *The Works of That Learned and Judicious Divine Mr. Richard Hooker, with an Account of His Life and Death by Isaac Walton*, arr. John Keble, 7th ed., rev. R. W. Church and F. Paget (Oxford: Clarendon Press, 1888), Vol. 1, 342 (3.1.7); Cf. Vol. 2, 214 (5.49.2).

107  *Laws*: pref.4.2: 20.
108  *Laws*: 1.14.2: 113–14.
109  *Laws*: 1.14.2: 113.
110  *Laws*: 1.8.8: 81; 1.8.9: 81; cf. 1.3.1: 58; 1.8.10: 82. See Tulloch, *Rational Theology*, Vol. 1, 51: "This unity of nature and life and Scripture, as all equally true, if not equally important, revelations of the divine will, lies as the foundation of Hooker's whole argument."
111  *Laws*: 1.8.9: 82.
112  *Laws*: 1.8.10: 83, emphasis original.
113  Much of the next two paragraphs summarize Insole, *The Politics of Human Frailty*, 73–74.
114  *Laws*: 1.2.3: 56. Locke's sense that societies may be tolerant, differing, and adaptable (given the nature of reasoned preferences concerning nonessential matters) bears some parallel with his ecclesial views. Cf. Tulloch, *Rational Theology*, Vol. 1, 52.
115  *Laws*: 1.3.1: 58.
116  Marshall, *John Locke: Resistance*, 114n62, claims that Hooker's "works supported *jure divino* episcopacy but only *jure humano* monarchy."
117  Insole, *The Politics of Human Frailty*, 74.
118  *Laws*: 1.10.8: 93: "for any Prince or potentate of what kind soever upon earth" to impose laws without express divine commission "or else by the authority derived at the first from their consent upon whose persons they impose laws … is no better than mere tyranny." However Marshall, *John Locke: Resistance*, 209, rightly differentiates between Hooker's construction of consent-based politics and Locke's construction.
119  *Laws*: 1.10.7: 92.
120  Locke, "Ecclesia," 80.
121  The "Great Tew Circle" often met in the home of Lucius Cary, second Lord Viscount Falkland (1610?–1643). Cary's house was located at Great Tew in Oxfordshire: thus the nickname "Tew Circle." For more, see Trevor-Roper, *Catholics, Anglicans, and Puritans*, 166–230.
122  For the link between Latitudinarianism and the Tew Circle, see Griffin, *Latitudinarianism in the Seventeenth Century Church of England*, 15; Cranston, *John Locke*, 127n.1.
123  See Nathan Guy, "Giving Locke Some Latitude: Locke's Theological Influences from Great Tew to the Cambridge Platonists," in *Revisioning Cambridge Platonism*, ed. Douglas Hedley, Sarah Hutton, and David Leech, The International Archives of the History of Ideas (Berlin/Heidelberg: Springer, forthcoming). See ftn. 3 above for a record of Locke's library, noting his familiarity with both groups. John Edwards (Edwards, *Some Thoughts*, 104–05) noted a clear similarity between the *RC* and Taylor's works. Near the end of his life, Locke recommended reading

Chillingworth carefully and often (John Locke, "Some Thoughts Concerning Reading and Study for a Gentleman," 351). Tetlow ("The Theological Context of Locke's Political Thought," 30) claims "there is a similarly of tone, argument, and intention" between Chillingworth and Locke and that comparison of arguments in Locke's *Second Vindication* and Chillingworth's *The Religion of Protestants* shows that "the substance of their arguments … were essentially the same." Locke considered Barrow "a very considerable friend" (Marshall, *John Locke: Resistance*, 80) and called John Tillotson (another major Latitudinarian figure) a "great" man and "a friend of many years, steadfast, candid, and sincere" (L1826 in COR, Vol. 5: 237–39).

124 See Jeremy Taylor, *A Discourse of the Liberty of Prophesying, with Its Just Limits and Temper: Shewing the Unreasonableness of Prescribing to Other Men's Faiths, and the Inquity of Persecuting Differing Opinions*, in *the Whole Works of the Right Rev. Jeremy Taylor, D.D.*, Rev. ed. M. A. Charles Page Eden (London: Printed for Richard Royston, 1647), Vol. 5. Locke's library contains a copy of Taylor's *Works* (LL, 244), which he purchased in 1650. See Cranston, *John Locke*, 24n.2. The Great Tew Circle would often read first-hand accounts of religious violence, such as Jacob Acontius's *Darkness Discovered*. On this see Loconte, *God, Locke, and Liberty*, 21; Trevor-Roper, *Catholics, Anglicans, and Puritans*, 190.

125 For the connection between Taylor's work and Locke's LCT, see Loconte, *God, Locke, and Liberty*, 106.

126 William Chillingworth, *The Religion of Protestants, a Safe Way to Salvation*, a new and complete edition (1638; Covent Garden: George Bell & Sons, 1888), 5.

127 Locke, "A Vindication of the Reasonableness of Christianity", 7–10, 20.

128 Isaac Barrow, "Sermon XXXII. Of A Peaceable Temper and Carriage," in *The Theological Works of Isaac Barrow, D.D., in 9 Volumes*, ed. Alexander Napier (Cambridge: Cambridge University Press, 1859), Vol. 2, 435–36, 438–39.

129 Taylor, *A Discourse of the Liberty of Prophesying*, 368.

130 Taylor, *A Discourse of the Liberty of Prophesying*, 368. On his use of this in the RC, as well as the complexity of Locke's singular proposition, see Chapter 6 of this book.

131 Chillingworth, *The Religion of Protestants*, 49–50.

132 Chillingworth, *The Religion of Protestants*, 50. On Hammond's minimal message, see Lettinga, "Covenant Theology and the Transformation of Anglicanism," 212; Tetlow, "The Theological Context of Locke's Political Thought," 23–25.

133 Locke, "A Vindication of the Reasonableness of Christianity", esp. 14–16.

134 Taylor, *A Discourse of the Liberty of Prophesying*, 377.

135 Chillingworth, *The Religion of Protestants*, 194, 50.

136 See Gilbert Burnet, *A Rational Method for Proving the Truth of the Christian Religion, as It Is Professed in the Church of England* (London: Printed for Richard Royston, 1675); Spellman, *John Locke*, 56.

137 See Martin Greig, "The Reasonableness of Christianity? Gilbert Burnet and the Trinitarian Controversy of the 1690's," *Journal of Ecclesiastical History* 44, no. 4 (October 1993): 637–38.
138 Burnet, *Bishop Burnet's History of His Own Time*, 323.
139 Burnet, *Bishop Burnet's History of His Own Time*, 323.
140 Burnet, *Bishop Burnet's History of His Own Time*, 323; Cf. Douglas Hedley, "Should Divinity Overcome Metaphysics? Reflections on John Milbank's Theology beyond Secular Reason and Confessions of a Cambridge Platonist," *The Journal of Religion* 80, no. 2 (April 2000): 277.
141 Colie, *Light and Enlightenment*, 22.
142 See David Pailin, "Reconciling Theory and Fact: The Problem of 'Other Faiths' in Lord Herbert and the Cambridge Platonists," in *Platonism at the Origins of Modernity: Studies on Platonism and Early Modern Philosophy*, ed. Douglas Hedley and Sarah Hutton, International Archives of the History of Ideas 196 (Dordrecht, Netherlands: Springer, 2008), 94.
143 Charles Taliaferro, *Evidence and Faith: Philosophy and Religion since the Seventeenth Century* (Cambridge: Cambridge University Press, 2005), 106.
144 Pailin, "Reconciling Theory and Fact," 93–112.
145 For example, see Graham A. J. Rogers, "Locke, Newton, and the Cambridge Platonists on Innate Ideas," in *Philosophy, Religion, and Science in the Seventeenth and Eighteenth Centuries*, ed. John W. Yolton (Rochester, NY: University of Rochester Press, 1990), 351–65; G. A. J. Rogers, "Locke, Plato and Platonism," in *Platonism at the Origins of Modernity*, 193–207; Victor Nuovo, "Reflections on Locke's Platonism," in *Platonism at the Origins of Modernity*, 207–23; Sarah Hutton, "Some Thoughts Concerning Ralph Cudworth," in *Studies on Locke: Sources, Contemporaries, and Legacy, in Honour of G.A.J. Rogers*, ed. Sarah Hutton and Paul Schuurman (Dordrecht, The Netherlands: Springer, 2008), 143–57; Sarah Hutton, "Damaris Cudworth, Lady Masham, between Platonism and Enlightenment," *British Journal for the History of Philosophy* 1, no. 1 (February 1993): 29–54; Sarah Hutton, "Damaris Masham (1658–1708)," in *The Bloomsbury Companion to Locke*, eds. S.-J. Savonius-Wroth, Paul Schuurman, and Jonathan Walmsley, gen. (London: Bloomsbury, 2014), esp. 74; Guy, "Giving Locke Some Latitude."
146 Wolterstorff, *John Locke and the Ethics of Belief*, xiv–xv.
147 Wolterstorff, *John Locke and the Ethics of Belief*, xv.
148 For Locke's use, see Locke, *The Reasonableness of Christianity as Deliver'd in the Scriptures*, ed. John C. Higgins-Biddle (Oxford: Clarendon Press, 1999), 140n.1. For its use among the Cambridge Platonists, see Nathaniel Culverwell, *An Elegant and Learned Discourse of the Light of Nature*, ed. Robert A. Greene and Hugh MacCallum (1652; Toronto: University of Toronto Press, 1971), 13; Robert A. Greene and Hugh MacCallum, "Introduction," in Culverwell, *An Elegant and*

*Learned Discourse of the Light of Nature*, li; Robert A. Greene, "Whichcote, the Candle of the Lord, and Synderesis," *Journal of the History of Ideas* 52, no. 4 (October–December 1991): 640.

149  See Rogers, "Locke, Plato and Platonism," 202, for this phrase.

150  Benjamin Whichcote, "Appendix: Moral and Religious Aphorisms," in *The Cambridge Platonists*, ed. C. A. Patrides (1703; 1753; Cambridge, MA: Harvard University Press, 1970), 326, 327, 331 (aphorism #33, #76, #99, and #460). See also *The Cambridge Platonists*, 58–59. I am indebted to Rogers, "Locke, Plato and Platonism," 202, for these references.

151  Pailin, "Reconciling Theory and Fact," 111.

152  See L684, L687, L688, L696, L699 (*COR*, Vol 2: 484–85, 488–90, 500–01, 503–05). Cf. Woolhouse, *Locke*, 175–77.

153  L699 (*COR*, Vol. 2: 503–05).

154  Whichcote, "Appendix: Moral and Religious Aphorisms," 330 (aphorism #349).

155  Henry More, "Enthusiasmus Triumphatus; or, a Brief Discourse of the Nature, Causes, Kinds, and Cure of Enthusiasm," in *A Collection of Several Philosophical Writings of Dr. Henry More*, 4th ed. corrected and much enlarged (London: Printed by Joseph Downing in Bartholomew-Close near West-Smithfield, 1712), 1. More's influence continues in Book IV of the *Essay*. When Locke expresses doubt concerning one's ability to discover the essence of a substance, he seems to be sharing in More's epistemological skepticism about the subject and even shares verbal cues. Compare Henry More, *The Immortality of the Soul, So Farre Forth as It Is Demonstrable from the Knowledge of Nature and the Light of Reason*, ed. Alexander Jacob, International Archives of the History of Ideas 122 (1662; Dordrecht: Nijhoff, 1987), 26–27 with *E*: 4.1.2: 525; 4.4.1: 562–63; 4.4.3: 563. On this, see G. A. J. Rogers, "Locke and the Latitude-men: ignorance as a ground for toleration," in *Philosophy, Science and Religion in England (1640–1700)*, ed. R. Ashcraft, R. Kroll, and P. Zagorin (Cambridge: Cambridge University Press, 1992), 238.

156  See Lydia Gysi, *Platonism and Cartesianism in the Philosophy of Ralph Cudworth* (Bern: Herbert Lang, 1962), 102–03; Ayers, *Locke*, Vol. 2, 168–83; Nuovo, *Christianity, Antiquity, and Enlightenment*, 214n.30.

157  For Cudworth, see Ralph Cudworth, *True Intellectual System of the Universe: The First Part, Wherein All the Reason and Philosophy of Atheism Is Confuted; And Its Impossibility Demonstrated* (London: Printed for Richard Royston, bookseller to his most sacred majesty, 1678) (*TIS*): 200, 210, 636, 645, 646, 652; for Locke, see *E*: 4.10.6: 621; 4.10.7: 621; *STCE*, 136; Locke, *An Early Draft of Locke's Essay*, 116–18.

158  *TIS*: 652; *E*: 1.1.4.16: 95.

159  *TIS*: 474, 683–84, 834; *E*: 4.10: 619–30.

160  *TIS*: 647, 717; Ralph Cudworth, *A Treatise of Free Will*, now first edited from the original manuscript, and with notes, by John Allen (London: John W. Parker,

1838), 34; Ralph Cudworth, *A Treatise Concerning Eternal and Immutable Morality*, with a preface by the Right reverend Father in God, Edward Lord Bishop of Durham (London: Printed for James and John Knapton, at the Crown in St. Paul's Church-yard, 1731), 27.

161 Cudworth, *A Treatise of Free Will*, 16–17, 53.
162 See Cudworth, *A Treatise Concerning Eternal and Immutable Morality*, 77; Cudworth, *A Treatise of Free Will*, 77, 78.
163 On free will, compare Cudworth's approach with *E*: 2.21.17–19: 242–43. Cf. John Arthur Passmore, *Ralph Cudworth: An Interpretation* (Cambridge: Cambridge University Press, 1951), 93–94.
164 *TIS*: 896.
165 *TIS*: 697–98; 895–98; Cudworth, *A Treatise Concerning Eternal and Immutable Morality*, 26–27; Cudworth, *A Treatise of Free Will*, 31. Cf. Gysi, *Platonism and Cartesianism*, 129, 131, who describes the "absolute values that carry universal obligation" as "all modifications of … love."
166 For "one community of nature," see *2nd T*: 4, 6. For "one divine mind," see Gysi, *Platonism and Cartesianism*, 130.
167 See Robert Crocker, *Henry More, 1614–1687: A Biography of the Cambridge Platonist* (Dordrecht: Kluwer Academic Publishers, 2003), 122, who uses the phrase "dogmatic Calvinism" to describe what Henry More, along with most of the Royal Society, rejected.
168 Henry Hammond, *A practicall catechisme* (1644; Oxford: [publisher not identified], 1645); cf. Lettinga, "Covenant Theology and the Transformation of Anglicanism," 6, 158, 214, 222.
169 Henry Hammond, *Charis kai Eirēnē, or, A pacifick discourse of God's grace and decrees: in a letter of full accordance written to the reverend and most learned Dr. Robert Sanderson: to which are annexed the extracts of three letters concerning Gods prescience reconciled with liberty and contingency* (London: Printed for R. Davis, 1600).
170 See, for example, Patrides, *The Cambridge Platonists*, 38n.38, citing Whichcote's *Several Discourses* (1701), Vol. 1: 364.
171 For the *RC*'s critique of hyper-Calvinism, see Chapter 6 of this book.
172 *TIS*: 873. Cf. 203.
173 *TIS*: 873; Cudworth, *A Treatise of Free Will*, 78. Cf. Gysi, *Platonism and Cartesianism*, 126–28.
174 *TIS*: 202, 203, 205, 406, 661; Cudworth, *A Treatise of Free Will*, 50.
175 On God's providential care, see *RC*: 40, 129, 133; *E*: 2.1.10: 108. On rejecting hyper-Calvinism, see *RC*: 4 and Chapter 6 of this book.
176 John Smith, *Select Discourses* (1660; repr., London: Garland Publishing, 1978), 383.
177 For example, *RC*: 142–45; *E*: 4.19.14: 704. For a fuller treatment, see Chapter 6 of this book.

178 John Tillotson, *The Rule of Faith: Or, an Answer to the Treatise of Mr. I. S. entituled, Sure-footing, &c., to Which is Adjoined A REPLY to Mr. I.S. His 3d Appendix &c. by Edw. Stillingfleet*, 1666, 2nd ed. (London: Printed by H.C. for O. Gellibrand, at the Golden-Ball in St. Paul's Church-yard, 1676), 67–70; John Locke, *A Discourse of Miracles*, in *Writings on Religion*, by John Locke, ed. Victor Nuovo (1706; Oxford: Clarendon Press, 2002). 48. Cf. *RC*: 32–33, 82, 135, 138, 143, 146–47.

179 Compare Benjamin Whichcote, *Theophoroumēna dogmata, or, Some Select Notions of that learned and Reverend Divine of the Church of England, Benj. Whitchcot, D.D., Lately Deceased* (London: Printed and are to be sold by Israel Harrison at Lincoln's-Inn Gate, 1685), 85–86 and Cudworth, *A Treatise Concerning Eternal and Immutable Morality*, 26–27, with Locke (*LN*: 186–87; *QLN*: 101). Spellman, *John Locke*, 75, notes that Whichcote "adopted the Aristotelian-Thomist definition of man as a rational creature, one whose unique defining characteristic was the ability, and hence the obligation, to exercise his reason and to discover God's eternal law in the nature of things." By reason alone, Whichcote thought, a human could acquire and comply with God's eternal law. Whichcote, *Theophoroumēna dogmata*, 85–86.

180 *STCE*, 193. Cf. Hutton, "Some Thoughts Concerning Ralph Cudworth," 154.

181 For more on Locke's use of happiness, see Chapter 5 of this book.

182 *RC*: 10, 78, 88, 98, 100, 122–23, 139, 147, 149–51; *Ethic*: 1; *LCT*: 28, 43, 47, 48; *E*. 1.3.3: 67; 2.7.5: 130; 2. 21.51: 266; 2.21.53: 268; 2.21.60: 273–74; 4.10.1: 619. Cf. *LN*: 157.

183 Cudworth, *A Treatise of Free Will*, 28, 30.

184 Ralph Cudworth, *A Sermon Preached before the Honourable House of Commons at Westminster, March 31, 1647*, reproduced from the original edition (Cambridge, 1647; repr. New York: The Facsimile Text Society, 1930), 19.

# Chapter 4

1 *LN*: 173.

2 Locke, *An Early Draft of Locke's Essay*, 116. Cf. *STCE*, 135 and 136: "There ought very early to be imprinted on his Mind a true Notion of *God*" (136). This true notion involves not only God's infinity, independence, Supremacy, and authorship of all Creation but also his goodness, love, and generosity. Locke speaks of the "one true God" repeatedly in the *RC* (e.g., *RC*, 26, 135, 137, *passim*).

3 Cf. Chapter 1, note 76. John Edwards, *The Socinian Creed, or, a Brief Account of the Professed Tenents and Doctrines of the Foreign and English Socinians Wherein Is shew'd the Tendency of Them to Irreligion and Atheism, with Proper Antidotes against Them* (London: Printed for J. Robinson and J. Wyat, 1697), esp. 120 and 128, attacks "the one article men" who claim "Jesus is the Messiah" is the only necessary article of the Christian faith.

4   I am grateful to Victor Nuovo for raising this point in personal correspondence.
5   See J. C. D. Clark, *English Society 1688–1832* (Cambridge: Cambridge University Press, 1985), 280: "Locke's significance for the eighteenth century was not chiefly in introducing contractarianism into political theory, but heterodox theology into religious speculation." Philip Dixon, *Nice and Hot Disputes: The Doctrine of the Trinity in the Seventeenth Century* (London: T&T Clark, 2003), 162: "John Locke was not a trinitarian believer." Considering "the trinitarian controversies of the decade," writes Dixon, Locke's "silence implies lack of belief rather than lack of concern" (163). See also J. A. I. Champion, *The Pillars of Priestcraft Shaken* (Cambridge: Cambridge University Press, 1992), 112n.27. Even Nuovo, *Christianity, Antiquity, and Enlightenment*, 47, makes a similar claim: "On the doctrine of the Trinity, he was not silent or indecisive. What he wrote in his notes and published works seems to contradict or at very least comes short of Athanasian orthodoxy."
6   Edward Stillingfleet, *A Discourse in Vindication of the Doctrine of the Trinity: With an Answer to the Late Socinian Objections against It from Scripture, Antiquity and Reason. And a Preface Concerning the Different Explications of the Trinity, and the Tendency of the Present Socinian Controversie* (London: Printed by J. H. for Henry Mortlock, 1697); Edward Stillingfleet, *The Bishop of Worcester's Answer to Mr. Locke's Letter, Concerning Some Passages Relating to His Essay of Humane Understanding, Mention'd in the Late Discourse in Vindication of the Trinity with a Postscript in Answer to Some Reflections Made on That Treatise in a Late Socinian Pamphlet* (London: Printed by J. H. for Henry Mortlock, 1697); Edward Stillingfleet, *The Bishop of Worcester's ANSWER to Mr. Locke's Second Letter; Wherein His NOTION of IDEAS Is prov'd to Be Inconsistent with It Self, and with the ARTICLES of the CHRISTIAN FAITH* (London: Printed by J. H. for Henry Mortlock at the Phoenix in St. Paul's Church-Yard, 1698).
7   See the last chapter in Stillingfleet, *A Discourse in Vindication of the Doctrine of the Trinity*. Summarized in Dixon, *Nice and Hot Disputes*, 145–46.
8   Dixon, *Nice and Hot Disputes*, 149.
9   See Stillingfleet, *The Bishop of Worcester's ANSWER to Mr. Locke's Letter*; Stillingfleet, *The Bishop of Worcester's ANSWER to Mr. Locke's Second Letter*. Noted in Dixon, *Nice and Hot Disputes*, 157.
10  Dixon, *Nice and Hot Disputes*, 139.
11  Wainwright, "Introduction," 38.
12  Dixon, *Nice and Hot Disputes*, 154: "His silence on the topic is all the more eloquent when set beside his eagerness to join in almost every other hot issue of his day, even if anonymously." Instead, one is "left with Locke's uncharacteristic and awkward silence" (164). The "contention that this reticence was due to Locke's reluctance to engage in complex theological speculation sits uneasily with the breadth and depth of Locke's reading and competence in theology" (164).

13  Dixon, *Nice and Hot Disputes*, 1697.
14  See *RC*: 157: "The writers and wranglers in religion fill it with niceties, and dress it up with notions, which they make necessary and fundamental parts of it; as if there were no way into the church, but through the academy or lyceum. The greatest part of mankind have not leisure for learning and logic, and superfine distinctions of the schools." According to Dixon, *Nice and Hot Disputes*, 164, "it is difficult not to construe" this "as a dismissive comment" upon the "Trinitarian controversies of the 1690s … On such a view, the 'niceties' of the doctrine of the Trinity are rendered the preserve of dilettante churchmen and cannot possibly be relevant to common Christian experience."
15  For discussion of Locke's correspondence with Limborch, see Mario Montuori, *John Locke on Toleration and the Unity of God* (Amsterdam: J. C. Gieben, 1983), 175–219; Dixon, *Nice and Hot Disputes*, 165–66.
16  John Locke, "Mr. Locke's Reply to the Right Reverend," in *The Works of John Locke*, 10th ed. (London: Printed for J. Johnson, 1801), Vol. 4, 343.
17  Locke, *Mr. Locke's Reply to the Right Reverend the Lord Bishop of Worcester's Answer to his Second Letter*, 343.
18  John Locke, "Adversaria Theologica," in John Locke, *Writings on Religion*, ed. Victor Nuovo (1794; Oxford: Clarendon Press, 2002), 19–33.
19  For example, see John C. Higgins-Biddle, "Introduction," in John Locke, *The Reasonableness of Christianity as Delivered in the Scriptures*, ed. John C. Higgins-Biddle (Oxford: Clarendon Press, 1999); Alan P. F. Sell, *John Locke and the Eighteenth Century Divines* (1997; Eugene, OR: Wipf & Stock, 2006), 203, speaks of "the doctrine of the Trinity, in which he believed, and did not deny, but did not affirm with fervor or examine in detail." Aaron, *John Locke*, 298: "The Reasonableness does not deny the doctrine of the Trinity, but it does stress the unity of the Godhead, and it omits the doctrine of the Trinity from the list of reasonable doctrines … he definitely states that he is no Socinian, that he does not deny Christ's divinity, nor any of the main Mysteries of the Christian Religion." Though Locke's Christology "did not fit the pattern of any existing school," warns Wainwright, "Introduction," 39, "the extent to which he deviated from the traditional doctrine of Christ can be exaggerated" (38). Nuovo, *Christianity, Antiquity, and Enlightenment*, 29, argues there is hardly any evidence that Locke "was pursuing a Socinian agenda or an Arian one, or that he was motivated by sympathies for one or the other."
20  *STCE*, 159.
21  *STCE*, 159: "There are some parts of the scripture, which may be proper to be put into the hands of a child to engage him to read … But the reading of the whole scripture indifferently, is what I think very inconvenient for children, till, after having been made acquainted with the plainest fundamental parts of it, they have got some kind of general view of what they ought principally to believe

and practice, which yet, I think, they ought to receive in the very words of the scripture, and not in such as men, prepossessed by systems and analogies, are apt in this case to make use of, and force upon them." See John Worthington, *A Form of Sound Words: Or, a Scripture Catechism; Shewing What a Christian Is to Believe and Practice, in Order to Salvation*, 6th ed. (London: R. Hett, 1733). In his Scripture Catechism, John Worthington orders his catechism in a Q&A format. In answer to the question, "What doth the Scripure affirm of the Father, the Son and the Holy Ghost?" Worthington offers the Johannine Comma (1 John 5:7): "The Scripture saith that there are three that bear Record in Heaven, the Father, the Word (or the Son) and the Holy Ghost; and these three are one" (16).

22   Catharine Cockburn, "A vindication of Mr. Locke's Christian Principles, from the Injurious Imputations of Dr. Holdsworth. Now First published," in *The Works of Mrs. Catharine Cockburn, Theological, Moral, Dramatic, and Poetical*. Several of them now first printed, revised and published, with an account of the life of the author, by Thomas Birch, in two volumes (London: Printed for J. and P. Knapton, in Ludgate-Street, 1751), Vol. 1, 188. Cited in Sell, *John Locke and the Eighteenth Century Divines*, 200.

23   Nuovo, *Christianity, Antiquity, and Enlightenment*, 22. Upon receiving the book, Locke replied to Limborch: "I think that I should now have leisure enough to devote myself for the most part to these studies," which Nuovo claims might refer to serious consideration of the arguments presented in the book (*COR*, Vol. 5, 237; translation by Nuovo).

24   Nuovo, *Christianity, Antiquity, and Enlightenment*, 28. Although Peter King's arrangement leaves the impression of "gathering the evidence pro and con in unequal columns on a single page, so that the whole looks like a score sheet waiting to be tallied," comparison of other examples in Locke's own hand suggests a regular note-taking pattern (27). "The disputational form seems to have been used as a convenient way of taking notes from a work that presents arguments supporting contrary positions" (27). Besides, writes Nuovo, the number of arguments on either side need not suggest endorsement (29). The fifth entry considers whether Christ was a mere man; Locke's list provides seven proofs for the affirmative and only one for the negative. However, Locke initials the negative argument and later affirms Christ's preexistence.

25   Nuovo, *Christianity, Antiquity, and Enlightenment*, 22: "Narration seems to me a more appropriate method of expounding on Locke's theology than a systematic presentation of it, for Locke's thoughts on theology were not all expressed as considered opinions, nor did he manifest a tendency to give assent where Scripture or reason did not require it. His thoughts on theological themes varied from suppositions to queries to preferences to clear and certain judgments. These differences in propositional attitude, to use current jargon, would be lost in a mere systematic account."

26  See Nuovo, *Christianity, Antiquity, and Enlightenment*, 22. For more on the complexity of Locke's singular proposition, see Chapter 6 of this book.
27  Nuovo, *Christianity, Antiquity, and Enlightenment*, 24.
28  See Dixon, *Nice and Hot Disputes*, 159–60, citing, as one example, Francis Gastrell, *Some Considerations Concerning the Trinity: and the Ways of Managing that Controversie* (London: E. Whitlock, 1696).
29  John Locke, "A Second Vindication of the Reasonableness of Christianity," in *Vindications of the Reasonableness of Christianity*, by John Locke, ed. Victor Nuovo (1697; Oxford: Clarendon Press, 2012), 107–15, though his version does not contain the line "descended into hell." Cf. Wainwright, "Introduction," 34.
30  See Locke's replies to Stillingfleet, cited above.
31  Toland, *Christianity Not Mysterious*, 6. Toland is the object of Stillingfleet's ire in Stillingfleet, *A Discourse in Vindication of the Doctrine of the Trinity*, chapter 10.
32  See Chapter 3 and Chapter 6 for citations.
33  Wainwright, "Introduction," 34.
34  Wainwright, "Introduction," 38–39.
35  Tetlow, "The Theological Context of John Locke's Political Thought," 456.
36  Tetlow, "The Theological Context of John Locke's Political Thought," 456.
37  *RC*; Locke, *Paraphrase and Notes*. Cf. Wainwright, "Introduction," 38.
38  Nuovo, *Christianity, Antiquity, and Enlightenment*, 98.
39  *E*: 1.1.4.16: 95. Cf. 1.1.5: 45; 1.3.5: 69.
40  *E*: 4.10.1: 621.
41  *E*: 4.10.1: 619. Cf. 1.4.17: 95; 4.10.6: 621.
42  *E*: 2.17.20: 222.
43  *E*: 1.1.5: 45.
44  *E*: 1.4.9: 89.
45  *E*: 1.4.11: 90.
46  Principally in *E*: 4.10: 619–30, but elsewhere as well.
47  *TIS*; Smith, *Select Discourses*, 41–55; More, *The Immortality of the Soul*. See also Boyle, *The Philosophical Works*, 150–59.
48  *E*: 4.8.6: 614.
49  *E*: 1.1.5: 45. Locke is skeptical of arbitrary "species" distinctions. Locke believes any being with the kind of rational awareness that would lead them a knowledge God and duties stemming from his knowledge of God would classify that being as a "man." For the language of God as "the maker and father of this universe," see Plato, *Timaeus*, in *Plato: Timaeus and Critias*, trans. A. E. Taylor (London: Methuen & Co., 1929), 28c.
50  *E*: 1.4.9: 89.
51  *E*: 1.1.5: 45. See also 2.23.12: 302: "We are furnished with Faculties (dull and weak as they are) to discover enough in the Creatures, to lead us to the Knowledge of the Creator, and the Knowledge of our Duty … These … are our Business in this world."

52  E: 1.4.12: 91.
53  See Forster, *John Locke's Politics of Moral Consensus*, 101: "The dependence of Locke's philosophy on God's existence can hardly be overstated ... It is not for nothing that Locke so frequently asserts that the existence of God is beyond dispute—if that existence were subject to any serious doubt, Locke's philosophy could not function."
54  Forster, *John Locke's Politics of Moral Consensus*, 101.
55  E: 4.10: 619–30.
56  See Waldron, *God, Locke, and Equality*, 234; Forster, *John Locke's Politics of Moral Consensus*, 102.
57  For negative appraisals, see Dunn, *The Political Thought of John Locke*, 21–22; Wolterstorff, "Locke's Philosophy of Religion," esp. 189; Michael P. Zuckert, "An Introduction to Locke's First Treatise," *Interpretation: A Journal of Political Philosophy* 8, no. 1 (January 1979): 69–70. For a positive appraisal, see Forster, *John Locke's Politics of Moral Consensus*, 102–03; Nuovo, *Christianity, Antiquity, and Enlightenment*, 212.
58  See the explanation provided by Jonathan Bennett, "Locke's Philosophy of Mind," in *The Cambridge Companion to Locke*, ed. Vere Chappell (Cambridge: Cambridge University Press, 1994), 102–04.
59  Edwin McCann, "Locke's Philosophy of Body," in *The Cambridge Companion to Locke*, ed. Vere Chappell (Cambridge: Cambridge University Press, 1994), 75.
60  J. B. Schneewind, "Locke's Moral Philosophy," in *The Cambridge Companion to Locke*, ed. Vere Chappell (Cambridge: Cambridge University Press, 1994), 207. See also Forster, *John Locke's Politics of Moral Consensus*, 103. In this regard, see C. S. Lewis, "Mere Christianity," in *The Complete C. S. Lewis Signature Classics* (New York: HarperOne, 2002), 24, who makes an interesting distinction: the classical philosophical arguments leading to a moral lawgiver (behind the moral law) may suggest "goodness" as an essential attribute in the strictest sense, but there is little empirical reason to suppose that the moral lawgiver is "indulgent, or soft, or sympathetic" (or what Locke calls "a bountiful and merciful Father"). A number of authors in the patristic period, however—beginning with Philo—connect God's essential goodness with his providential care, suggesting the correlation may be discovered through natural reason. See Wayne Hankey, "Natural Theology in the Patristic Period," in *The Oxford Handbook of Natural Theology*, ed. Russell Re Manning (Oxford: Oxford University Press, 2013), 38–56. In addition to goodness, several have noted that "justice" is not clearly proved as an essential aspect of God's nature. See Tuckness, "The Coherence of a Mind," 83; Marshall, *John Locke: Resistance*, 384; Harris, *The Mind of John Locke*, 270–72. Ultimately, the issue may be a moot point; as I will argue in Chapter 6, revelation in scripture—which provides the narrative whereby one graciously interprets the effects of natural law—is indispensable for tying together Locke's moral and political theory.

61 David Hume, *A Treatise of Human Nature*, ed. David Fate Norton and Mary J. Norton (Oxford: Oxford University Press, 2000), 56–58 (1.3.3). For arguments exonerating the philosophers addressed by Hume, see D. G. C. Macnabb and E. J. Khamara, "Hume and His Predecessors on the Causal Maxim," in *David Hume: Bicentenary Papers*, ed. G. P. Morice (Austin: University of Texas, 1977), 153n.4; Edward J. Khamara, "Hume against Locke on the Causal Principle," *British Journal for the History of Philosophy* 8, no. 2 (2000): 339–43.

62 *E*: 4.1.3: 620; 4.10.8: 622. Khamara, "Hume against Locke on the Causal Principle," 341. In fact, Khamara rightly notes that Locke's claim that "nonentity cannot produce a real being" is a "dispensable" proposition, an "extra" rather than an "explicit" premise in his argument. What is further, Hume summarizes the Lockean causal principle as advocating "everything must have a cause" when Locke, in fact, claims such is *not* a principle of reason; "Everything *that has a beginning* must have a cause" is a principle of reason. Cf. Locke, *The Works of John Locke: A New Edition, Corrected, in Ten Volumes*, Vol. 4, 61–62.

63 Khamara, "Hume against Locke on the Causal Principle," 342–43. Khamara calls it a "Lewis Carroll" reading of Locke's argument to think "X is produced by nothing" means "X has a cause which is 'nothing,'" rather than "X has no cause whatever" (341). See also Locke, *The Works of John Locke: A New Edition, Corrected, in Ten Volumes*, Vol. 4, 62, where Locke speaks of "*something operating*, which we call a *cause*." A reified "nothing" cannot fill the space of "something operating" in Locke's approach.

64 Zuckert, "An Introduction to Locke's First Treatise," 69–70.

65 *E*: 4.10.19: 629–30; cf. 4.11.1: 630.

66 Zuckert, "An Introduction to Locke's First Treatise," 69–70.

67 For example, Emile du Châtelet, the great Leibniz advocate, sought to build her cosmological argument from Lockean premises, supplemented with Leibnizian metaphysics. See the discussion in Marcy P. Lascano, "Emile du Châtelet on the Existence and Nature of God: An Examination of Her Arguments in Light of Their Sources," *British Journal for the History of Philosophy* 19, no. 4 (2011): 743–45, citing (and translating) Gabrielle-Emilie Le Tonnelier de Breteuil, Marquise du Châtelet, *Institutions de physique* (Paris: Chez Prault Fils, 1740), 39–40.

68 Dunn, *The Political Thought of John Locke*, 194, is simply mistaken to assert that Locke "feels it necessary only to demonstrate the existence of a God to feel that he has established the existence of a substantially Christian God." See also John Dunn, *Locke* (Oxford: Oxford University Press, 1984), 84.

69 *E*: 4.2.6: 621; he further suggests "all those other attributes" that "we ought to ascribe" to a perfect Being may be delineated from the idea of perfection.

70 LN: 90, 108–09, and throughout.

71 Horwitz, "Introduction," 57. Cf. 55–59.

72 Horwitz, "Introduction," 58: "One is led to conclude ... that when the editor replaces *deus* by *Deus*, he intends us to understand that Locke is speaking of the God of

Sacred Scripture, the God of whom Aquinas, Culverwell, Sanderson, Cumberland, and countless others in that host of Christian natural law writers were speaking, and 'under whose influence' Locke's work is understood by the author to have been fundamentally shaped." But the first paragraph of Locke's first essay lends itself to just such a conclusion. Shortly before speaking of "god, best and greatest" (as Horwitz translates it), Locke describes this god as one who presented himself to humanity through "the once frequent testimony of miracles" and declares "he ... has fixed limits to the unruly sea itself," which is an allusion to Proverbs 8:29 (*QLN*: 95). As Horwitz admits in a footnote, this text is "often adduced by writers on the theory of natural law," citing Aquinas, Suarez, Hooker, and Culverwell. Not only are these Christian natural law theorists, they represent the trajectory of Locke's Theo-philosophical perspective.

73 Thomas Burnet, *Second Remarks upon an Essay Concerning Humane Understanding, in a Letter Address'd to the Author* (1697; repr., New York: Garland, 1984), 11, charges Locke with fostering "a Manichean God (or a God without Moral Attributes)."

74 Here, I borrow a phrase from Janet Martin Soskice, "Naming God: A Study in Faith and Reason," in *Reason and the Reasons of Faith*, ed. Paul Griffiths and Reinhard Hütter (London: T&T Clark, 2005), 254; however, Soskice affirms that "Locke was not a Deist" but rather "a man of deep Christian convictions" (247fn.16).

75 *RC*: 8.

76 In addition to the *RC* references in this paragraph, see *E*: 1.4.15: 93.

77 *RC*: 135, 137; 106; 137.

78 *RC*: 26. Locke speaks repeatedly of the "one true God" (26, 135, 136, 137), eternal (137) and invisible (106, 137).

79 *RC*: 137, 136.

80 Locke speaks often of the "true" God (*E*: 1.4.13: 92; 1.4.15: 93) and bemoans widespread false notions of God (1.4.12: 92; 1.4.14: 93). For example, polytheists and idolaters are aware of God but are "mistaken about Him" (1.4.15: 93). Yet even among Christians one may find "absurd and unfit notions" of God (1.4.16: 94). Locke traces the prevalence of wrong notions of deity—even within the disparate denominations of Christianity—to custom, education and "the constant din of their party" (2.33.18: 400–01).

81 *STCE*, 136; Locke, *An Early Draft of Locke's Essay*, 116–18.

82 *RC*: 5.

83 *RC*: 8: "and other attributes of the supreme Being, which he has declared of himself; and reason, as well as revelation, must acknowledge to be in him."

84 *RC*: 16–17.

85 *E*: 4.10.6: 621.

86 *RC*: "supreme" (8, 148); eternal, infinite, and invisible (106, 137, 148); "most powerful" (17, 82, 84); "most knowing Being" (84, 129). *2nd T*: God is "sovereign,"

"Lord," "Master," "Almighty," and "infinitely wise" (4, 6, 56, 79, 195), as well as "omnipotent" (6). *LCT*: "Almighty" (27, 56), "Master" (32), "Supreme" (32), and speaks of the "eternal and infinite wisdom of God" (58). *E*: "incomprehensible" (2.1.15: 113; 2.13.18: 174; 2.15.8: 200); "eternal" (2.27.2: 329; 2.14.31: 196; 4.3.6: 541; 4.3.27: 558; cf. 2.15.3: 197; 2.17.1: 210; 2.17.20: 221–22); "infinite" (2.1.10: 108; 2.13.18: 174; 2.14.31: 196); omnipresent (2.27.2: 329); omnipotent (1.3.13: 75; 2.13.22: 75; 2.13.22: 177); "infinitely wise" (1.4.12: 91; 2.23.12: 302; etc.); "superior" and "supreme" (1.4.10: 89; 1.3.13: 302).

87  *RC*: 11, 112. Locke speaks of God as the "law-giver" in the *Essay* as well (*E*: 1.3.5: 69; 1.3.13: 75).
88  *RC*: 4, 5, 6, though "some things belong to the unalterable purpose of the divine justice" (10).
89  *2nd T*: 241.
90  *LN*: 183; *RC*: 113, 114, 125, 126, 127; *LCT*: 32, 49; *2nd T*: 21, 241.
91  *RC*: 4, 5, 133; 7; 133, 157; 130, 132, 133. See also references in the *Essay*: "Goodness" (2.27.13: 338; 2.32.14: 388; 2.7.4: 129; 2.9.12: 148; 2.23.12: 302); "bountiful" (1.1.5: 45); "kind and merciful father" (2.21.53: 268). Locke offers combinations in the Essay: "wisdom and goodness" (2.7.4: 129; 2.9.12: 148) or "wisdom, power, and goodness" (2.23.12: 302, and with reference to creation)—suggesting the kind of interrelationship expressed by Cudworth and others.
92  *RC*: 129.
93  *RC*: 40, 129, 133. God not only provides for all things but preserves all things (*E*: 2.1.10: 108).
94  *RC*: 129.
95  *RC*: 133.
96  *STCE*, 136, 137; *E*: 2.21.53: 268. The notion of God as the "Supreme Being" should not be interpreted as "the biggest being" or the one at the end of a cosmic chain. This basic orientation toward the good can be found in Plato and Aristotle, as well as later Christian tradition. Cf. Lloyd Gerson, "Plotinus on Akrasia: The Neoplatonic Synthesis," in *Akrasia in Greek Philosophy: From Socrates to Plotinus*, ed. Christopher Bobonich and Pierre Destrée, Philosophia Antiqua 106 (Leiden: Brill, 2007), esp. 278.
97  Besides, natural law theory is incompatible with a deistic metaphysic.
98  This is why the Christian vision of God is crucial for Locke; philosophical reflection solely on God's power must be balanced by theological reflection on his wisdom, goodness, and covenant-keeping faithfulness.
99  Janet Martin Soskice, "Creation ex nihilo: Its Jewish and Christian Foundations," in *Creation and the God of Abraham*, ed. David B. Burrell, Carlo Cogliati, Janet M. Soskice and William R. Stoeger (Cambridge: Cambridge University Press, 2010), 24. For more on *creatio ex nihilo*, see *Creation and the God of Abraham*, ed. David B. Burrell, Carlo Cogliatti, Janet M. Soskice, and William R. Stoeger (Cambridge: Cambridge University Press, 2010).

100   Soskice, "Creatio ex nihilo," 24.
101   Soskice, "Creatio ex nihilo," 25.
102   Soskice, "Creatio ex nihilo," 25, who notes though the doctrine is not explicitly named in the Bible, it is eminently biblical, since the metaphysical claim is driven by scripture.
103   Soskice, "Naming God."
104   Soskice, "Naming God," 248–49.
105   David Sedley, *Creationism and Its Critics in Antiquity* (Berkeley: University of California Press, 2009), xvii; cf. Soskice, "Creatio ex nihilo," 24.
106   Soskice cites *E*: 3.9: 490.
107   This approach lumps Locke into a larger narrative about the Enlightenment. Cf. Alexander Broadie, "Scotistic Metaphysics and Creation ex nihilo," in *Creation and the God of Abraham*, ed. David B. Burrell, Carlo Cogliati, Janet M. Soskice, and William R. Stoeger (Cambridge: Cambridge University Press, 2010), 53: "In the High Middle Ages all the major theologians of the Christian West teach that God created our world *ex nihilo* … During the Age of Enlightenment the concept of the creation of the world modulates to a distant key."
108   *LN*: 187.
109   *ST* IaIIae q21 art 4, ad 3um. In addition, Locke's description of God and creation in the *LN* are not relegated to Locke's early and former notions, which were soon to give way in his mature writings to a radically different conception altogether. Compare essay VI of *LN* with *2nd T*: 4–6.
110   *E*: 4.10.18: 629: "The Creation or Beginning of any one SUBSTANCE out of nothing, being once admitted, the Creation of all other, but the CREATOR himself, may, with the same ease, be supposed." Cf. 2.21.2: 234, where God is described as the "Author" of matter; 4.3.27: 558: "Father of all Spirits, the eternal independent Author of them and us and all Things." Cf. 2.1.10: 108, where God is the "infinite author and preserver of all things."
111   *E*: 2.26.2: 325. For God as the "Creator," see *E*: 2.1.15: 112–13; 2.7.3: 129; 2.23.12: 302–03; 4.3.6: 541–43; 4.3.23: 554; 4.4.14: 570; 4.10.18: 628–29; 4.16.12: 665–66. For these references, I am indebted to Vivienne Brown, "The 'Figure' of God and the Limits to Liberalism: a rereading of Locke's *Essay* and *Two Treatises*," *Journal of the History of Ideas* 60 (1999): 88.
112   Keith Ward, *Rational Theology and the Creativity of God* (Oxford: Basil Blackwell, 1982), 214–27.
113   *E*: 2.16.8: 209; 2.17.5: 212.
114   *E*: 2.29.16: 371. Cf. 2.15.12: 204: "Finite of any Magnitude, holds not any proportion to infinite."
115   *E*: 2.13.18: 174.
116   *E*: 2.15.8: 200. Cf. 2.1.15: 113; 2.13.18: 174. While Locke does at times lapse into language such as "a most Perfect Being" (4.10.7: 621, though, to his credit,

hypothetically and in the context of negation), his conception of God is consistent with the definition of Anselm as that "than which nothing greater can be thought" (*aliquid quo maius nihil cogitari potest*)—that is, beyond classification or qualification. See Anselm, *Proslogion*, in *Complete Philosophical and Theological Treatises of Anselm of Canterbury*, trans. Jasper Hopkins and Herbert Richardson (Minneapolis: Arthur J. Banning Press, 2000), par. 2. For the distinction, as well as a discussion of how one may speak analogously of God (as does Locke) without doing violence to Anselm's definition, see Ian McFarland, *From Nothing: A Theology of Creation* (Louisville: Westminster John Knox Press, 2014), 29–33.

117  Locke, *The Works of John Locke: A New Edition, Corrected, in Ten Volumes*, Vol. 9, 251; Cf. *STCE*, 136.

118  This suggests that Locke's category language concerning God's attributes is by means of analogy in which naming attributes that flow from perfection "are literally true ... of God; but they add nothing positive to our knowledge of God. On the contrary, they merely restate God's essential unknowability" (McFarland, *From Nothing*, 33). Cf. *ST*: Ia 13.1–12.

119  McFarland, *From Nothing*, 29–158. For particular reflection on how this implies God's goodness, see 135–37, 140–42, 188–89.

120  McFarland, *From Nothing*, 189.

121  McFarland, *From Nothing*, 189.

122  McFarland, *From Nothing*, 189.

123  McFarland, *From Nothing*, 33; Victor Preller, *Divine Science and the Science of God: A Reformulation of Thomas Aquinas* (Princeton, NJ: Princeton University Press, 1967), 167.

124  See the various chapters in Burrell, *Creation and the God of Abraham*.

125  See Norman Kretzmann, *The Metaphysics of Theism: Aquinas' Natural Theology in Summa Contra Gentiles I* (Oxford: Clarendon Press, 1997), esp. 113, who claims that, according to Aquinas, the first cause must be "the transcendent, personal, omniscient, omnipotent, perfectly good creator and governor of the universe." However, Kretzman incorrectly claims that Aquinas begins with perfection, rather than creation. For more, see discussion in Brian Hebblethwaite, *Philosophical Theology and Christian Doctrine* (Oxford: Blackwell, 2005), 35–36.

126  *E*: 2.17.1: 210.

127  See Soskice, "Creatio ex nihilo," 38–39, for three ways the doctrine of *creatio ex nihilo* continues to provide a position for open dialogue with those across the religious spectrum, as well as with disciplines outside the field of religion, such as modern cosmology.

128  *LN*: 173. Cf. *E*: 2.28.6: 351.

129  *E*: 4.3.6: 542.

130  *LCT*: 32.

131  *LCT*: 49.

132 *2nd T*: 20, 21, 168, 176, 241–42.
133 *RC*: 113, 114, 125, 126, 127; *E*: 1.3.12: 74.
134 John Locke, "Understanding [8 Feb 1677]," in *Political Essays*, by John Locke, ed. Mark Goldie (1677; 1997; repr., Cambridge: Cambridge University Press, 2006), 263; *E*: 2.21.70: 281–82. Cf. discussion in Tuckness, "The Coherence of a Mind," 87–88.
135 On Locke's Christology, see Nuovo, *Christianity, Antiquity, and Enlightenment*, esp. 75–101.
136 Compare *2nd T*: 241, with *RC*: 113–14.
137 *2nd T*: 20–21, 168, 176, 241–42.
138 On Locke's use of the Hebrew Bible, see Yechiel J. M. Leiter, *John Locke's Political Philosophy and the Hebrew Bible* (Cambridge: Cambridge University Press, 2018). Though his claim that Locke was a political Hebraist is not persuasive, his attention to the connections between Locke's political outcomes and the ground for such outcomes found in the Hebrew scriptures makes his work an ally in both the "religious turn" as well as the "theological turn" in Locke scholarship.
139 *RC*: 113–14.
140 *RC*: 125, 126. Cf. 126–27, where Locke cites John 5:28–30; Matt. 7:22–23; 13:41, 49; 16:24; 25:31–46; Lk. 13:26. "These, I think, are all the places where our Saviour mentions the last judgment, or describes his way of proceeding in that great day" (127).
141 *2nd T*: 6, emphasis added.
142 Locke accepts the Pauline authorship of Ephesians. Cf. Locke, *A Paraphrase and Notes*, title page; Vol. 2, 607–61, 668–71; Wainwright, "Introduction," 3.
143 Luke 2:49, KJV.
144 Plato, *Timaeus*, 28c.
145 Forde, "Natural Law," 78, 399, noting Locke's emphasis on the "providence" of God. By "providence," Forde has in mind the moral character of God. For more on following habit and custom, see *E*: 1.3.24–25: 82–83; 2.28.12: 356–57; 4.16.4: 659–61; cf. *LN*: 127–34.
146 *E*: 2.28.2–4: 349–51.
147 *E*: 2.28.4: 351.
148 *E*: 2.28.5: 351.
149 *E*: 2.28.5: 351.
150 *E*: 2.28.16: 360; 2.28.8: 352; 2.28.14: 358.
151 *E*: 2.28.8: 352.
152 *E*: 2.28.10: 353. In fact, "The true boundaries of the Law of Nature … ought to be the Rule of Vertue and Vice" (2.28.11: 356).
153 *E*: 1.3.2: 66.
154 *E*: 1.3.19: 79.
155 *E*: 2.28.11: 356.

156  *E*: 2.28.12: 357.
157  *E*: 4.12.4: 641.
158  *E*: 1.3.18: 78.
159  *E*: 2.21.53: 268.
160  *E*: 4.10.7: 622. See also *RC*: 150.
161  In the *LCT*, Locke lists the following central societal virtues: charity (23, 25, 31, 33, 34), love (25), peace (31, 33, 34, 43, 54), meekness/meekness of Spirit (23, 34), goodwill (23, 25, 34), friendship (31, 43), honesty (54), industry (54), bounty (31), liberality (31), justice (26), equity (26, 31), and "equal justice" (43). With clear reference to the religious, Locke also speaks against "Covetousness, Uncharitableness, Idleness, and many other … sins," and for "Peace, Friendship, Faith and equal Justice" (43), "Holiness of Life, Purity of Manners, and Benignity and Meekness of Spirit" (23), and "the Duties of Peace, and Good-will towards all men" (34).
162  *LCT*: 44.
163  *LCT*: 56.
164  *LCT*: 54.
165  *2nd T*: 107.
166  *2nd T*: 93. For the earlier quote "love of himself," see 94. On dishonesty, see 46, 51.
167  *2nd T*: 130.
168  *2nd T*: 107.
169  *QLN*: 211: "power."
170  *QLN*: 211: "God, who is best and greatest."
171  *LN*: 184–86.
172  *LN*: 186.
173  *LN*: 183; *QLN*: 117.
174  *E*: 4.11.13: 638.
175  *E*: 1.3.12: 74.
176  *E*: 1.4.8: 87.
177  *E*: 1.3.12: 74.
178  *2nd T*: 195.
179  *2nd T*: 135.
180  *2nd T*: 56, 66; see also 80; 118.
181  *2nd T*: 66; see also 169.
182  *2nd T*: 77.
183  *2nd T*: 5, 6.
184  *RC*: 13, 14, 15, 122.
185  *RC*: 112.
186  *RC*: 142.
187  *RC*: 144.
188  *E*: 4.12.4: 642.

189   *Quod si nihil cum potentiore iuris humani relinquitur inopi, at ego ad deos vindices humanae superbiae confugiam.* Cf. Livy, *History of Rome*, trans. B. O. Foster, Loeb Classical Library (London: Heinemann, 1926), 9.1.8, where *intolerandae* replaces *humanae*. For this reference and translation, I am indebted to David Wootton, "Introduction," in John Locke, *Political Writings*, ed. David Wootton (Indianapolis: Hackett, 2003), 6.
190   *LN*: 183; *RC*: 113, 114, 125, 126, 127; *LCT*: 32, 49; *2nd T*: 21, 241.
191   *2nd T*: 241: "But farther, this Question (*Who shall be Judge?*) cannot mean, that there is no Judge at all. For where there is no Judicature on Earth, to decide Controversies amongst Men, *God* in Heaven is *Judge*: He alone, 'tis true, is Judge of the Right."
192   *2nd T*: 20, 21, 176, 242.
193   *2nd T*: 176; see also 242 for a similar warning, though measured in tone.
194   For more on Locke's rhetoric, see Torrey Shanks, *Authority Figures: Rhetoric and Experience in John Locke's Political Thought* (University Park: University of Pennsylvania Press, 2014).
195   *2nd T*: 6.
196   *2nd T*: 6, 7, 8; cf. 11.
197   *2nd T*: 8.
198   *2nd T*: 8.
199   *2nd T*: 9.
200   *2nd T*: 8, 10, 11.
201   *2nd T*: 13.
202   *2nd T*: 11.
203   *2nd T*: 12.
204   *2nd T*: 130.
205   *2nd T*: 176.
206   *LCT*: 49.
207   *2nd T*: 4, 6.
208   *2nd T*: chapter XVIII "Of Tyranny" (199–210), and chapter XIX "Of the Dissolution of Government" (211–43).
209   *2nd T*: 222.
210   *2nd T*: 241–42. See also 20–21, 168, and 176.
211   I am indebted to Greg Forster for pointing out this connection in private correspondence.

# Chapter 5

1   *2nd T*: 6.
2   *2nd T*: 4, 5, 6.

3   In addition to Laslett, see Brown, "The 'Figure' of God and the Limits of Liberalism," 98–99, who argues "the figure of God" in Locke's *Essay* and the *Two Treatises* "is constituted metaphorically" and functions "as a master trope, a 'figure of thought' according to the categories of classical rhetoric"; thus Locke is not intending to provide "a literal description of God's attributes."
4   Peter Laslett, "The Social and Political Theory of Two Treatises of Government," in John Locke, *Two Treatises of Government, A Critical Edition with an Introduction and Apparatus Criticus*, ed. Peter Laslett, 2nd ed. (1960; 1967; repr., Cambridge: Cambridge University Press, 1988), 92.
5   Laslett, "The Social and Political Theory," 92.
6   Lamprecht, *The Moral and Political Philosophy of John Locke*; for an earlier work at least addressing the topic, see Curtis, *An Outline of Locke's Ethical Philosophy*.
7   LN. These Latin essays, composed between 1660 and 1664, were discovered among Locke's papers housed in Oxford's Bodleian Library.
8   Some, such as Strauss, *Natural Right and History*, 204, 220, have argued that Locke has no deontic notion of natural law and should not be considered a promulgator of the Christian natural law tradition. Cf. Rabieh, "The Reasonableness of Locke," 951, who argues that according to the logic of Locke's writings, "there is no law of nature." For a general take on Locke's natural law theory similar to the one presented in this chapter, see Lenz, "Locke's Essays on the Law of Nature," 105–13; Francis Oakley and Elliot W. Urdang, "Locke, Natural law, and God," *Natural Law Forum* 11 (1966): 92–109; Sparkes, "Trust and Teleology," 263–73; Drury, "John Locke, Natural Law and Innate Ideas," 531–45; Oakley, "Locke, Natural Law, and God—Again," 624–51; Tuckness, "The Coherence of a Mind," 73–90; Flage, "Locke and Natural Law," 435–60; Waldron, *God, Locke, and Equality*; Francis Oakley, *Natural Law, Laws of Nature, Natural Rights: Continuity and Discontinuity in the History of Ideas* (London: Continuum, 2005); Nuovo, *Christianity, Antiquity, and Enlightenment*.
9   Flage, "Locke and Natural Law," 435: "virtually no one denies" Locke was a proponent of a natural law theory of ethics and politics. Cf. Forde, "Natural Law," 398: even those who espouse that "there is no natural law teaching according to Locke" usually mean that Locke fails to adequately address the scope and content of it. In support, see Tuckness, "The Coherence of a Mind," 90: "Locke presents one of the most intricate theistic theories of the natural law tradition."
10  *LN*: 237–39.
11  John Gordon Clapp, "Locke, John," in *The Encyclopedia of Philosophy*, ed. Paul Edwards (New York: Macmillan/Free Press, 1967), Vol. 4, 492: "Locke was extremely vague about the Law of Nature." Dunn, *The Political Thought of John Locke*, 187, claims Locke never got around to providing the particulars of the law of nature or setting out an argument in this regard. Cf. Harris, *The Mind of John Locke*, 268; Locke, *The Reasonableness of Christianity as deliver'd in the Scriptures*,

140n.2. Tuckness, "The Coherence of a Mind," 74, admits "Locke never produced a proof of the law of nature." Wootton, "Introduction," 117, claims that Locke "went on believing the arguments of the *Second Treatise* were plainly true even after he knew he could not properly ground them in natural law." Cf. David Wootton, "John Locke: Socinian or Natural law Theorist?" in *Religion, Secularization and Political Thought: Thomas Hoobes to J. S. Mill*, ed. James E. Crimmins (London: Routledge, 1990), esp. 40, 62.

12  While Locke claims in the *Essay* (*E*: 4.3.18: 549) that morality is capable of demonstration, he does not provide any delineated demonstration, the absence of which is noticeable not only in the *Essay* but also in a manuscript (*Ethic*) intended to more fully develop his thinking in this area. Two years after publishing the *Essay*, Locke wrote to Molyneux the following: "Though by the view I had of moral ideas, whilst I was considering that subject, I thought I saw that morality might be demonstratively made out, yet whether I am able so to make it out is another question" (L1538, *COR*, Vol. 4: 524). In this letter he remained optimistic of accomplishing such a task, however, and even four years later still seemed open to the possibility (L2059, *COR*, Vol 5: 595). For discussion, see Colman, *John Locke's Moral Philosophy*, 138, 140.

13  Speaking of the *Two Treatises*, Tuckness, "The Coherence of a Mind," 90, writes the following: "The question can be put to Locke's critics: given the purposes for which he was writing, why should Locke have included a complicated proof of something his opponents would most likely have granted?" Such a move "would have alienated more readers than it persuaded … Such a strategy would have been rhetorically and polemically foolish."

14  Cf. Tuckness, "The Coherence of a Mind," 74: "Locke's theory of natural law is more coherent than his critics have allowed."

15  For references in this section to Aquinas, I am especially indebted to Mark Murphy, "The Natural Law Tradition in Ethics," in *The Stanford Encyclopedia of Philosophy*, Winter 2011 edition, ed. Edward N. Zalta, http://plato.stanford.edu/archives/win2011/entries/natural-law-ethics/.

16  Oakley, "Locke, Natural Law and God—Again," 624–51.

17  Oakley, "Locke, Natural Law and God—Again," 649.

18  This will be argued in Caleb Clanton and Kraig Martin, *Nature and Command* (Knoxville: University of Tennessee Press, forthcoming).

19  *ST*: IaIIae 91.1–2.

20  *ST*: IaIIae 91.2.

21  *ST*: IaIIae 91.2.

22  *ST*: IaIIae 94.2, emphasis original.

23  The title line of Essay I in *LN*: 108: "An Detur Morum Regula Sive Lex Naturae? Affirmatur"; *RC*: 142: "It is true there is a law of nature." Cf. *2nd T*: 6, 11, 135, passim; *LCT*: 43; see also hints at *LCT*: 42, 46, 49, 51, 55.

24  *QLN*: 95–97.
25  *RC*: 10; *QLN*: 103. Cf. *2nd T*: 135: "Thus the law of nature stands as an eternal rule to all men."
26  *LN*: 109–11; cf. *E*: 2.28.11: 356: "The true boundaries of the Law of Nature, which ought to be the Rule of Vertue and Vice." It also appears closely related to "the Law(s) of Equity," referencing how humans view and treat one another. See *LCT*: 43, 55.
27  According to Aquinas, "certain most general precepts" of natural law "are known to all" (*ST*: IaIIae 94.6). Cf. *ST*: IaIIae 93.2: While "no one can know the eternal law, as it is in itself" (except God), "every rational creature knows it in its reflection ... (f) or every knowledge of truth is a kind of reflection and participation of the eternal law ... Now all men know the truth to a certain extent, at least as to the common principles of the natural law." These general principles, referring to natural law "in the abstract," are universally known at all times by all rational creatures through the use of reason (*ST*: IaIIae 94.6). Such knowledge cannot be removed since natural law, for Aquinas, is a providential gift constituting the basic principles of practical rationality (*ST*: IaIIae 94.4; 94.6). According to Aquinas, these general precepts, discerned by human reason, "can nowise be blotted out from men's hearts" (94.6). However, Aquinas does immediately acknowledge (at 94.6) that it may be "blotted out in the case of a particular action, in so far as reason is hindered from applying the general principle to a particular point of practice," due to the passions. Cf. *ST*: IaIIae 77.2. However, Aquinas adds that "certain secondary and more detailed precepts" are "conclusions following closely from first principles" (*ST*: IaIIae 94.6). These secondary principles or conclusions can be "blotted out from the human heart" by vice, on account of "evil persuasions ... vicious customs and corrupt habits" (*ST*: IaIIae 94.6).
28  *RC*: 10; *QLN*: 101; cf. *LN*: Essays II and IV.
29  *QLN*: 103.
30  This statement accords with what Murphy, "The Natural Law Tradition in Ethics," calls the two "key features" of natural law, according to Aquinas (*ST*: IaIIae 94.1–6): (1) natural law is one aspect of divine providence, and (2) it constitutes the basic principles of practical rationality. Cf. IaIIae.90.4, where "law," for Aquinas, refers to "an ordinance of reason for the common good, made by him who has care of the community."
31  *RC*: 157.
32  Locke speaks often in the *RC* of those who do not follow the "light" of nature due to inward emotions or evil inclinations and yet are culpable of violating the law of nature, which they can and ought to perceive.
33  *RC*: 11.
34  *QLN*: 101.
35  *2nd T*: 6, 11.

36  LN: 186–87: "The law of nature (*legem naturae*) is binding on all men"; *2nd T*: 135.
37  *ST*: IaIIae 94.4.
38  *RC*: 11; *QLN*: 101.
39  Locke believes he has provided an account of this in Book IV of the *Essay*.
40  Cf. *ST*: IaIIae 91.2.
41  *RC*: 11.
42  *RC*: 11; *QLN*: 95. By "suitable to man's nature," Locke may only have "rationality" in mind, which agrees with Aquinas (*ST*: IaIIae 94.2). However, Locke's insistence on teleology and his explanation of the role of virtue may more fully accord with Aquinas's more protracted view: that the precepts of natural law not only bind humanity (IaIIae 94.2) but also direct them toward the "good," which, given human nature, is what is perfective of humans (Ia 5.1). For this observation, I am indebted to Murphy, "The Natural Law Tradition in Ethics."
43  *QLN*: 101, 95.
44  *QLN*: 103; *LN*: 187.
45  *2nd T*: 135: "be conformable to the law of nature, i.e. to the will of God."
46  *LN*: 187. Cf. 184–86.
47  Tuckness, "The Coherence of a Mind," 75. Cf. *E*: 1.3.6: 69, "the true ground of Morality; which can only be the Will and Law of … God." On the question of voluntarism, see Tuckness, "The Coherence of a Mind," 74–78; cf. John W. Yolton, *John Locke and the Compass of Human Understanding: A Selective Commentary on the "Essay"* (Cambridge: Cambridge University Press, 1970), 168–69; Colman, *John Locke's Moral Philosophy*, 32; Ward, "Divine Will," 209–12; Stephen Buckle, *Natural Law and the Theory of Property: Grotius to Hume* (Oxford: Oxford University Press, 1991), 125–49.
48  *ST*: IaIIae 94.4.
49  *ST*: IaIIae 94.2.
50  *ST*: IaIIae 94.4.
51  *ST*: IaIIae 91.4.
52  *RC*: 15.
53  *RC*: 13, 14, 15, 122.
54  *RC*: 130, 131.
55  *RC*: 131.
56  *RC*: 156.
57  *RC*: 132.
58  *RC*: 133.
59  *RC*: 140.
60  *RC*: 133.
61  *QLN*: 109–11; *RC*: 112, 122, 151.
62  Cf. Thomas Aquinas, *Commentary on Aristotle's Nichomachean Ethics*, trans. C. I. Litzinger (Notre Dame: Dumb Ox Books, 1993), 258–59 (2.2).

63  Waldron, *God, Locke, and Equality*, 111.
64  However, acknowledging there is content to the natural law, knowable and available, is not to claim to offer a catalog. Waldron, *God, Locke, and Equality*, 97, states that Locke doesn't claim to offer the content of natural law but only to show that it is reasonable and available and that reason gives us the tools for evaluating revelation. The *RC* allows us to be more precise. For Locke, providing a precise catalog is now irrelevant in the light of revelation, which has provided it for us (at least, as much as is necessary to glorify God and achieve ultimate happiness).
65  *RC*: 15. Locke's natural law is not identical to God's positive law; the latter includes doctrines to be believed, shared only by revelation; the former includes moral obligation, which includes ethical duties enshrined in scripture. See *E*: 2.25.8: 322–23; Yolton, "Locke on the Law of Nature," 477–78; Drury, "John Locke, Natural Law and Innate Ideas," 531–45.
66  Contra John Wild, *Plato's Modern Enemies and the Theory of Natural Law* (Chicago: University of Chicago Press, 1953), 131; on this, see Lenz, "Locke's Essays on the Law of Nature," 105–13; Drury, "John Locke, Natural Law and Innate Ideas," 531–45.
67  Thus, Locke need not spell out a catalog of basic goods but only declares that the law of nature is (1) whatever right reason would affirm and (2) whatever God prescribes. These are never in contradiction, but the particular practical requirements for a given person are judged, by the lawgiver, "according to the promises they had received, and the dispensations they were under" (*RC*: 132).
68  *E*: 2.28.7: 352. Cf. 2.28.7–10: 352–54.
69  *E*: 2.28.10: 353. Cf. *E*: 2.28.8: 352 (cited on p. 2 of this book) with *QLN*: 95 ("it seems proper to ask if man alone has come into this world entirely outside some Jurisdiction, with no law proper to him, without plan, without law, without a rule for his life—something he who has given thought to god, best and greatest, or … to himself or his own conscience, will not easily believe").
70  *E*: 2.28.16: 360; 2.28.14: 358. For "Rule of Right," see *E*: 2.28.11: 356; 2.28.16: 359.
71  *E*: 2.28.14: 358. cf. *E*: 1.3.5: 69.
72  *E*: 2.28.8: 352.
73  *E*: 1.3.13: 75: "I think they … forsake the Truth, who … deny that there is a Law, knowable by the light of Nature, i.e. without the help of positive Revelation." Locke is, however, skeptical of producing a catalog of particular moral rules to which all men subscribe simply from reflecting on the law of nature (*E*: 1.3.14: 76). Yet this will not suffice, since repentance cannot be expected if one is unaware of what actions have caused offense (*E*: 1.3.19: 79).
74  However, note *2nd T*: 136: "for the law of nature being unwritten, and so nowhere to be found but in the minds of men." While it is possible Locke changed his mind, there are two alternative readings to show consistency: (1) Locke may be assuming there is no written code to which all in the society would naturally ascribe, or (2)

Locke is speaking specifically about the law of nature concerning political and legislative matters, the specifics of which are not to be found in the New Testament.
75  *RC*: 143.
76  *RC*: 122.
77  *RC*: 147. This is precisely the converse of Hancey, "John Locke and the Law of Nature," 450, who claims "it is doubtful that [Locke] ever had a clear idea of a complete code of the law of nature. In this respect he leaves us no better off than we were with the classics."
78  Tuckness, "The Coherence of a Mind," 81. Cf. L2059.
79  Locke spends several pages listing the various moral duties given by Jesus on this occasion (*RC*: 114–16). Jesus "confirms, and at once re-inforces all the moral precepts in the Old Testament" but also gives those eternal precepts a clear exposition. Locke explains the Matt. 5:21 reference to "righteousness" as "i.e. your performance of the eternal law of right," and the Matt. 5:17 reference to Christ coming to complete the law as "viz. by giving its full and clear sense, free from the corrupt and loosening glosses of the scribes and Pharisees" (15). "Thus we see," writes Locke, "our Savior … only confirmed the moral law; and clear[ed] it from the corrupt glosses of the scribes and Pharisees, [and] showed the strictness as well as obligation of its injunctions" (122).
80  *RC*: 50.
81  See *E*: 4.18.5: 691–92.
82  See *RC*: 112 for a succinct quote. This one paragraph contains claims that turn out to be central in Locke's discussion of the law of nature, discussed in this book. (1) There exists an eternal law of right, which is in effect for man as a rational creature. (2) The prescriptive power and authority of this law is in some respect essentially dependent on the existence and nature of God. (3) The descriptive explication of this law is in accordance with, and arises from, man's nature as a rational creature. (4) The eternal law of right (i.e., the law of nature) cannot be removed without removing any basis for the exercise of morality. (5) This law of nature, which applies to all humans (including Christians), finds ultimate adjudication (and thus motivation) in a final judgment, namely, the judgment of Christ. That (6) this law can be known by rational creatures seems implicit. These positions reasonably place Locke in the Christian tradition as a natural law theorist. For a description of paradigmatic natural law theory, see Murphy, "The Natural Law Tradition in Ethics." This is not to say that Locke is a Thomist or even that Locke would satisfy every criteria offered by natural law theorists. However, see Simmons, *The Lockean Theory of Rights*, 16n.3: "Locke's theory of natural law can be positioned at least largely within the Thomist tradition." Contra William Carl Lindahl, "A Critical Commentary on John Locke's Essays on the Law of Nature" (PhD diss., University of Dallas, Dallas, 1986), 15; Perry, *The Pretenses of Loyalty*, 93. Perry claims Locke rejects "the basis of Thomistic natural law" when Locke admits that every "Mind

has a different relish" and thus "the Philosophers of old did in vain enquire" of what does "the *Summum bonum*" consist (whether in money, bodily pleasure, virtue, or contemplation). But Locke is describing what people *claim* brings *pleasure* with regard to *temporal* affairs (irrespective of concerns for the afterlife); in the same chapter, Locke urges that "we should take pains to suit the relish of our Minds to the true intrinsick good or ill, that is in things" (*E*: 2.21.53: 268) and connects this with the claim that what one presently desires for enjoyment "is a false way of judging, when apply'd to the happiness of another life," which is most important; "the Manna in Heaven will suit every one's Palate" (*E*: 2.21.65: 277). Reflection on rewards and punishments in another life means a man "must own himself to judge very much amiss, if he does not conclude, That a virtuous Life ... is to be preferred to a vicious one" noting "This is evidently so, though the virtuous Life here had nothing but Pain, and the vicious continual pleasure" (*E*: 2.21.70: 282).

83 On the ordering of human nature, see *E*: 2.7.4: 129–30. Patricia Sheridan, "Locke's Ethics and the British Moralists: The Lockean Legacy in Eighteenth Century Moral Philosophy" (PhD diss., University of Western Ontario, London, Ontario, 2001), iii–iv, claims later moralists "maintaining a metaphysics of morality that relates moral law to the general teleological order of the universe ... can all be seen to be working within a broadly Lockean frame of reference."

84 *RC*: 149.

85 His use of the term elsewhere is also provocative. See John Locke, "Of Ethick in General," in *Writings on Religion*, by John Locke, ed. Victor Nuovo (1687; Oxford: Clarendon Press, 2002), 9 (par. 1), where Locke begins with the following line: "Happyness & misery are the two great springs of humane actions ... they all aime at happynesse & desire to avoid misery." That Locke here as well as in the *RC* has in mind more than Benthamite pleasure and pain is obvious in both contexts. If a closer connection ought to be made, it is still helpful to note that Locke distinguishes obligation (which is rooted in God) from motivation (in which pleasure and pain could motivate one toward their obligations). See Singh, "John Locke and the Theory of Natural Law," 105–18; Yolton, "Locke on the Law of Nature," 477–98. Also, West, "The Ground of Locke's Law of Nature," 1–50, notes that the *Essay* claims that human common goods are elements or conditions of happiness but cannot constitute complete happiness.

86 *RC*: 78.
87 *RC*: 100.
88 *RC*: 122.
89 *RC*: 123.
90 *RC*: 147.
91 *RC*: 139.
92 *RC*: 149.
93 *RC*: 10, or, "a state of happy immortality" (98).

94  *RC*: 98.
95  *RC*: 88.
96  *RC*: 150–51.
97  *RC*: 150.
98  *LCT*: 28.
99  *LCT*: 43.
100 *LCT*: 47.
101 *LCT*: 47.
102 *LCT*: 48.
103 *E*: 1.3.3: 67. And, furthermore, that which moves desire is "happiness and that alone" (*E*: 2.21.41: 258).
104 *E*: 2.21.53: 268.
105 *E*: 2.21.51: 266. Compare the language of "careful and constant pursuit of happiness" with "keep[ing] constantly and steadily in our course towards Heaven, without ever standing still, or directing our actions to any other end" (2.21.38: 255).
106 *E*: 4.10.1: 619.
107 *E*: 2.21.60: 274. Cf. 2.21.43: 260.
108 *E*: 2.21.60: 273–74. See also *E*: 2.21.38: 255, where Locke speaks of "the eternal condition of a future state infinitely out-weighing … any … worldly pleasure." This helps explain *E*: 2.21.55: 269 and 2.21.65: 277, where Locke downplays agreement on what constitutes personal temporal happiness in which people "relish," since "the Manna in Heaven will suit every one's Palate" (277). See Wolterstorff, *John Locke and the Ethics of Belief*, 226.
109 *E*: 2.21.60: 274. Even when Locke wishes to speak neutrally with respect to the afterlife (such as when he states "I have foreborn to mention any thing of the certainty, or the probability of a future State"), he offers Pascal's Wager as the reasonable position with respect to the prospect of infinite misery vs. infinite happiness. See *E*: 2.21.70: 281–82. For a similar treatment of happiness in Aquinas, see *ST*: IaIIae 1.8.
110 With Aquinas, Locke appears to hold an Aristotelian account of natural goodness (as opposed to a transcendent Platonic or a subjective Hobbesian theory of the good) in that what makes it true that something is good is that it is somehow perfective or completing of a being, based on the nature of that being. For an interesting defense of the view that Locke's teaching on the law of nature is grounded in his understanding of the conditions for human happiness, see West, "The Ground of Locke's Law of Nature," 1–50.
111 *E*: 2.7.5: 130.
112 *LN*: 157.
113 Tuckness, "The Coherence of a Mind," 80.

114 This may help explain two passages in the *Two Treatises*, where Locke claims God "planted ... a strong desire for Self-preservation" in man (*1st T*: 86) and that the death penalty for murder is "writ in the Hearts of all Mankind" (*2nd T*: 11). These passages speak to instincts or inclinations that accord with right reason, but knowledge of the law of nature requires study (*2nd T*: 124). See Tuckness, "The Coherence of a Mind," 88–89. For references to *1st T*, see John Locke, "First Treatise of Government," in *Two Treatises of Government: A Critical Edition with an Introduction and Apparatus Criticus*, ed. Peter Laslett, 2nd ed. (Cambridge: Cambridge University Press, 1967).
115 Sparkes, "Trust and Teleology," 263.
116 Sparkes, "Trust and Teleology," 263.
117 Sparkes, "Trust and Teleology," 265.
118 Sparkes, "Trust and Teleology," 263.
119 Sparkes, "Trust and Teleology," 263.
120 Sparkes, "Trust and Teleology," 273.
121 *E*: 4.10.18: 628.
122 *E*: 4.10.12: 625.
123 *1st T*: 86.
124 *1st T*: 30.
125 *1st T*: 40. The word "image" is not found in Gen 1:28, but Locke finds it so important that he borrows from the larger context (Gen. 1:26–27).
126 *1st T*: 40.
127 *2nd T*: 6.
128 Cf. Locke's use of "image" as a representative, a stand-in for someone else (*2nd T*: 151; Wootton, "Introduction," 56, 73).
129 Especially *1st T*: 30.
130 *E*: 2.23.12: 302.
131 *2nd T*: 6.
132 *2nd T*: 56.
133 *E*: 1.4.13: 92.
134 *RC*: 106.
135 *RC*: 106.
136 *RC*: 106.
137 Col. 1:15, 18.
138 *RC*: 106.
139 *RC*: 106–07.
140 Citing Rom. 8:29.
141 *RC*: 107.
142 *RC*: 107.
143 *RC*: 107.

144 *RC*: 9.
145 Rom. 8:23; 1 Cor. 15:42–44, 49, 54. Locke immediately follows up with Luke 20:35–36 and Acts 13:32–33.
146 *RC*: 108.
147 *RC*: 108.
148 See Jonathan L. Kvanvig and Hugh McCann, "Divine Conservation and the Persistence of the World," in *Divine and Human Action: Essays in the Metaphysics of Theism*, ed. Thomas V. Morris (Ithaca, NY: Cornell University Press, 1988), 13–49.
149 *E*: 2.15.12: 204, emphasis added. For other language of dependence, see *E*: 4.3.18: 549; 4.10.12: 625.
150 Oakley, *Natural Law*, 82–86.
151 For example, Nuovo, *Christianity, Antiquity, and Enlightenment*, 253–54, cites Catharine Trotter Cockburn, "A defence of Mr. Locke's *Essay of Human Understanding*, wherein its principles, with reference to morality, revealed religion, and the immortality of the soul, are considered and justified: in answer to Some remarks on that Essay. First printed in the year 1702," in *The Works of Mrs. Catharine Cockburn, Theological, Moral, Dramatic, and Poetical*. Several of them now first printed, revised and published, with an account of the life of the author, by Thomas Birch, in two volumes (London: Printed for J. and P. Knapton, in Ludgate-Street, 1751), Vol. 1, 48–69. Cockburn found the *Essay* to represent an "Anti-voluntarist" moral rationalism with which she was in sympathy. According to Cockburn (56–57), Locke founded morality on the nature rather than mere will of God. Nuovo agrees with this Stoic strain in Locke but also acknowledges an Epicurean hedonism in Locke's work.
152 Oakley, *Natural Law*, 86. Cf. 83, where Oakley advocates approaching Locke's works "with the late medieval voluntarist tradition in mind, the dialectic between omnipotence and covenant characteristic of that tradition, and with the use made accordingly of the distinction between God's power conceived as absolute and ordained." Cf. Oakley, "Locke, Natural Law, and God—Again," 643–48. Rather than engaging in the voluntarist/intellectualist debate, this book emphasizes Locke's biblical (especially Pauline) language and his willingness to borrow language from several schools of thought to offer a general defense for his theological approach to the law of nature.
153 Tetlow, "The Theological Context of Locke's Political Thought," 453. Cf. 373–452.
154 Tetlow, "The Theological Context of Locke's Political Thought," 454.
155 Tetlow, "The Theological Context of Locke's Political Thought," 386: "Locke's political theology is covenantal as he finds the law of nature at creation to be the linchpin of his conception of an ordered polity, and the moral law suffused in Scripture to be a clear promulgation to all mankind of divine positive law."
156 Tetlow, "The Theological Context of Locke's Political Thought," 458.

157 See Michael J. Perry, *Toward a Theory of Human Rights: Religion, Law, Courts* (Cambridge: Cambridge University Press, 2007), 141: "The claim that every human being has inherent dignity and is inviolable is deeply problematic for many secular thinkers, because the claim is difficult—perhaps to the point of being impossible—to align with one of [the] reigning intellectual convictions" in secular thought—that there is neither a God nor a metaphysical order. On the problem in ethics, see Ian Carter, "Respect and the Basis of Equality," *Ethics* 121, no. 3 (April 2011): 539; Louis J. Pojman, "A Critique of Contemporary Egalitarianism: A Christian Perspective," *Faith and Philosophy* 8, no. 4 (October 1991): 481–504; Peter Singer, *Unsanctifying Human Life: Essays on Ethics*, ed. Helga Kuhse (Oxford: Blackwell, 2002), 80–94.
158 *2nd T*: 4, 6, 27.
159 *E*: 3.6.36–37: 462.
160 *E*: 3.11.16: 517.
161 *E*: 3.11.16: 517.
162 *E*: 4.4.13: 569. For the entire section on changelings, see *E*: 4.4.13–16: 569–73.
163 *E*: 4.4.14: 570.
164 *E*: 4.4.15: 570.
165 On nonhuman animals, see *E*: 2.11.10: 160; on early stages of life, see *E*: 2.1.21: 116–17; on mental deficiency, see *2nd T*: 60 and *E*: 2.11.13: 161; on memory and reasoning late in life, see *E*: 2.9.14: 148–49.
166 *E*: 4.20.5: 709.
167 *2nd T*: 4, 5, 6.
168 *E*: 2.27.17: 341. Cf. Aristotle, *Politics*, trans. H. Rackham, Loeb Classical Library (1932; repr., London: Heinemann, 1967), 1253a; Aristotle, *Nicomachean Ethics*, trans. and ed. Roger Crisp, Cambridge Texts in the History of Philosophy (Cambridge: Cambridge University Press, 2000), 1110a–15a; Immanuel Kant, *Groundwork for the Metaphysics of Morals*, ed. Mary Gregor, Cambridge Texts in the History of Philosophy (Cambridge: Cambridge University Press, 1997), Vol. 4, 428.
169 *E*: 1.1: 45.
170 *E*: 1.1: 45.
171 Waldron, *God, Locke, and Equality*.
172 *2nd T*: 6.
173 Cf. Pailin, "Reconciling Theory and Fact," 94n.4, where Pailin cites Whichcote.
174 Waldron, *God, Locke, and Equality*, 113.
175 *2nd T*: 55; Waldron, *God, Locke, and Equality*, 113.
176 Waldron, *God, Locke, and Equality*, 114. See *2nd T*: 6, 55–56.
177 *2nd T*: 6.
178 Tate, "Dividing Locke from God," 140.
179 *E*: 2.21.14: 240. I am indebted to Polin, "John Locke's Conception of Freedom," 1–18, for many Locke references in this section.

180  *E*: 2.21.14: 240; cf. 2.21.16: 241.
181  *E*: 2.21.8: 237; 2.21.15: 241.
182  *E*: 2.21.8: 238.
183  *E*: 2.21.2: 234.
184  *E*: 4.17.16: 685.
185  *E*: 2.21.47: 263–64.
186  *E*: 2.21.47: 263.
187  *2nd T*: 4.
188  See *2nd T*: 6, 23, 87 and 123.
189  *2nd T*: 135.
190  *2nd T*: 57.
191  See, for example, *2nd T*: 135.
192  *2nd T*: 22, 96, 98, 135.
193  *2nd T*: 87, 96.
194  *2nd T*: 119, 134, 175.
195  *2nd T*: 122.
196  *2nd T*: 122.
197  *2nd T*: 223, 230.
198  *2nd T*: 240, 242.
199  *RC*: 4.
200  *RC*: 4.
201  *RC*: 4.
202  See *E*: 2.27.13: 338; 2.27.21: 343; 2.27.26: 347.
203  *RC*: 12, 26, 28, 42, 123, *passim*.
204  *E*: 1.3.14: 76–77.
205  Polin, "John Locke's Conception of Freedom," 1–18.
206  Polin, "John Locke's Conception of Freedom," 17.
207  Polin, "John Locke's Conception of Freedom," 3. See *E*: 2.21.54: 268.
208  This claim, at first, poses a problem for voluntarism, since God is not obligated to anything superior to Himself. This language (of God being "bound" by the good) was readily available in Locke's context and was often on the lips of Cambridge Platonists such as Cudworth (see *TIS*: 716, 873; Cudworth, *A Treatise Concerning Eternal and Immutable Morality*, 26), though Locke's *Essay* sought to critique rather than condone the intellectualist position this language was meant to espouse. See Crocker, *Henry Moore*, 82: "Since the divine law which bound each person through his or her conscience was also taken to be determined in its ends by the goodness of the deity, it was argued repeatedly (and more controversially) that God himself was also to a great extent 'bound' in his relations with his creatures by this 'rule' of his own goodness." Crocker cites George Rust, *A Discourse of the Use of Reason in Matters of Religion: Shewing, That Christianity Contains Nothing Repugnant to Right Reason; Against Enthusiasts*

*and Deists … Translated into English, with Annotations upon It, by Hen. Hallywell* (London: Printed by Hen. Hills, jun. for Walter Kettilby, 1683). However, at *E*: 2.21.49–50: 265, Locke writes, "If it were fit for such poor finite Creatures as we are, to pronounce what infinite Wisdom and Goodness could do, I think, we might say, That God himself cannot choose what is not good; the Freedom of the Almighty hinders not his being determined by what is best." This is because "God Almighty himself is under the necessity of being happy," and happiness is found only in the good. Locke's hesitant language here ("if … I think… we might …") may reflect a practical point concerning God's self-limiting action rather than a philosophical point about God's sense of obligation. Locke makes a similar claim in *2nd T*: 195, claiming that the obligations enjoined in making promises are so great "omnipotency itself can be tied by them. *Grants, promises*, and *oaths*, are *bonds* that *hold the Almighty*." I follow Tuckness, "The Coherence of a Mind," 77, who offers a charitable and convincing reading: "Locke's point is not that it is morally wrong for God to break promises but rather that if the King of Kings always keeps promises we have no reason to believe that human kings are exempt from that obligation." However, if Locke is indeed making a philosophical claim (rather than a practical one), this may simply be a reference to the proper end of right reason—that rationality (which is present in humanity by virtue of our being made in the image of God) is in accord with certain obligations. Were God to act contrary to right reason, he would be irrational, and thus a system of natural law centered on the nature of God would be unintelligible. On this see Tuckness, "The Coherence of a Mind," 77n14, who claims this is in keeping with the view of Aquinas. Note that Cudworth used this language specifically in attacking the Calvinistic notion of God's arbitrary will (*TIS*: 873). Cf. Ward, "Divine Will," 218, who claims that a voluntarist is able to affirm that God is bound by logical consistency.

209 *E*: 2.21.50–51: 265–66. This language is consistent with generic Christian natural law theory. As Tuckness, "The Coherence of a Mind," 89, explains, Locke intimates that certain inclinations are given to humanity as "a Principle of Action by God himself," and then by the use of reason ("which was the voice of God in him"), one can "[realize] that this inclination and God's will are in harmony. This implies that not all desires and inclinations can legitimately be satisfied." Cf. *E*: 1.3.3: 67; 1.3.13: 75; and *1st T*: 86.

210 *2nd T*: 22, 61.
211 Polin, "John Locke's Conception of Freedom," 3.
212 Polin, "John Locke's Conception of Freedom," 4.
213 Polin, "John Locke's Conception of Freedom," 4.
214 *E*: 2.21.53: 268.
215 Polin, "John Locke's Conception of Freedom," 5.
216 *E*: 2.21.52: 266–67.

217 Polin, "John Locke's Conception of Freedom," 5.
218 Polin, "John Locke's Conception of Freedom," 5.
219 Polin, "John Locke's Conception of Freedom," 10.
220 *2nd T*: 6.
221 Polin, "John Locke's Conception of Freedom," 7.
222 *2nd T*: 135. Polin, "John Locke's Conception of Freedom," 8, 9.
223 Polin, "John Locke's Conception of Freedom," 9.
224 See Polin, *La politique morale de John Locke*, 155–62.
225 Polin, "John Locke's Conception of Freedom," 13.
226 Polin, "John Locke's Conception of Freedom," 15.
227 See *LCT*.
228 Polin, "John Locke's Conception of Freedom," 17.
229 *RC*: 4.
230 *RC*: 15.
231 Cf. Kelly, *Locke's Second Treatise of Government*, 33–35.
232 For more on the religious dimension of Locke's account of free agency, see Nuovo, *Christianity, Antiquity, and Enlightenment*, 236–37.

# Chapter 6

1 Forde, "Natural Law," 406, claims the *Essay* "leaves no doubt about the difficulty if not impossibility of confirming revelation and the danger of relying on it implicitly," citing *E*: 4.16–19: 657–706.
2 On the one hand, as Parker, *The Biblical Politics of John Locke*, 2, notes, "The idea that scripture does not bear directly on political questions would have seemed very strange to most Christians before the eighteenth century." On the other hand, Locke wishes to build a political theory that can survive the religious pluralism of his day.
3 Polin, "John Locke's Conception of Freedom," 14–15.
4 Waldron, *God, Locke, and Equality*, 132. Cf. Jeremy Waldron, *Dignity of Legislation* (Cambridge: Cambridge University Press, 1999), 68–85.
5 *LCT*: 23–25, citing Luke 22:25.
6 *E*: 4.18.2: 689.
7 *E*: 4.10.1: 619.
8 Rom. 1:18–22. Romans speaks specifically of God's eternal nature as well as the magnitude of His power; thus it is not surprising that, for Locke, reason alone can bring us "to the knowledge of this certain and evident truth, *that there is an eternal, most powerful, and most knowing Being*" who is God (*E*: 4.10.6: 621). Locke continues, suggesting that from this idea "will easily be deduced all those other attributes, which we ought to ascribe to this eternal being."

9   This is evident in the next paragraph of the *Essay*, where Locke alludes to considerations of "a most perfect being" as if such a discussion naturally follows from his arguments above (*E*: 4.10.7: 621). If certain key aspects of the nature of God may be deduced through reason, certain key principles of morality may likewise follow suit (*E*: 4.3.18, 549; 4.3.20: 552).

10  Tuckness, "The Coherence of a Mind," 89, wisely cautions that "Locke was not writing to convince twentieth century critics. The *Two Treatises* is a fundamentally political work designed to promote a definite political end; we should not be surprised that the rhetorical demands of Locke's purpose substantially affect which arguments he thought it relevant to pursue and which ones he did not."

11  See Conrad, "Locke's Use of the Bible." Locke makes eighty-six direct biblical references within the *1st T* (including eight NT passages), twenty-five within the *2nd T* (including two NT passages), and 558 within the *RC* (most of which are NT passages).

12  As Dunn, *The Political Thought of John Locke*, 99, states, "Jesus Christ (and St. Paul) may not appear in the text of the *Two Treatises*, but their presence can hardly be missed"; both texts are "saturated with Christian assumptions." According to Tuckness, "The Coherence of a Mind," 89–90, this might be due to the fact that "Locke's opponents ... were people who would readily accept that New Testament morality and the content of natural law were roughly equivalent."

13  *E*: 3.9.23: 490.

14  Spellman, *John Locke*, 54: "It cannot be stressed enough that Locke considered it to be a fundamental Christian duty that each person read and study the Bible. It was, in addition to a moral life, part of one's work of obedience to God."

15  L787 (*COR*, Vol. 2: 640): "I cannot but Fancie by your Letter that you have learnt more Scripture there then ever you Knew in your whole life before, whom I little thought once would ever have writ me a letter not to be understood without turning to St Paul, and St Peters Epistles."

16  On the former, see David James Foster, "John Locke's Critique of the Bible in the *First Treatise of Government*" (PhD diss., University of Toronto, Toronto, 1991), who claims that in the *1st T* "Locke intends ... to attack the Bible" since "Locke defines his views on reason ... freedom ... government ... property, and the family in opposition to the Bible" (Abstract). On the latter, see Marshall, *John Locke: Resistance*, 338. Loconte, *God, Locke, and Liberty*, 132–34, suggests Le Clerc may have ignored questions of inspiration for reasons of persuasion, emphasizing the practical nature of religion.

17  *E*: 3.9.23: 489.

18  *2nd T*: 52, 65. Cf. 136n., where Locke provides the following quote from Hooker: "*Humane Laws are measures in respect of Men, whose actions they must direct, howbeit such measures they are as have also their higher Rules to be measured by, which Rules are two, the Law of God and the Law of Nature; so that Laws Humane must be made according to the general Laws of Nature, and without contradiction to any positive Law of Scripture, otherwise they are ill made.*" (*2nd T*: 136). The twin

forms of revelation—"the law of nature" and the (positive, scriptural) "law of God" are worth noting. Locke speaks of the "law of nature" fifty-one times in the *2nd T*, and it appears obvious that this law of nature is something that can be apprehended by use of reason (alone). But at times Locke speaks of "the law of God and nature" (*2nd T*: 66, 142), or "God and nature" allowing or not allowing something (*2nd T*: 168). Given the Hooker footnote, it appears likely that "law of God" or even the term "God" in such contexts is a reference to positive law in scripture. In the opening of the *2nd T*, Locke speaks of "there being no law of nature nor positive law of God" on a subject (*2nd T*: 1).

19   *RC*: 143, 122, 147.
20   *RC*: 15, 156.
21   *RC*: 147.
22   *RC*: 56.
23   *RC*: 135.
24   *RC*: 68, 75, 101.
25   *RC*: 154–55.
26   *RC*: 156.
27   *RC*: 25.
28   *RC*: 25.
29   For this definition of fideism, see Richard Amesbury, "Fideism," in *The Stanford Encyclopedia of Philosophy*, Winter 2012 edition, ed. Edward N. Zalta, http://plato.stanford.edu/archives/entries/fideism/. For the general claim that Locke abandoned his belief in a law of nature discoverable by reason in favor of a fideistic acceptance of revelation, see Harris, "The Mind of John Locke," 279; Wootton, "Introduction," 117; Spellman, *John Locke*, 49. Cf. Marshall, *John Locke: Resistance*, 441, who speaks of a "practical fideism." For a response, see Colman, *John Locke's Moral Philosophy*, 138–40; Tuckness, "The Coherence of a Mind," 79–82.
30   See Locke, *Of the Conduct of the Understanding*, par. 22: "The Works of Nature, and the Words of Revelation, display ... to Mankind" our knowledge of God and duty to others. See also Locke's 1696 letter to Molyneaux (L2059, *COR*, Vol. 5: 595) in which he claims that a science of morals is possible (and he is still interested in pursuing it); however, the endeavor may prove unnecessary as a practical matter, since "the Gospel contains so perfect a body of Ethics, that reason may be excused from that inquiry, since she may find man's duty clearer and easier in revelation than in herself."
31   *RC*: 135.
32   *RC*: 138. Locke has in mind Julian the Apostate.
33   *RC*: 147.
34   *RC*: 146, 147.
35   *RC*: 146.
36   *RC*: 147.

37  Locke, *A Discourse of Miracles*.
38  Stanley J. Grenz, *Theology for the Community of God* (Grand Rapids, MI: Eerdmans, 2000), 251–60. Cf. N. T. Wright, *The Resurrection of the Son of God* (Minneapolis: Fortress, 2003), as noted by Forster, *John Locke's Politics of Moral Consensus*, 142.
39  See Parker, *The Biblical Politics of John Locke*, 7.
40  Nuovo, *Christianity, Antiquity, and Enlightenment*, 125: "It should also be kept in mind that in all of Locke's writings on politics, philosophy and theology, there is an equal reliance upon reason and revelation and a mixing of them. This important feature of Locke's writings has rarely been noticed and never, to my mind, been explained." For Locke, "Reason is natural Revelation … [and] Revelation is natural Reason enlarged" (*E*: 4.19.4: 698).
41  *RC*: 143.
42  *E*: 4.19.14: 704.
43  Locke, *Of the Conduct of the Understanding*, pars.1, 3.
44  For example, Pearson, "The Religion of John Locke," 251; Forde, "Natural Law," 406.
45  *E*: 4.19.14: 704.
46  *E*: 4.18.5: 691–93.
47  Burnet, *Bishop Burnet's History of His Own Time*, 323–24.
48  *E*: 4.19.14: 704–05.
49  Locke, *A Second Vindication of the Reasonableness of Christianity*, 36.
50  *E*: 4.18.8: 694; see also *E*: 4.16.14: 667–68; *E*: 3.9.23: 489–90.
51  *E*: 4.7.11: 598–603; 4.18.2: 689; 4.18.4: 690–91.
52  *E*: 4.18.7: 694.
53  *RC*: 144. Locke emphasizes epistemic humility in the light of human weakness and limited capacity (129, 133, 134, 151, 157–58). By itself, this argument would challenge any notion that Locke grounds the law of nature—or even his defense of toleration—in man's reasoning capacities.
54  *RC*: 145.
55  *RC*: 145.
56  *RC*: 142. Cf. Locke, "Of Ethick in General," 12 (par. 9).
57  *RC*: 142.
58  *RC*: 143.
59  *RC*: 139, 140, 146–47.
60  Motivation includes knowledge of rewards and punishments (*RC*: 148–51). Thus the role of judgment and "consideration of another life" play a crucial juridical role in Locke's schema (149). By knowing that Christ links virtue with reward in the afterlife, "virtue now is visibly the most enriching purchase, and by much the best bargain" (150).
61  *RC*: 144, emphasis added.
62  *RC*: 144, emphasis added.
63  *RC*: 150.

64 *RC*: 112.
65 *RC*: 150.
66 *RC*: 150.
67 *RC*: 150.
68 *RC*: 151, emphasis added. Cf. Locke, "Of Ethick in General," 12 (par. 9).
69 *E*: 4.10.7: 622.
70 *E*: 4.12.4: 641; *E*: 2.21.53: 268.
71 *RC*: 151.
72 *RC*: 128–34.
73 *E*: 4.18.5: 691–93.
74 It is striking that Locke imagines one could perceive, apart from revelation, an expected state of immortality, complete with rewards: "It being highly rational to think, even were Revelation silent in the Case, That as Men employ those Talents, God has given them here, they shall accordingly receive their Rewards at the close of the day, when their Sun shall set, and Night shall put an end to their Labours" (*E*: 4.14.2: 652).
75 *RC*: 130–33, 140, 156.
76 Ian Harris claims Locke is concerned with revelation establishing authority and normativity, not content to the law of nature (Harris, "The Mind of John Locke," 309). But this ignores the fact that, for Locke, some truths are not accessible by unassisted reason (*RC*: 144).
77 *RC*: 128–34.
78 *RC*: 128–32.
79 *RC*: 129–31.
80 *RC*: 130. Cf. 131.
81 *RC*: 131.
82 *RC*: 132–34.
83 *RC*: 132.
84 *RC*: 133.
85 *RC*: 133.
86 *RC*: 117, 123.
87 *RC*: 13.
88 For an example of this mistaken view, see Norman Sykes, *The English Religious Tradition: Sketches of Its Influence on Church, State, and Society* (London: SCM Press, 1953), 55; Waldron, *God, Locke, and Equality*, 181n65. Throughout the *RC*, Locke holds a thick conception of what "Jesus is the Messiah" means, and thus Locke's claims for a simple assent must be read in the light of a laundry list of elements involved in this proposition. In fact, he speaks of "concomitant articles" of faith necessary for justification, such as Christ's resurrection and coming judgment (Wainwright, "Introduction," 33). In addition, Locke conceives of biblical faith as one that is never devoid of obedient, ethical activity.

89  *RC*: 117, 123.
90  *2nd T*: 25–51.
91  *2nd T*: 27.
92  In addition to Brubaker's work, see Steven Forde, *Locke, Science, and Politics* (Cambridge: Cambridge University Press, 2013). Forde notes that the *Second Treatise*'s discussion of property leaves no room for charity (177). This, however, is not incompatible with Locke's larger sense of one's obligation to charity, as Forde acknowledges (173). Forde's reconstruction of Locke's moral epistemology is interesting, but what such a philosophical reconstruction leaves wanting can be (and is) filled by a consideration of Locke's approach to revelation in scripture.
93  Stanley C. Brubaker, "Coming into One's Own: John Locke's Theory of Property, God, and Politics," *The Review of Politics* 74 (2012): 207. It is interesting to note that Locke's explicitly religious works come at the end of his life, suggesting that the Brubakerian kind of "awakening" to one's own mind in contradistinction to dependence on revelation is a path Locke himself refused to tread.
94  Brubaker, "Coming into One's Own," 216; cf. *2nd T*: 25–51.
95  Brubaker, "Coming into One's Own," 212n10.
96  Brubaker, "Coming into One's Own," 231, 232.
97  Brubaker, "Coming into One's Own," 208.
98  Brubaker, "Coming into One's Own," 214.
99  Brubaker, "Coming into One's Own," 214.
100 Waldron, *God, Locke, and Equality*, 151–87.
101 *2nd T*: 5.
102 *RC*: 115–16.
103 Locke, *Of the Conduct of the Understanding*, par. 41. For more, see Harris, "The Mind of John Locke," 309 and 389n50.
104 *E*: 1.3.4: 68.
105 *2nd T*: 6.
106 Waldron, *God, Locke, and Equality*, 159.
107 *1st T*: 86; *2nd T*: 26. See Waldron, *God, Locke, and Equality*, 159–60.
108 Waldron, *God, Locke, and Equality*, 162.
109 For restrictions such as not to destroy the product of one's labor or to let it perish due to neglect, see *2nd T*: 6. and 31. See also Waldron, *God, Locke, and Equality*, 163.
110 Waldron, *God, Locke, and Equality*, 177–87.
111 *1st T*: 42.
112 Waldron, *God, Locke, and Equality*, 180–81.
113 Waldron, *God, Locke, and Equality*, 181.
114 *2nd T*: 6.
115 *RC*: 127, 128, 141. Locke's clearest statement (127) comes in the context of reflection on the judgment scene of Matt. 25.
116 *RC*: 141.

117  *RC*: 141–47.
118  *1st T*: 42n.
119  This high emphasis on charity is reminiscent of Aquinas (*ST*: IaIIae 66.6).
120  Loconte, *God, Locke, and Liberty*, 136.
121  John Locke, *Selected Correspondence*, ed. Mark Goldie, from the Clarendon edition by E. S. deBeer (New York: Oxford University Press, 2002), 192; Fox Bourne, *The Life of John Locke*, Vol. 2, 8; Colie, *Light and Enlightenment*, 30.
122  Woolhouse, *Locke*, 198–99.
123  Luisa Simonutti, "Political Society and Religious Liberty: Locke at Cleves and in Holland," *British Journal for the History of Philosophy* 14, no. 3 (2006): 425–32; Loconte, *God, Locke, and Liberty*, 139–48.
124  *LCT*: 23.
125  *LCT*: 54.
126  *LCT*: 51. Cf. *LCT*: 54 and Chapter 2 of this book.
127  Some Locke scholars suggest Locke's chief justification for his doctrine of toleration centers on instrumental rationality (Richard H. Popking and Mark Goldie, "Scepticism, Priestcraft, and Toleration," in *The Cambridge History of Eighteenth Century Political Thought*, ed. Mark Goldie and Robert Wolker [Cambridge: Cambridge University Press, 2006], 102) or pragmatic concerns (Jeremy Waldron, "Locke: Toleration and the Rationality of Persecution," in *John Locke: A Letter Concerning Toleration in Focus*, ed. John Horton and Susan Mendus [New York: Routledge, 1991], 120) rather than any religious, theological, or even moral grounds. This section of the book argues that Locke's concern was religious and theological, as well as moral and rational. For an excellent defense of Locke's moral and theological justification for his doctrine of toleration, see Loconte, *God, Locke, and Liberty*, esp. 159–236.
128  *LCT*: 25, 27, 35, 37.
129  *LCT*: 48, 49.
130  *LCT*: 25, 45, 58.
131  *LCT*: 54.
132  *LCT*: 37, 40, 41.
133  *LCT*: 39.
134  Loconte, *God, Locke, and Liberty*, esp. 233–34.
135  Loconte, *God, Locke, and Liberty*, 10.
136  *RC*: 8.
137  *RC*: 5.
138  On reason as a "primary intellectual virtue," see Rogers, "Locke, Plato and Platonism," 202.

# Bibliography

## Primary Sources

Barrow, Isaac. "Sermon XXXII. Of A Peaceable Temper and Carriage." In *The Theological Works of Isaac Barrow, D.D., in 9 Volumes. Volume II: Containing Twenty-One Sermons on Several Occasions*, edited by Alexander Napier, 433–66. Cambridge: Cambridge University Press, 1859.

Beconsall, Thomas. *The Grounds and Foundation of Natural Religion, Discover'd, in the Principal Branches of it, in Opposition to the Prevailing Notions of the Modern Scepticks and Latitudinarians. With an Introduction Concerning the Necessity of Revealed Religion*. London: Printed by W. O. for George West, bookseller, in Oxford, 1698.

Boyle, Robert. *The Excellency of Theology, Compar'd with Natural Philosophy, (as Both Are Objects of Men's Study), Discours'd of in a Letter to a Friend, by T. H. R. B. E., Fellow of the Royal Society, to Which Are Annex'd Some Occasional Thoughts about the Excellency and Grounds of the Mechanical Hypothesis by the Same Author*. London: Printed by T.N. for Henry Herringman, 1674.

Boyle, Robert. *A Disquisition about the Final Causes of Natural Things: Wherein It Is Inquir'd, Whether and (If at All) with What Cautions, a Naturalist Should Admit Them?, to Which Are Subjoyn'd, by Way of Appendix Some Uncommon Observations about Vitiated Sight by the Same Author*. London: Printed by H. C. for John Taylor, at the Ship in St. Paul's Church-Yard, 1688.

Boyle, Robert. *The Philosophical Works of the Honourable Robert Boyle, Esq; Abridged, Methodized, and Disposed under the General Heads Of Physics, Statics, Pneumatics, Natural-History, Chymistry, and Medicine, the Whole Illustrated with Notes, Containing the Improvements Made in the Several Parts of Natural and Experimental Knowledge, since His Time*. Ed. Peter Shaw. 2 vols. London: Printed for W. and J. Innys, at the West-End of St. Paul's; and J. Osborn, and T. Longman, in Pater-Noster-Row, 1725.

Boyle, Robert. *The Works of the Honourable Robert Boyle in Six Volumes, to Which Is Prefixed the Life of the Author*. A new edition. London: Printed for J. and F. Rivington, L. Davis, W. Johnston, S. Crowder, T. Payne, G. Kearsley, J. Robson, B. White, T. Becket and P. A. De Hont, T. Davies, T. Cadell, Robinson and Roberts, Richardson and Richardson, J. Knox, W. Woodfall, J. Johnson, and T. Evans, 1772.

Burnet, Gilbert. *A Rational Method for Proving the Truth of the Christian Religion, as It Is Professed in the Church of England*. London: Printed for Richard Royston, 1675.

Burnet, Gilbert. *Bishop Burnet's History of His Own Time: With the Suppressed Passages of the First Volume, and Notes by the Earls of Dartmouth and Hardwicke and Speaker

Onslow, Hitherto Unpublished. To Which Are Added the Cursory Remarks of Swift, and Other Observations. Ed. Martin J. Routh. Vol. 1. 1724. Oxford: Clarendon Press, 1823.

Burnet, Thomas. *Second Remarks upon an Essay Concerning Humane Understanding, in a Letter Address'd to the Author*. 1697. Reprint. New York: Garland, 1984.

Chillingworth, William. *The Religion of Protestants, a Safe Way to Salvation*. A new and complete edition. 1638. Covent Garden: George Bell & Sons, 1888.

Cockburn, Catharine Trotter. "A defence of Mr. Locke's *Essay of Human Understanding*, wherein its principles, with reference to morality, revealed religion, and the immortality of the soul, are considered and justified: in answer to Some remarks on that Essay. First printed in the year 1702." In *The Works of Mrs. Catharine Cockburn, Theological, Moral, Dramatic, and Poetical. Several of Them Now First Printed*. Revised and published, with an account of the life of the author, by Thomas Birch, in 2 Volumes. Volume 1, 43–111. London: Printed for J. and P. Knapton, in Ludgate-Street, 1751.

Cockburn, Catharine Trotter. "A vindication of Mr. Locke's Christian principles, from the injurious imputations of Dr. Holdsworth. Now first published." In *The Works of Mrs. Catharine Cockburn, Theological, Moral, Dramatic, and Poetical*. Several of them now first printed, revised and published, with an account of the life of the author, by Thomas Birch, in 2 Volumes. Volume 1, 155–378. London: Printed for J. and P. Knapton, in Ludgate-Street, 1751.

Cudworth, Ralph. *True Intellectual System of the Universe: The First Part, Wherein All the Reason and Philosophy of Atheism Is Confuted; and Its Impossibility Demonstrated*. London: Printed for Richard Royston, bookseller to his most sacred majesty, 1678.

Cudworth, Ralph. *A Treatise Concerning Eternal and Immutable Morality*, with a preface by the Right reverend Father in God, Edward Lord Bishop of Durham, 27. London: Printed for James and John Knapton, at the Crown in St. Paul's Church yard, 1731.

Cudworth, Ralph. *A Treatise of Free Will*, now first edited from the original manuscript, and with notes, by John Allen. London: John W. Parker, 1838.

Cudworth, Ralph. *A Sermon Preached before the Honourable House of Commons at Westminster, March 31, 1647*. Cambridge, 1647. Reproduced from the original edition. New York: The Facsimile Text Society, 1930.

Culverwell, Nathaniel. *An Elegant and Learned Discourse of the Light of Nature*. Ed. Robert A. Greene and Hugh MacCallum. 1652. Toronto: University of Toronto Press, 1971.

du Châtelet, Gabrielle-Emilie Le Tonnelier de Breteuil, Marquise. *Institutions de physique*. Paris: Chez Prault Fils, 1740.

Edwards, John. *Some Thoughts Concerning the Several Causes and Occasions of Atheism, Especially in the Present Age, with Some Brief Reflections on Socinianism: And on a Late Book Entitled The Reasonableness of Christianity as Delivered in the Scriptures*. London: Printed for J. Robinson at the Golden Lyon, and J. Wyat at the Rose in S. Paul's Churchyard, 1695.

Edwards, John. *The Socinian Creed, or, a Brief Account of the Professed Tenents and Doctrines of the Foreign and English Socinians Wherein Is shew'd the Tendency of Them to Irreligion and Atheism, with Proper Antidotes against Them*. London: Printed for J. Robinson and J. Wyat, 1697.

Gastrell, Francis. *Some Considerations Concerning the Trinity: And the Ways of Managing that Controversie*. London: E. Whitlock, 1696.

Hammond, Henry. *A practicall catechisme*. 1644. Oxford: [publisher not identified], 1645.

Hammond, Henry. *Charis kai Eirēnē, or, A pacifick discourse of God's grace and decrees: in a letter of full accordance written to the reverend and most learned Dr. Robert Sanderson: to which are annexed the extracts of three letters concerning Gods prescience reconciled with liberty and contingency*. London: Printed for R. Davis, 1660.

Hooker, Richard. *Of the Laws of Ecclesiastical Polity*, Preface, Book I, Book VIII, edited by Arthur Stephen McGrade. Cambridge: Cambridge University Press, 1989, rep. 1997.

Hooker, Richard. *The Works of That Learned and Judicious Divine Mr. Richard Hooker, with an Account of His Life and Death by Isaac Walton*. Arr. John Keble. 7th ed. Rev. R. W. Church and F. Paget. 3 vols. Oxford: Clarendon Press, 1888.

Limborch, Philip van. *A Compleat System, or Body of Divinity, Both Speculative and Practical, Founded on Scripture and Reason, Written Originally in Latin, by Philip Limborch, with Improvements, from Bishop Wilkins, Arch-Bishop Tillotson, Doctor Scott, and Several Other Divines of the Church of England*. Trans. William Jones. 2 vols. London: Printed for J. Taylor and A. Bell, 1702.

Locke, John. *Mr. Locke's Reply to the Right Reverend the Lord Bishop of Worcester's Answer to His Letter*. In *The Works of John Locke*. Vol. 4. 10th ed. London: Printed for J. Johnson, 1801.

Locke, John. *Mr. Locke's Reply to the Right Reverend the Lord Bishop of Worcester's Answer to His Second Letter. Wherein, besides Other Incident Matters, What His Lordship Has Said Concerning Certainty by Reason, Certainty by Ideas, and Certainty by Faith; the Resurrection of the Body; the Immateriality of the Soul; the Inconsistency of Mr. Locke's Notions with the Articles of the Christian Faith, and Their Tendency to Scepticism; Is Examined*. In *The Works of John Locke*. Vol. 4. 10th ed. London: Printed for J. Johnson, 1801.

Locke, John. *A Second Letter Concerning Toleration*. In *The Works of John Locke in Ten Volumes*, new edition, corrected, Vol. 6, 59–138. 1690. London: Thomas Tegg, 1823.

Locke, John. "A Third Letter for Toleration: To the Author of the Third Letter Concerning Toleration." In *The Works of John Locke in Ten Volumes*, new edition, corrected, Vol. 6, 139–516. 1692. London: Thomas Tegg, 1823.

Locke, John. *The Works of John Locke: A New Edition, Corrected, in Ten Volumes*. London: Thomas Tegg, 1823.

Locke, John. *The Reasonableness of Christianity as Delivered in the Scriptures*, in *The Works of John Locke in Nine Volumes*, 12th ed. London: C. Baldwin, 1824, Vol. 6, 1–158.

Locke, John. *An Early Draft of Locke's Essay, Together with Excerpts from His Journals.* Ed. Richard I Aaron and Jocelyn Gibb. Oxford: Clarendon Press, 1936.

Locke, John. *Essays on the Law of Nature* [1664]: *The Latin Text with a Translation, Introduction, and Notes, Together with Transcripts of Locke's Shorthand in His Journal for 1676.* Ed. and trans. W. von Leyden. Oxford: Clarendon Press, 1954, reissued 1988.

Locke, John. "First Tract on Government." In *John Locke: Two Tracts on Government*, edited and trans. Philip Abrams, 117–81. 1660. Cambridge: Cambridge University Press, 1967.

Locke, John. "Second Tract on Government." In *John Locke: Two Tracts on Government*, edited and trans. Philip Abrams, 185–241. 1662. Cambridge: Cambridge University Press, 1967.

Locke, John. *A Paraphrase and Notes on the Epistles of St. Paul to the Galatians, 1 and 2 Corinthians, Romans, Ephesians.* 2 vols. Ed. Arthur W. Wainwright. 1707. Oxford: Clarendon Press, 1987.

Locke, John. *Some Thoughts Concerning Education* [1693]. Ed. with introduction, notes, and critical apparatus by John W. Yolton and Jean S. Yolton. Oxford: Clarendon Press, 1989.

Locke, John. "An Essay Concerning the Understanding, Knowledge, Opinion & Assent [Draft B]." In *Drafts for the Essay Concerning Human Understanding, and Other Philosophical Writings, Volume I: Drafts A and B*, edited by Peter H. Nidditch and G. A. J. Rogers, 87–270. 1671. Oxford: Clarendon Press, 1990.

Locke, John. *Questions Concerning the Law of Nature* [1664]: *With an Introduction, Text, and Translation.* Trans. Robert Horwitz, Jenny Strauss Clay, and Diskin Clay. Ithica, NY: Cornell University Press, 1990.

Locke, John. "Sic Cogitavit de Intellectu humano [Draft A]." In *Drafts for The Essay Concerning Human Understanding, and Other Philosophical Writings, Vol. 1: Drafts A and B*, edited by Peter H. Nidditch and G. A. J. Rogers, 1–83. 1671. Oxford: Clarendon Press, 1990.

Locke, John. *Of the Conduct of the Understanding.* Reprint from the 1706 edition of the *Posthumous Works of Mr. John Locke.* 2nd impression. Key Texts: Classic Studies in the History of Ideas. 1706. Bristol: Thoemmes Press, 1996. Citations are by paragraph.

Locke, John. *The Reasonableness of Christianity as Deliver'd in the Scriptures.* Ed. John C. Higgins-Biddle. 1695. Oxford: Clarendon Press, 1999.

Locke, John. "A Discourse of Miracles." In John Locke, *Writings on Religion*, edited by. Victor Nuovo, 44–50. 1706. Oxford: Clarendon Press, 2002.

Locke, John. "Adversaria Theologica." In John Locke, *Writings on Religion*, edited by Victor Nuovo, 19–33. 1794. Oxford: Clarendon Press, 2002.

Locke, John. "Ecclesia." In John Locke, *Writings on Religion*, edited by Victor Nuovo, 80. 1682. Oxford: Clarendon Press, 2002.

Locke, John. "Of Ethick in General." In John Locke, *Writings on Religion*, edited by Victor Nuovo, 9–14. 1687. Oxford: Clarendon Press, 2002.

Locke, John. *Selected Correspondence.* Ed. Mark Goldie. From the Clarendon edition by E. S. de Beer. New York: Oxford University Press, 2002.

Locke, John. *Writings on Religion*. Ed. Victor Nuovo. Oxford: Clarendon Press, 2002.
Locke, John. "An Essay Concerning Toleration." In John Locke, *An Essay Concerning Toleration and Other Writings on Law and Politics, 1667–1683*, edited by J. R. Milton and Philip Milton. 1667. Oxford: Clarendon Press, 2006.
Locke, John. "Pacific Christians." In John Locke, *Political Essays*, edited by Mark Goldie, 304–06. 1688. 1997. Reprint. Cambridge: Cambridge University Press, 2006.
Locke, John. *Political Essays*. Ed. Mark Goldie. 1997. Reprint. Cambridge: Cambridge University Press, 2006.
Locke, John. "Some Thoughts Concerning Reading and Study for a Gentleman." In John Locke, *Political Essays*, edited by Mark Goldie, 348–55. 1703. 1997. Reprint. Cambridge: Cambridge University Press, 2006.
Locke, John. "The Fundamental Constitutions of Carolina." In John Locke, *Political Essays*, edited by Mark Goldie, 160–81. 1669. 1997. Reprint. Cambridge: Cambridge University Press, 2006.
Locke, John. "Understanding." In John Locke, *Political Essays*, edited by Mark Goldie, 260–65. 1677. 1997. Reprint. Cambridge: Cambridge University Press, 2006.
Locke, John. *A Second Vindication of the Reasonableness of Christianity*. In John Locke, *Vindications of the Reasonableness of Christianity*, edited by Victor Nuovo, 27–233. 1697. Oxford: Clarendon Press, 2012.
Locke, John. "A Vindication of the Reasonableness of Christianity." In John Locke, *Vindications of the Reasonableness of Christianity*, edited by Victor Nuovo, 7–26. 1695. Oxford: Clarendon Press, 2012.
More, Henry. "Enthusiasmus Triumphatus; or, a Brief Discourse of the Nature, Causes, Kinds, and Cure of Enthusiasm." In *A Collection of Several Philosophical Writings of Dr. Henry More*. 4th ed. Corrected and much enlarged. London: Printed by Joseph Downing in Bartholomew-Close near West-Smithfield, 1712.
More, Henry. "The Immortality of the Soul, So Farre Forth as It Is Demonstrable from the Knowledge of Nature and the Light of Reason." In *International Archives of the History of Ideas*, edited by Alexander Jacob, 122, 1662. Dordrecht: Nijhoff, 1987.
Patrides, C. A. ed. *The Cambridge Platonists*. Cambridge: Harvard University Press, 1970.
Rust, George. *A Discourse of the Use of Reason in Matters of Religion: Shewing, That Christianity Contains Nothing Repugnant to Right Reason; Against Enthusiasts and Deists ... Translated into English, with Annotations upon It, by Hen. Hallywell*. London: Printed by Hen. Hills, jun. for Walter Kettilby, 1683.
Smith, John. *Select Discourses*. London, 1660, rep. London: Garland Publishing, 1978.
Stillingfleet, Edward. *A Discourse in Vindication of the Doctrine of the Trinity: With An Answer to the Late Socinian Objections against It from Scripture, Antiquity and Reason. And a Preface Concerning the Different Explications of the Trinity, and the Tendency of the Present Socinian Controversie*. London: Printed by J. H. for Henry Mortlock, 1697.
Stillingfleet, Edward. *The Bishop of Worcester's Answer to Mr. Locke's Letter, Concerning Some Passages Relating to His Essay of Humane Understanding, mention'd in the Late*

*Discourse in Vindication of the Trinity with a Postscript in Answer to Some Reflections Made on That Treatise in a Late Socinian Pamphlet*. London: Printed by J. H. for Henry Mortlock, 1697.

Stillingfleet, Edward. *The Bishop of Worcester's ANSWER to Mr. Locke's Second Letter; Wherein his NOTION of IDEAS Is prov'd to be Inconsistent with It Self, and with the ARTICLES of the CHRISTIAN FAITH*. London: Printed by J. H. for Henry Mortlock at the Phoenix in St. Paul's Church-Yard, 1698.

Taylor, Jeremy. *A Discourse of The Liberty of Prophesying, with Its Just Limits and Temper: Shewing the Unreasonableness of Prescribing to Other Men's Faiths, and the Inquity of Persecuting Differing Opinions*. Vol. 5, in *The Whole Works of the Right Rev. Jeremy Taylor, D.D.*, Rev. Charles Page Eden, M.A., London: Printed for Richard Royston, 1647.

Tillotson, John. *The Rule of Faith: Or, an ANSWER to the TREATISE of Mr. I.S. entituled, Sure-Footing &c., to Which Is Adjoined A REPLY to Mr. I.S. His 3d Appendix &c. by Edw. Stillingfleet*. 1666. 2nd ed. London: Printed by H.C. for O. Gellibrand, at the Golden-Ball in St. Paul's Church-yard, 1676.

Toland, John. *Christianity Not Mysterious: Or, a Treatise Shewing, That There Is Nothing in the Gospel Contrary to Reason, Nor Above It: And That No Christian Doctrine Can Be Properly Call'd a Mystery*. 2nd ed, enlarged. London: Printed for Sam Buckley at the Dolphin over against St. Dunstans Church in Fleetstreet, 1696.

Whichcote, Benjamin. *Theophoroumēna Dogmata, or, Some Select Notions of That Learned and Reverend Divine of the Church of England, Benj. Whitchcot, D.D., Lately Deceased*. London: Printed and are to be sold by Israel Harrison at Lincoln's-Inn Gate, 1685.

Whichcote, Benjamin. "Appendix: Moral and Religious Aphorisms," taken from *Moral and Religious Aphorisms*, revised by Samuel Salter (1753) from the edition by John Jeffery (1703). In *The Cambridge Platonists*, edited by C. A. Patrides, 326–36. Cambridge, MA: Harvard University Press, 1970.

Worthington, John. *A Form of Sound Words: Or, a Scripture Catechism; Shewing What a Christian Is to Believe and Practice, in Order to Salvation*. 6th ed. London: printed for R. Hett, 1733.

## Secondary Sources

Aaron, Richard I. *John Locke*. 3rd ed. Oxford: Oxford University Press, 1971.

Aarsleff, Hans. "Locke's Influence." In *The Cambridge Companion to Locke*, edited by Vere Chappell, 252–89. Cambridge: Cambridge University Press, 1994.

Amesbury, Richard. "Fideism." In *The Stanford Encyclopedia of Philosophy*. Winter 2012 edition, edited by Edward N. Zalta. http://plato.stanford.edu/archives/entries/fideism/.

Anselm. *Proslogion*. In *Complete Philosophical and Theological Treatises of Anselm of Canterbury*. Trans. Jasper Hopkins and Herbert Richardson, 88–112. Minneapolis: Arthur J. Banning Press, 2000. Citations are by paragraph.

Aquinas, Thomas. *Commentary on Aristotle's Nicomachean Ethics*. Trans. C. I. Litzinger. Notre Dame: Dumb Ox Books, 1993.

Aquinas, Thomas. *Summa Theologiae*. Trans. Fr. Laurence Shapcote, ed. John Mortensen and Enrique Alarcón, in *Latin/English Edition of the Works of St. Thomas Aquinas*. Lander, WY: The Aquinas Institute for the Study of Sacred Doctrine, 2012, Vols. 13–18.

Aristotle. *Politics*. Trans. H. Rackham. Loeb Classical Library. 1932. Reprint. London: Heinemann, 1967.

Aristotle. *Nicomachean Ethics*. Trans. and ed. Roger Crisp. Cambridge Texts in the History of Philosophy. Cambridge: Cambridge University Press, 2000.

Armitage, David. "John Locke, Carolina and the Two Treatises of Government." *Political Theory* 32 (2004): 602–26.

Ashcraft, Richard. "Faith and Knowledge in Locke's Philosophy." In *John Locke: Problems and Perspectives: A Collection of New Essays*, edited by John W. Yolton, 194–223. Cambridge: Cambridge University Press, 1969.

Ashcraft, Richard. *Revolutionary Politics and Locke's "Two Treatises of Government."* Princeton, NJ: Princeton University Press, 1986.

Ashcraft, Richard. *Locke's "Two Treatises of Government."* London: Unwin Hyman, 1987.

Ashcraft, Richard. Review of *The Mind of John Locke*, by Ian Harris. *The American Historical Review* 100, no. 4 (October 1995): 1247–48.

Ayers, Michael. *Locke*. 2 vols. *Vol. I: Epistemology, Vol II: Ontology*. London: Routledge, 1991.

Barzun, Jacques. *From Dawn to Decadence: 500 Years of Cultural Life, 1500 to the Present*. New York: HarperCollins, 2000.

Bennett, Jonathan. *Locke, Berkeley, Hume*. Oxford: Oxford University Press, 1971.

Bennett, Jonathan. "Locke's Philosophy of Mind." In *The Cambridge Companion to Locke*, edited by Vere Chappell, 89–114. Cambridge: Cambridge University Press, 1994.

Bennett, Jonathan. *Learning from Six Philosophers: Descartes, Spinoza, Leibniz, Locke, Berkeley, Hume*. 2 vols. Oxford: Oxford University Press, 2001.

Biddle, John C. "Locke's Critique of Innate Principles and Toland's Deism." *Journal of the History of Ideas* 37, no. 3 (July–September 1976): 411–22.

Bluhm, William T., Neil Wintfeld, and Stuart H. Teger. "Locke's Idea of God: Rational Truth or Political Myth?" *Journal of Politics* 42, no. 2 (1980): 414–38.

Broadie, Alexander. "Scotistic Metaphysics and Creation *ex nihilo*." In *Creation and the God of Abraham*, edited by David B. Burrell, Carlo Cogliati, Janet M. Soskice, and William R. Stoeger, 53–64. Cambridge: Cambridge University Press, 2010.

Brown, Vivienne. "The 'Figure' of God and the Limits to Liberalism: A Rereading of Locke's *Essay* and *Two Treatises*." *Journal of the History of Ideas* 60 (1999): 83–100.

Brown, Stuart. "The Sovereignty of the People." In *Studies on Locke: Sources, Contemporaries, and Legacy, in Honour of G.A.J. Rogers*, edited by Sarah Hutton and Paul Schuurman, 45–57. Dordrecht, The Netherlands: Springer, 2008.

Brubaker, Stanley C. "Coming into One's Own: John Locke's Theory of Property, God, and Politics." *The Review of Politics* 74 (2012): 207–32.

Buckle, Stephen. *Natural Law and the Theory of Property: Grotius to Hume*. Oxford: Oxford University Press, 1991.

Burnyeat, Myles F. "Sphinx without a Secret." *New York Review of Books* 32, no. 9 (May 30, 1985): 30–36.

Burrell, David. B., Carlo Cogliatti, Janet M. Soskice, and William R. Stoeger, eds. *Creation and the God of Abraham*. Cambridge: Cambridge University Press, 2010.

Carlin, Laurence. "The Importance of Teleology to Boyle's Natural Philosophy." *British Journal for the History of Philosophy* 19, no. 4 (2011): 665–82.

Carter, Ian. "Respect and the Basis of Equality." *Ethics* 121, no. 3 (April 2011): 538–71.

Champion, J. A. I. *The Pillars of Priestcraft Shaken*. Cambridge: Cambridge University Press, 1992.

Clanton, Caleb and Kraig Martin. *Nature and Command*. Knoxville: University of Tennessee Press, forthcoming.

Clapp, John Gordon. "Locke, John." In *The Encyclopedia of Philosophy*. Vol. 4, edited by Paul Edwards, 492. New York: Macmillan/Free Press, 1967.

Clark, J. C. D. *English Society 1688–1832*. Cambridge: Cambridge University Press, 1985.

Coby, Patrick. "The Law of Nature in Locke's Second Treatise: Is Locke a Hobbesian?" *The Review of Politics* 49, no. 1 (1987): 3–28.

Colie, Rosalie L. *Light and Enlightenment: A Study of the Cambridge Platonists and the Dutch Arminians*. Cambridge: Cambridge University Press, 1957.

Colman John. *John Locke's Moral Philosophy*. Edinburgh: Edinburgh University Press, 1983.

Costello, William T. *The Scholastic Curriculum in Early Seventeenth-Century Cambridge*. Cambridge, MA: Harvard University Press, 1958.

Cox, Richard H. *Locke on War and Peace*. 1960. Reprint. Washington, DC: University Press of America, 1982.

Cranston, Maurice. *John Locke: A Biography*. London: Longmans, Green, & Co., 1957.

Crocker, Robert. *Henry More, 1614–1687: A Biography of the Cambridge Platonist*. Dordrecht: Kluwer Academic Publishers, 2003.

Crowe, Michael Bertram. *The Changing Profile of the Natural Law*. The Hague: Nijhoff, 1977.

Curran, Eleanor. "An Immodest Proposal: Hobbes Rather than Locke Provides a Forerunner for Modern Rights Theory." *Law and Philosophy* 32 (2013): 515–38.

Curtis, Mattoon Monroe. *An Outline of Locke's Ethical Philosophy*. Leipzig: Gustav Fock, 1890.

De Beer, E. S. "Introduction." In *The Correspondence of John Locke*, edited by E. S. de Beer, Vol. 1, xv–lxxix. Oxford: Clarendon Press, 1976.

Dixon, Philip. *Nice and Hot Disputes: The Doctrine of the Trinity in the Seventeenth Century*. London: T&T Clark, 2003.

Dreyer, Frederick. "Edmund Burke and John Wesley: The Legacy of Locke." In *Religion, Secularization and Political Thought: Thomas Hobbes to J. S. Mill*, edited by James E. Crimmins, 111–29. London: Routledge, 1990.

Drury, S. B. "John Locke, Natural Law and Innate Ideas." *Dialogue* 19, no. 4 (December 1980): 531–45.

Dunn, John. *The Political Thought of John Locke: An Historical Account of the Argument of the "Two Treatises of Government."* Cambridge: Cambridge University Press, 1969.

Dunn, John. "The Politics of Locke in England and America in the Eighteenth Century." In *John Locke: Problems and Perspectives, A Collection of New Essays*, edited by John W. Yolton, 45–80. Cambridge: Cambridge University Press, 1969.

Dunn, John. *Locke*. Oxford: Oxford University Press, 1984.

Dunn, John. "What Is Living and What Is Dead in the Political Theory of John Locke?" In *Interpreting Political Responsibility: Essays 1981–1989*, edited by John Dunn, 9–25. Cambridge: Polity Press, 1990.

Dupré, Louis. *Passage to Modernity: An Essay in the Hermeneutics of Nature and Culture*. New Haven, CT: Yale University Press, 1993.

Dworetz, Stephen M. *The Unvarnished Doctrine: Locke, Liberalism and the American Revolution*. Durham, NC: Duke University Press, 1990.

Eisenach, Eldon J. *Two Worlds of Liberalism: Religion and Politics in Hobbes, Locke, and Mill*. Chicago: The University of Chicago Press, 1981.

Eisenach, Eldon J. "Religion and Locke's *Two Treatises*." In *John Locke's 'Two Treatises: New Interpretations*, edited by Edward J. Harpham, 50–81. Lawrence: University Press of Kansas, 1992.

Faulkner, Robert K. *Richard Hooker and the Politics of a Christian England*. Berkeley: University of California Press, 1981.

Flage, Daniel E. "Locke and Natural Law." *Dialogue* 39, no. 3 (June 2000): 435–60.

Forde, Steven. "Natural Law, Theology, and Morality in Locke." *American Journal of Political Science* 45, no. 2 (April 2001): 396–409.

Forde, Steven. *Locke, Science and Politics*. Cambridge: Cambridge University Press, 2013.

Forster, Greg. *John Locke's Politics of Moral Consensus*. Cambridge: Cambridge University Press, 2005.

Fox Bourne, H. R. *The Life of John Locke*. 2 vols. London: Henry S. King and Co., 1876.

Franklin, Julian H. Review of *John Locke: Resistance, Religion, and Responsibility*, by John Marshall. *The American Historical Review* 101, no. 2 (April 1996): 479–80.

Gerson, Lloyd. "Plotinus on *Akrasia*: The Neoplatonic Synthesis." In *Akrasia in Greek Philosophy: From Socrates to Plotinus*, edited by Christopher Bobonich and Pierre Destrée, Philosophia Antiqua 106, 165–82. Leiden: Brill, 2007.

Gibbs, Lee W. "Richard Hooker: Prophet of Anglicanism or English Magisterial Reformer?" *Anglican Theological Review* 84, no. 4 (Fall 2002): 943–60.

Gierke, Otto. *Natural Law and the Theory of Society: 1500–1800*. Trans. Ernest Barker. 1934. Reprint. Cambridge: Cambridge University Press, 1950.

Gill, Michael B. *The British Moralists on Human Nature and the Birth of Secular Ethics*. Cambridge: Cambridge University Press, 2006.

Glendon, Mary Ann. *Rights Talk: The Impoverishment of Political Discourse*. New York: Free Press, 1991.

Goldwin, Robert. "John Locke." In *History of Political Philosophy*, edited by Leo Strauss and Joseph Cropsey, 451–86. 2nd ed. Chicago: Rand McNally, 1972.

Grant, Ruth W., and Nathan Tarcov. "Introduction." In John Locke, *Some Thoughts Concerning Education and of the Conduct of the Understanding*, edited by Ruth W. Grant and Nathan Tarcov, vii–xix. Indianapolis: Hackett, 1996.

Grayling, A. C. *The Age of Genius: The Seventeenth Century and the Birth of the Modern Mind*. London: Bloomsbury, 2016.

Greene, Robert A., and Hugh MacCallum. "Introduction." In Nathaniel Culverwell, *An Elegant and Learned Discourse of the Light of Nature*, edited by Robert A. Greene and Hugh MacCallum, ix–lv. 1652. Toronto: University of Toronto Press, 1971.

Greene, Robert A. "Whichcote, the Candle of the Lord, and Synderesis." *Journal of the History of Ideas* 52, no. 4 (October–December 1991): 617–44.

Greig, Martin. "The Reasonableness of Christianity? Gilbert Burnet and the Trinitarian Controversy of the 1690's." *Journal of Ecclesiastical History* 44, no. 4 (October 1993): 631–51.

Grenz, Stanley J. *Theology for the Community of God*. Grand Rapids, MI: Eerdmans, 2000.

Griffin, Martin I. J., Jr. *Latitudinarianism in the Seventeenth Century Church of England*. Leiden: E. J. Brill, 1992.

Guy, Nathan. "Giving Locke Some Latitude: Locke's Theological Influences from Great Tew to the Cambridge Platonists." In *Revisioning Cambridge Platonism*, edited by Douglas Hedley, Sarah Hutton, and David Leech. The International Archives of the History of Ideas. Berlin/Heidelberg: Springer, forthcoming.

Gysi, Lydia. *Platonism and Cartesianism in the Philosophy of Ralph Cudworth*. Bern: Herbert Lang, 1962.

Hancey, James O. "John Locke and the Law of Nature." *Political Theory* 4, no. 4 (November 1976): 439–54.

Hankey, Wayne. "Natural Theology in the Patristic Period." In *The Oxford Handbook of Natural Theology*, edited by Russell Re Manning, 38–56. Oxford: Oxford University Press, 2013.

Harris, Tim. "Introduction: Revising the Restoration." In *The Politics of Religion in Restoration England*, edited by Tim Harris, Paul Seaward, and Mark Goldie, 1–28. Oxford: Blackwell, 1990.

Harris, Ian. *The Mind of John Locke: A Study of Political Theory in Its Intellectual Setting*. Cambridge: Cambridge University Press, 1994.

Harrison, John and Peter Laslett, *The Library of John Locke* [1965], 2nd ed. Oxford: Clarendon Press, 1971.

Hebblethwaite, Brian. *Philosophical Theology and Christian Doctrine*. Oxford: Blackwell, 2005.

Hedley, Douglas. "Should Divinity Overcome Metaphysics? Reflections on John Milbank's Theology beyond Secular Reason and Confessions of a Cambridge Platonist." *The Journal of Religion* 80, no. 2 (April 2000): 271–98.

Higgins-Biddle, John C. "Introduction." In John Locke, *The Reasonableness of Christianity as Delivered in the Scriptures*, edited by John C. Higgins-Biddle, xv–cxv. Oxford: Clarendon Press, 1999.

Holmes, Stephen. *The Anatomy of Antiliberalism*. Revised Edition. Cambridge, MA: Harvard University Press, 1996.

Horwitz, Robert. "Introduction." In John Locke, *Questions Concerning the Law of Nature* [1664]: *With an Introduction, Text, and Translation*. Trans. Robert Horwitz, Jenny Strauss Clay, and Diskin Clay, 1–62. Ithaca, NY: Cornell University Press, 1990.

Hume, David. *A Treatise of Human Nature*. Ed. David Fate Norton and Mary J. Norton. Oxford: Oxford University Press, 2000.

Hutton, Sarah. "Damaris Cudworth, Lady Masham, Between Platonism and Enlightenment." *British Journal for the History of Philosophy* 1, no. 1 (February 1993): 29–54.

Hutton, Sarah. "Some Thoughts Concerning Ralph Cudworth." In *Studies on Locke: Sources, Contemporaries, and Legacy, in Honour of G.A.J. Rogers*, edited by Sarah Hutton and Paul Schuurman, 143–57. Dordrecht, The Netherlands: Springer, 2008.

Hutton, Sarah. "Damaris Masham (1658–1708)." In *The Bloomsbury Companion to Locke*, edited by S.-J. Savonius-Wroth, Paul Schuurman, and Jonathan Walmsley, 72–75. London: Bloomsbury, 2014.

Im Hof, Ulrich. *The Enlightenment*. Trans. William E. Yuill. Oxford: Oxford University Press, 1994.

Insole, Christopher J. *The Politics of Human Frailty: A Theological Defence of Political Liberalism*. Notre Dame: University of Notre Dame Press, 2004.

Israel, Jonathan I. *Radical Enlightenment: Philosophy and the Making of Modernity 1650–1750*. Oxford: Oxford University Press, 2001.

Kant, Immanuel. *Groundwork for the Metaphysics of Morals*. Ed. Mary Gregor. Cambridge Texts in the History of Philosophy. Cambridge: Cambridge University Press, 1997.

Kelly, Paul. *Locke's Second Treatise of Government: A Readers Guide*. London: Continuum, 2007.

Kelly, Paul. "Liberalism, Secularism and the Challenge of Religion—Is There a Crisis?" In *Cultural Politics in a Global Age: Uncertainty, Solidarity, and Innovation*, edited by Henrietta Moore and David Held, 124–31. London: OneWorld, 2008.

Khamara, Edward J. "Hume against Locke on the Causal Principle." *British Journal for the History of Philosophy* 8, no. 2 (2000): 339–43.

Kretzmann, Norman. *The Metaphysics of Theism: Aquinas' Natural Theology in Summa Contra Gentiles I*. Oxford: Clarendon Press, 1997.

Kvanvig, Jonathan L. and Hugh McCann. "Divine Conservation and the Persistence of the World." In *Divine and Human Action: Essays in the Metaphysics of Theism*, edited by Thomas V. Morris, 13–49. Ithaca, NY: Cornell University Press, 1988.

Lake, Peter. *Anglicans and Puritans? Presbyterianism and English Conformist Thought from Whitgift to Hooker*. London: Unwin Hyman, 1988.

Lamb, Matthew L. "Inculturation and Western Culture: The Dialogical Experience between Gospel and Culture." *Communio* 21 (1994): 124–44.

Lamprecht, Sterling Power. *The Moral and Political Philosophy of John Locke*. 1918. Reprint. New York: Russell and Russell, 1962.

Lascano, Marcy P. "Emile du Châtelet on the Existence and Nature of God: An Examination of Her Arguments in Light of Their Sources." *British Journal for the History of Philosophy* 19, no. 4 (2011): 741–58.

Laslett, Peter. "The Social and Political Theory of *Two Treatises of Government*." In John Locke, *Two Treatises of Government: A Critical Edition with an Introduction and Apparatus Criticus*, edited by Peter Laslett, 2nd ed., 92–120. 1960. 1967. Reprint. Cambridge: Cambridge University Press, 1988.

Leiter, Yechiel J. M. *John Locke's Political Philosophy and the Hebrew Bible*. Cambridge: Cambridge University Press, 2018.

Lenz, John W. "Locke's Essays on the Law of Nature." *Philosophy and Phenomenological Research* 17, no. 1 (September 1956): 105–13.

Levering, Matthew. *Biblical Natural Law: A Theocentric and Teleological Approach*. Oxford: Oxford University Press, 2008.

Lewis, C. S. *Mere Christianity*. In *The Complete C. S. Lewis Signature Classics*. New York: HarperOne, 2002.

Livy. *History of Rome. Vol. IV: Books 8–10*. Trans. B. O. Foster. Loeb Classical Library. London: Heinemann, 1926.

Loconte, Joseph. *God, Locke, and Liberty: The Struggle for Religious Freedom in the West*. Plymouth: Lexington Books, 2014.

Mackie, John. *Problems from Locke*. Oxford: Oxford University Press, 1976.

Macnabb, D. G. C., and E. J. Khamara. "Hume and His Predecessors on the Causal Maxim." In *David Hume: Bicentenary Papers*, edited by G. P. Morice, 146–55. Austin: University of Texas, 1977.

MacPherson, C. B. *The Political Theory of Possessive Individualism: Hobbes to Locke*. Oxford: Oxford University Press, 1962.

Marshall, John. *John Locke: Resistance, Religion, and Responsibility*. Cambridge: Cambridge University Press, 1994.

Marshall, John. *John Locke, Toleration and Early Enlightenment Culture: Religious Intolerance and Arguments for Religious Toleration in Early Modern and "Early Enlightenment" Europe*. 2006. Reprint. Cambridge: Cambridge University Press, 2008.

McCann, Edwin. "Locke's Philosophy of Body." In *The Cambridge Companion to Locke*, edited by Vere Chappell, 56–88. Cambridge: Cambridge University Press, 1994.

McFarland, Ian A. *From Nothing: A Theology of Creation*. Louisville, KY: Westminster John Knox Press, 2014.

Milton, J. R. and Philip Milton. "Textual Introduction." In John Locke, *An Essay Concerning Toleration and Other Writings on Law and Politics, 1667–1683*, edited by J. R. Milton and Philip Milton, 162–263. Oxford: Clarendon Press, 2006.

Montuori, Mario. *John Locke on Toleration and the Unity of God*. Amsterdam: J. C. Gieben, 1983.
Murphy, Mark. "The Natural Law Tradition in Ethics." *The Stanford Encyclopedia of Philosophy*. Winter 2011 edition. ed. Edward N. Zalta. http://plato.stanford.edu/archives/win2011/entries/natural-law-ethics/.
Myers, Peter C. *Our Only Star and Compass: Locke and the Struggle for Political Rationality*. Lanham, MD: Rowman & Littlefield, 1998.
Newbigin, Leslie. *The Gospel in a Pluralist Society*. Grand Rapids, MI: Eerdmans, 1989.
Newbigin, Leslie. "The Trinity as Public Truth." In *The Trinity in a Pluralistic Age: Theological Essays on Culture and Religion*, edited by Kevin J. Vanhoozer, 1–8. Grand Rapids, MI: Eerdmans, 1997.
Nidditch, Peter H. "Foreward." In John Locke, *An Essay Concerning Human Understanding*, edited by Peter H. Nidditch, vii–xxvi. 1689. 1975. Revised edn. Reprint. Oxford: Clarendon Press, 1979.
Nuovo, Victor. "Introduction." In *John Locke: Writings on Religion*, edited by Victor Nuovo, xv–lvii. Oxford: Clarendon Press, 2002.
Nuovo, Victor. "Reflections on Locke's Platonism." In *Platonism at the Origins of Modernity: Studies on Platonism and Early Modern Philosophy*, edited by Douglas Hedley and Sarah Hutton. International Archives of the History of Ideas 196, 207–33. Dordrecht, Netherlands: Springer, 2008.
Nuovo, Victor. *Christianity, Antiquity, and Enlightenment: Interpretations of Locke*. Archives Internationales D'Histoire Des Idées. Vol. 203. Dordrecht: Springer, 2011.
Nuovo, Victor. *John Locke: The Philosopher as Christian Virtuoso*. Oxford: Clarendon Press, 2017.
O'Donovan, Oliver. *The Desire of the Nations: Rediscovering the Roots of Political Theology*. Cambridge: Cambridge University Press, 1996.
Oakley, Francis and Elliot W. Urdang. "Locke, Natural Law, and God." *Natural Law Forum* 11 (1966): 92–109.
Oakley, Francis. "Locke, Natural Law, and God—Again." *History of Political Thought* 18, no. 4 (Winter 1997): 624–51.
Oakley, Francis. *Natural Law, Laws of Nature, Natural Rights: Continuity and Discontinuity in the History of Ideas*. London: Continuum, 2005.
Pailin, David. "Reconciling Theory and Fact: The Problem of 'Other Faiths' in Lord Herbert and the Cambridge Platonists." In *Platonism at the Origins of Modernity: Studies on Platonism and Early Modern Philosophy*, edited by Douglas Hedley and Sarah Hutton, 93–112. International Archives of the History of Ideas 196. Dordrecht, Netherlands: Springer, 2008.
Pangle, Thomas L. *The Spirit of Modern Republicanism: The Moral Vision of the American Founders and the Philosophy of Locke*. Chicago: University of Chicago Press, 1988.
Parker, Kim Ian. *The Biblical Politics of John Locke*. Editions SR. Vol. 29. Waterloo, ON: Wilfrid Laurier University Press, 2004.

Passmore, John Arthur. *Ralph Cudworth: An Interpretation*. Cambridge: Cambridge University Press, 1951.

Pearson, Samuel. "The Religion of John Locke and the Character of His Thought." *Journal of Religion* 58 (1978): 244–62.

Perry, Michael J. *Toward a Theory of Human Rights: Religion, Law, Courts*. Cambridge: Cambridge University Press, 2007.

Perry, John. *The Pretenses of Loyalty: Locke, Liberal Theory, and American Political Theology*. Oxford: Oxford University Press, 2011.

Plato. *Timaeus*. In *Plato: Timaeus and Critias*. Trans. A. E. Taylor, 13–100. London: Methuen & Co, 1929.

Pojman, Louis J. "A Critique of Contemporary Egalitarianism: A Christian Perspective." *Faith and Philosophy* 8, no. 4 (October 1991): 481–504.

Polin, Raymond. *La politique morale de John Locke*. Paris: Presses universitaires de France, 1960.

Polin, Raymond. "Justice in Locke's Philosophy." In *Nomos VI: Justice*, edited by Carl J. Friedrich and J. W. Chapman, 262–83. New York: Atherton Press, 1963.

Polin, Raymond. "John Locke's Conception of Freedom." In *John Locke: Problems and Perspectives: A Collection of New Essays*, edited by John W. Yolton, 1–18. Cambridge: Cambridge University Press, 1969.

Popking, Richard H. and Mark Goldie. "Scepticism, Priestcraft, and Toleration." In *The Cambridge History of Eighteenth Century Political Thought*, edited by Mark Goldie and Robert Wolker, 79–109. Cambridge: Cambridge University Press, 2006.

Pratt, James Bisset. Review of *The Moral and Political Philosophy of John Locke*, by Sterling Power Lamprecht, *The American Political Science Review* 13, no. 2 (May 1919): 319–20.

Preller, Victor. *Divine Science and the Science of God: A Reformulation of Thomas Aquinas*. Princeton, NJ: Princeton University Press, 1967.

*Public Theology for a Global Society: Essays in Honor of Max L. Stackhouse*, edited by Deirdre King and Scott R. Paeth. Grand Rapids, MI: Eerdmans, 2010.

Quintana, Ricardo. *Two Augustans: Locke and Swift*. Madison: University of Wisconsin Press, 1978.

Rabieh, Michael S. "The Reasonableness of Locke, or the Questionableness of Christianity." *The Journal of Politics* 53, no. 4 (November 1991): 933–57.

Redwood, John. *Reason, Ridicule and Religions: The Age of Enlightenment in England, 1660–1750*. Cambridge, MA: Harvard University Press, 1976.

Reventlow, Henning Graf. *The Authority of the Bible and the Rise of the Modern World*. 1984. Philadelphia, PA: Fortress Press, 1985.

Rogers, G. A. J. "Introduction." In John Locke, *Drafts for the Essay Concerning Human Understanding and Other Philosophical Writings, Volume 1: Drafts A and B*, edited by Peter H. Nidditch and G. A. J. Rogers, xiii–xxvi. Oxford: Clarendon Press, 1990.

Rogers, G. A. J. "Locke, Newton, and the Cambridge Platonists on Innate Ideas." In *Philosophy, Religion, and Science in the Seventeenth and Eighteenth Centuries*, edited by John W. Yolton, 351–65. Rochester: University of Rochester Press, 1990.

Rogers, G. A. J. "Locke and the Latitude-Men: Ignorance as a Ground for Toleration." In *Philosophy, Science and Religion in England (1640–1700)*, edited by R. Ashcraft, R. Kroll, and P. Zagorin, 230–52. Cambridge: Cambridge University Press, 1992.

Rogers, G. A. J. "Locke, Plato and Platonism." In *Platonism at the Origins of Modernity: Studies on Platonism and Early Modern Philosophy*, edited by Douglas Hedley and Sarah Hutton. International Archives of the History of Ideas 196, 193–207. Dordrecht, Netherlands: Springer, 2008.

Schneewind, J. B. "Locke's Moral Philosophy." In *The Cambridge Companion to Locke*, edited by Vere Chappell, 199–225. Cambridge: Cambridge University Press, 1994.

Scott, Jonathan. "England's Troubles: Exhuming the Popish Plot." In *The Politics of Religion in Restoration England*, edited by Tim Harris, Paul Seaward, and Mark Goldie, 107–31. Oxford: Blackwell, 1990.

Scott, Jonathan. *England's Troubles: Seventeenth-century English Political Instability in European Context*. Cambridge: Cambridge University Press, 2000.

Sedley, David. *Creationism and Its Critics in Antiquity*. Berkeley: University of California Press, 2009.

Seliger, Martin. *The Liberal Politics of John Locke*. 1968. New York: Praeger, 1969.

Sell, Alan P. F. *John Locke and the Eighteenth Century Divines*. 1997. Eugene, OR: Wipf & Stock, 2006.

Shanks, Torrey. *Authority Figures: Rhetoric and Experience in John Locke's Political Thought*. University Park: University of Pennsylvania Press, 2014.

Sigmund, Paul E. "Jeremy Waldron and the Religious Turn in Locke Scholarship." *The Review of Politics* 67, no. 3 (Summer 2005): 407–18.

Simmons, A. John. *The Lockean Theory of Rights*. Princeton, NJ: Princeton University Press, 1992.

Simonutti, Luisa. "Political Society and Religious Liberty: Locke at Cleves and in Holland." *British Journal for the History of Philosophy* 14, no. 3 (2006): 413–36.

Simonutti, Luisa. "Circles of Virtuosi and 'Charity under Different Opinion': The Crucible of Locke's Last Writings." In *Studies on Locke: Sources, Contemporaries, and Legacy, in Honour of G.A.J. Rogers*, edited by Sarah Hutton and Paul Schuurman, 159–75. Dordrecht, The Netherlands: Springer, 2008.

Singer, Peter. *Unsanctifying Human Life: Essays on Ethics*, edited by Helga Kuhse. Oxford: Blackwell, 2002.

Singh, Raghuveer. "John Locke and the Theory of Natural Law." *Political Studies* 9 (1961): 105–18.

Soskice, Janet Martin. "Naming God: A Study in Faith and Reason." In *Reason and the Reasons of Faith*, edited by Paul Griffiths and Reinhard Hütter, 241–54. London: T&T Clark, 2005.

Soskice, Janet Martin. "Creatio ex nihilo: Its Jewish and Christian Foundations." In *Creation and the God of Abraham*, edited by David B. Burrell, Carlo Cogliati, Janet M. Soskice and William R. Stoeger, 24–39. Cambridge: Cambridge University Press, 2010.
Sparkes, A. W. "Trust and Teleology: Locke's Politics and His Doctrine of Creation." *Canadian Journal of Philosophy* 3, no. 2 (1973): 263–73.
Spellman, William M. *John Locke and the Problem of Human Depravity*. Oxford: Oxford University Press, 1988.
Spellman, William M. *John Locke*. London: Macmillan, 1997.
Stanton, Timothy. "Authority and Freedom in the Interpretation of Locke's Political Theory." *Political Theory* 39, no. 1 (2011): 6–30.
Stanton, Timothy. "On (Mis)interpreting Locke: A Reply to Tate." *Political Theory* 40, no. 1 (2012): 229–36.
Strauss, Leo. *Persecution and the Art of Writing*. Glencoe, IL: The Free Press, 1952.
Strauss, Leo. *Natural Right and History*. Chicago: University of Chicago Press, 1953.
Strauss, Leo. "Critical Note: Locke's Doctrine of Natural Law." *The American Political Science Review* 52, no. 2 (June 1958): 490–501.
Strauss, Leo. *What Is Political Philosophy? And Other Studies*. Glencoe, IL: The Free Press, 1959.
Sykes, Norman. *The English Religious Tradition: Sketches of Its Influence on Church, State, and Society*. London: SCM Press, 1953.
Taliaferro, Charles. *Evidence and Faith: Philosophy and Religion since the Seventeenth Century*. Cambridge: Cambridge University Press, 2005.
Tate, John William. "Locke, God and Civil Society: Response to Stanton." *Political Theory* 40, no. 2 (2012): 222–28.
Tate, John William. "Dividing Locke from God: The Limits of Theology in Locke's Political Philosophy." *Philosophy and Social Criticism* 39, no. 2 (2013): 133–64.
Taylor, Charles. *Sources of the Self: The Making of Modern Identity*. Cambridge, MA: Harvard University Press, 1989.
Trevor-Roper, Hugh. *Catholics, Anglicans, and Puritans: Seventeenth Century Essays*. 1987. Chicago: University of Chicago Press, 1988.
Tuck, Richard. *The Rights of War and Peace*. Oxford: Oxford University Press, 1999.
Tuckness, Alex Scott. "The Coherence of a Mind: John Locke and the Law of Nature." *Journal of the History of Philosophy* 37, no. 1 (January 1999): 73–90.
Tulloch, John. *Rational Theology and Christian Philosophy in England in the Seventeenth Century*. 2 Vols. Vol I: Liberal Churchmen; Vol II: The Cambridge Platonists. London: William Blackwood and Sons, 1872.
Tully, James. *A Discourse on Property: John Locke and His Adversaries*. Cambridge: Cambridge University Press, 1980.
Tully, James. "Note on the Text." 19. In John Locke, *A Letter Concerning Toleration*, [1689], edited by James H. Tully. Indianapolis, IN: Hackett, 1983.
Tully, James. *An Approach to Political Philosophy: Locke in Contexts*. Cambridge: Cambridge University Press, 1993.

Tully, James. "Rediscovering America: The Two Treatises and Aboriginal Rights." In *An Approach to Political Philosophy: Locke in Contexts*, edited by James Tully, 137–76. Cambridge: Cambridge University Press, 1993.
Von Leyden, W. "John Locke and Natural Law." *Philosophy* 31, no. 116 (January 1956): 23–35.
Vanhoozer, Kevin J., and Owen Strachan. *The Pastor as Public Theologian: Reclaiming a Lost Vision*. Grand Rapids, MI: Baker Academic, 2015.
Wainwright, Arthur W. "Introduction." In *A Paraphrase and Notes on the Epistles of St. Paul to the Galatians, 1 and 2 Corinthians, Romans, Ephesians*, Vol. 1, by John Locke, edited by Arthur W. Wainwright, 1–88. Oxford: Clarendon Press, 1987.
Waldron, Jeremy. "Locke: Toleration and the Rationality of Persecution." In *John Locke: A Letter Concerning Toleration in Focus*, edited by John Horton and Susan Mendus, 98–124. New York: Routledge, 1991.
Waldron, Jeremy. *Dignity of Legislation*. Cambridge: Cambridge University Press, 1999.
Waldron, Jeremy. *God, Locke, and Equality: Christian Foundations of Locke's Political Thought*. Cambridge: Cambridge University Press, 2002.
Waldron, Jeremy. "Response to Critics." *The Review of Politics* 67, no. 3 (Summer 2005): 495–513.
Ward, Keith. *Rational Theology and the Creativity of God*. Oxford: Basil Blackwell, 1982.
Ward, W. Randall. "Divine Will, Natural Law, and the Voluntarism/Intellectualism Debate in Locke." *History of Political Thought* 16, no. 2 (Summer 1995): 208–18.
Wardle, David L. "Reason to Ratify: The Influence of John Locke's Religious Beliefs on the Creation and Adoption of the United States Constitution." *Seattle University Law Review* 26 (2002): 291–308.
West, Thomas G. "The Ground of Locke's Law of Nature." *Social Science and Philosophy* 29, no. 2 (2012): 1–50.
Wild, John. *Plato's Modern Enemies and the Theory of Natural Law*. Chicago: University of Chicago Press, 1953.
Willcox, W. F. Review of *an Outline of Locke's Ethical Philosophy*, by Mattoon Monroe Curtis. *The Philosophical Review* 1, no. 2 (March 1892): 200–01.
Williams, Rowan. *Faith in the Public Square*. London: Bloomsbury Continuum, 2012.
Wolterstorff, Nicholas. "Locke's Philosophy of Religion." In *The Cambridge Companion to Locke*, edited by Vere Chappell, 172–98. Cambridge: Cambridge University Press, 1994.
Wolterstorff, Nicholas. *John Locke and the Ethics of Belief*. Cambridge Studies in Religion and Critical Thought, Vol. 2. Cambridge: Cambridge University Press, 1996.
Woolhouse, Roger. *Locke: A Biography*. Cambridge: Cambridge University Press, 2007.
Woolhouse, Roger and Timothy Stanton. "Contemporary Locke Scholarship." In *The Continuum Companion to Locke*, edited by S.-J. Savonius-Wroth, Paul Schuurman, and Jonathan Walmsley, 314–16. London: Continuum, 2010.
Wootton, David. "John Locke: Socinian or Natural Law Theorist?" In *Religion, Secularization and Political Thought: Thomas Hoobes to J. S. Mill*, edited by James E. Crimmins, 39–67. London: Routledge, 1990.

Wootton, David. "Introduction." In John Locke, *Political Writings*, edited by David Wootton, 6–122. 1993. Indianapolis: Hackett, 2003.
Wright, N. T. *The Resurrection of the Son of God*. Minneapolis: Fortress, 2003.
Yolton, John W. *John Locke and the Way of Ideas*. London: Oxford University Press, 1956.
Yolton, John W. "Locke on the Law of Nature." *The Philosophical Review* 67, no. 4 (October 1958): 477–98.
Yolton, John W. Review of *Locke on War and Peace*, by Richard H. Cox. *The Philosophical Review* 71, no. 2 (April 1962): 269–71.
Yolton, John W. *John Locke and the Compass of Human Understanding: A Selective Commentary on the "Essay."* Cambridge: Cambridge University Press, 1970.
Yolton, John W. *Locke: An Introduction*. Oxford: Basil Blackwell, 1985.
Zuckert, Michael P. "An Introduction to Locke's First Treatise." *Interpretation: A Journal of Political Philosophy* 8, no. 1 (January 1979): 58–74.
Zuckert, Michael P. *Natural Rights and the New Republicanism*. Princeton, NJ: Princeton University Press, 1994.
Zuckert, Michael P. *Launching Liberalism: On Lockean Political Philosophy*. Lawrence: University Press of Kansas, 2002.
Zuckert, Michael P. "Locke-Religion-Equality." *The Review of Politics* 67, no. 3 (Summer 2005): 419–31.

# Unpublished Sources

Conrad, Jonathan Donald. "Locke's Use of the Bible in 'The Two Treatises,' 'The Reasonableness of Christianity,' and 'A Letter Concerning Toleration.'" PhD diss., Northern Illinois University, DeKalb, IL, 2004.
Foster, David James. "John Locke's Critique of the Bible in the *First Treatise of Government*." PhD diss., University of Toronto, Toronto, 1991.
Lettinga, Corneilius H. "Covenant Theology and the Transformation of Anglicanism." PhD diss., The Johns Hopkins University, Baltimore, MD, 1987.
Lindahl, William Carl. "A Critical Commentary on John Locke's *Essays on the Law of Nature*." PhD diss., University of Dallas, Dallas, 1986.
Parker, Kim Ian. "A Critical Analysis of Filmer's and Locke's Use of Genesis in the Development of Their Political Philosophies." MA thesis, McMaster University, Hamilton, Ontario, 1982.
Sheridan, Patricia. "Locke's Ethics and the British Moralists: The Lockean Legacy in Eighteenth Century Moral Philosophy." PhD diss., University of Western Ontario, London, Ontario, 2001.
Tetlow, Joanne E. "The Theological Context of John Locke's Political Thought." PhD diss., The Catholic University of America, Washington, DC, 2006.
Windstrup, George Alan. "Politic Christianity: Locke's Theology of Liberalism." PhD diss., Princeton University, Princeton, NJ, 1978.

# People Index

Aaron, Richard 25, 172, 187
Allestree, Richard 54
Anselm 195
Aquinas, Thomas 7, 24, 27, 86, 89–91, 107–12, 114, 177, 192, 195, 200–2, 206, 211, 218
Aristotle 88–9, 114, 193, 202, 209
Ashcraft, Richard 25–6, 160, 162–3, 183
Ashley, Lord. *See* Cooper, Anthony Ashley
Ayers, Michael 163, 183

Barrow, Isaac 66–7, 71, 171, 181
Barzun, Jacques 153, 157
Beconsall, Thomas 157
Bennett, Jonathan 161, 190
Boyle, Robert 8, 55, 61–2, 173, 176–8, 189
Brown, Vivienne 194, 199
Brubaker, Stanley 144–5, 217
Burnet, Gilbert 63, 66, 68, 137, 171, 178, 181, 182, 215
Burnet, Thomas 192
Burrell, David 193–5

Calvin, John 25, 27
Carlin, Laurence 62, 176–7
Charles I 52
Chillingworth, William 66–8, 81, 171, 181
Coby, Patrick 153–4, 160
Cockburn, Catharine Trotter 79, 188, 208
Colie, Rosalie 68, 178, 182, 218
Colman, John 25, 29, 163, 200, 202, 214
Conrad, Jonathan Donald 153, 165, 213
Cooper, Anthony Ashley 56
Cox, Richard 20, 153, 159–60
Cranston, Maurice 53, 63, 157, 172–6, 178, 180, 181
Crocker, Robert 184, 210
Cromwell, Oliver 54
Crook, Samuel 52, 172
Crowe, Michael 159
Cudworth, Damaris 51, 58, 60, 68, 70, 174, 182

Cudworth, Ralph 81, 82, 134, 171, 182–5, 193, 210–11
Culverwell, Nathaniel 22, 68, 182, 192
Curran, Eleanor 155, 164
Curtis, Mattoon 22, 161, 199

d'Alembert, Jean Le Rond 18
De Beer, E S 173
Dixon, Philip 78, 186, 187, 189
Drury, S B 40, 168, 199, 203
Dunn, John 10, 18, 23–4, 26, 156, 158, 161–2, 167, 179, 190–1, 199, 213

Edwards, John 157, 163, 180, 185, 199
Eisenach, Eldon J 24, 163

Filmer, Robert 59, 144, 175
Flage, Daniel 155, 168, 199
Forde, Steven 40, 45, 49, 50, 155–6, 160, 166, 168–9, 170, 196, 199, 212, 215, 217
Forster, Greg ix, 7, 28, 50, 103, 153, 156, 165, 171, 190, 198, 215
Fowler, Edward 66, 171
Fox Bourne, H R 154, 172, 174–5, 218
Furly, Benjamin 59

Gastrell, Francis 189
Gibbs, Lee 179
Greene, Robert 182–3
Griffin, Martin 171, 180
Gysi, Lydia 183–4

Hales, John 66, 68, 171
Hammond, Henry 66, 67, 72, 81, 171, 181, 184
Hancey, James 161, 166, 204
Harris, Ian 160, 164, 190, 199, 214, 216–17
Hedley, Douglas viii, 182
Hobbes, Thomas 19–23, 45, 84, 129, 159, 160, 164, 206

## People Index

Hooker, Richard 8–9, 20, 33, 63–9, 74, 134, 145, 164, 171, 178–80, 192, 213–14
Horwitz, Robert 86, 153, 156, 191–2
Hume, David 22, 84, 159, 191
Hutton, Sarah 182, 185

Im Hof, Ulrich 153, 156
Insole, Christopher J 50, 64–5, 171, 179–80
Israel, Jonathan 18, 21, 157–8

Kant, Immanuel 6, 159, 209
Kelly, Paul viii, 159, 169, 212
Khamara, Edward 191
King, Richard 60

Lamprecht, Sterling Power 22, 106, 161, 199
Laslett, Peter 4, 105, 106, 147, 154, 199
Leibniz, Gottfried Wilhelm 57, 191
Lenz, John W 154, 161–2, 199, 203
Locke, Agnes 52
Locke, John (Sr.) 52, 54
Loconte, Joseph 28, 147, 149, 154, 165, 168, 173–4, 178, 181, 213, 218
Lettinga, Cornelius 178, 181, 184
Limborch, Philip van 58, 79–81, 147, 155, 174–5, 187–8

MacPherson, C B 20, 153, 160–1
Marshall, John 8, 25–6, 28–9, 54, 163, 165, 170, 173, 175, 178–81, 190, 213–14
Masham, Lady Damaris. *See* Cudworth, Damaris
McCann, Edwin 83, 190
McFarland, Ian 91, 195
More, Henry 68, 70, 82, 138, 171, 183–4, 189
Murphy, Mark 200–2, 204
Myers, Peter 153, 159

Newbigin, Leslie 5, 156
Newton, Isaac 18
Nidditch, Peter 2, 154, 174
Nuovo, Victor ix, 10, 27, 79–80, 82, 154, 161, 163–4, 169, 176, 178–9, 182–3, 186–90, 196, 199, 208, 212, 215

Oakley, Francis 108, 120, 154, 199–200, 208
O'Donovan, Oliver 6, 156
Owen, John 53–4, 172

Pailin, David 182–3, 209
Pangle, Thomas 153, 158
Parker, Kim 27, 136, 153, 165, 169, 176, 212, 215
Pascal, Blaise 57, 206
Patrick, Simon 171
Pearson, Samuel 162, 171, 215
Perry, John 6, 28, 50, 156, 165, 171, 204
Plato 19, 85, 88, 94, 123, 189, 193, 196, 206
Polin, Raymond 23, 126–31, 162, 209–12
Pufendorf, Samuel von 6, 57, 159

Rabieh, Michael 153, 155, 160, 199
Reventlow, Henning Graf 157, 162
Rogers, G. A. J. 154, 174–5, 178, 182–3, 218
Rousseau, Jean-Jacques 22, 159

Sedley, David 89, 194
Seliger, Martin 160, 162, 167
Sell, Alan 187–8
Shaftesbury, Earl of. *See* Cooper, Anthony Ashley
Sigmund, Paul 21, 153, 161
Simmons, A. John 155, 204
Simonutti, Luisa 175, 218
Singh, Raghuveer 40, 168, 205
Smith, John 60, 70, 73, 82, 171, 183, 189
Soskice, Janet viii, 89, 192–5
Sparkes, A. W. 24, 115–16, 162, 168, 199, 207
Spellman, William 8, 18–19, 25–6, 157–8, 162–4, 171, 181, 185, 213–14
Stanton, Timothy 24, 28, 162, 165
Stillingfleet, Edward 78–81, 171, 186, 189
Strauss, Leo 4, 19–21, 23–4, 144, 153, 155, 157, 159, 160–1, 165–6, 172, 199, 228

Tate, John William 8, 31, 34, 36, 40–1, 46–7, 52, 124, 154, 155, 165–9, 172, 209
Taylor, Jeremy 66–8, 81, 171, 180, 181
Tetlow, Joanne 28–9, 63, 81, 120–1, 154, 156, 164–5, 171, 175, 178, 181, 189, 208

Tillotson, John 73, 171, 175, 181, 185
Toinard, Nicolas 57, 174
Toland, John 17, 81, 157–8, 189
Trevor-Roper, Hugh 163, 164, 180–1
Tuckness, Alex Scott 112, 154, 165, 170, 190, 196, 199–200, 202, 204, 206–7, 211, 213–14
Tulloch, John 154, 171, 178, 180
Tully, James 155, 158, 160, 162, 165, 167
Tyrrell, James 154, 174

Voltaire 18, 22
von Leyden, W. 22, 23, 86, 90, 161

Wainwright, Arthur 78, 81, 164, 186, 187, 189, 196, 216
Waldron, Jeremy 1, 10, 26, 31, 123–4, 132, 145–6, 153, 161, 164–5, 167, 190, 199, 203, 209, 212, 216–18

Ward, Keith 90, 194
Ward, W. Randall 165, 202, 211
Wardle, David 173, 175
West, Thomas 44, 168, 205–6
Whichcote, Benjamin 29, 56, 68, 70, 72–3, 81, 123, 138, 171, 183–5, 209
Williams, Rowan 5, 170–1
Wolterstorff, Nicholas 69, 158, 176, 182, 190, 206
Woolhouse, Roger 24, 53, 55, 147, 162, 169, 172–3, 183, 218
Wootton, David 198, 200, 207, 214
Worthington, John 79, 188

Yolton, John 23, 25, 40, 160–2, 168, 202–3, 205

Zuckert, Michael 84, 153–4, 157, 159–60, 190–1

# Subject Index

Amsterdam 58
Anglicanism (also "Anglican church", "Church of England", and "Anglican communion") 3, 26, 51–6, 63–4, 66, 68, 81, 151, 172, 175
Arminianism 58, 147
Atheism 1, 5, 9, 20, 46–9, 63, 66, 70, 74, 82, 104, 129, 148, 151, 156–7, 169–70

Bible, the (or "Scripture"). *See* Theology, Revelation in Christian scripture

Calvinism (or "Reformed theology"; see also Puritanism) 3, 24, 26, 51, 52, 55, 64, 126, 172, 173, 179
   Anti-Calvinism 25, 59, 72, 79–80, 126, 129–130, 151, 162, 211
   Hyper-Calvinism (or "dogmatic Calvinism") 5, 9, 72, 74, 130, 151, 184
Cambridge 51–3, 68, 70, 72, 172
Cambridge Platonism 3, 9, 28, 51–2, 56, 58, 68–74, 162, 171, 178, 180, 182–4, 210
Christian political philosopher 4, 5–7, 49–50, 152
Church of England. *See* Anglicanism
Cleves 55–6, 173

Deism 1, 26, 63, 86, 88, 92, 103, 119, 137, 144–5, 149, 157, 192–3
Dominion founded in grace 34–6
Dutch (or "Netherlands") 18, 28, 54

Empiricism (and "Empirical") 62, 69, 131, 145, 190
English Civil War 52
Enlightenment, the 8, 15, 19, 28, 144, 158, 194
Enthusiasm. *See* Religious experience

Epistemology 2, 4, 17–18, 23, 25, 40, 42–4, 59, 61, 78, 80, 107, 135, 138, 141–2, 157, 163, 178, 183, 215, 217

Fideism 10, 68, 135–6, 166, 214

God. *See* Theology
Great Tew Circle (or "Oxford Tew Circle") 3, 51, 63–9, 72–4, 164, 171, 180–1

Happiness. *See* Political Philosophy, Eudaimonism
Heresy 17, 66, 79, 81, 166, 172
Heterodoxy 4–5, 16–17, 37, 52, 78, 81, 186

Islam 8, 46, 89, 148

Judaism 8, 46, 56, 89, 147

Latitudinarianism 3–4, 7–11, 26, 28–30, 51–74, 80–1, 104, 121, 130, 137, 138, 151–2, 156–7, 162–3, 171–2, 178, 180–1
London 8, 51, 56, 71, 155
Lutheranism 55, 173

Marxism 20

Natural Law 4–5, 8–11, 15, 19–20, 22–5, 29, 31, 41, 44, 65, 77, 83, 92, 98, 105–130, 135, 155, 159, 190, 192, 193, 199–204, 211, 213
   the basics 107–12
   Locke as Christian natural law theorist 105–30
   Teleology 112–16

Orthodoxy 17, 53, 54, 56, 77–81, 166, 186
Oxford 51, 53, 66, 161, 173, 180, 199
Oxford Tew Circle. *See* Great Tew Circle

Parliament 52, 53, 65
Platonism. *See* Cambridge Platonism
Political philosophy
    Authority 65, 90, 94, 99, 102–3, 125, 132–4, 139–40, 147, 149, 163, 172, 179–80, 204, 216
    Consent 21, 31–4, 49, 56, 65–6, 120, 125, 129–30, 148, 166, 180
    Divine right 18, 59
    Equality 3, 9, 16, 18, 26, 28, 29, 31, 34, 40, 48, 66–7, 74, 85, 94, 101–3, 105, 110, 120, 121–5, 130, 132, 145, 151, 197
    Eudaimonism 2, 10, 26, 30, 38, 60, 62, 77, 104, 112--15, 125, 127, 128, 130, 133–4, 151, 185, 203, 205–6, 211
    Freedom (and "free will" and "free agency") 9, 15–16, 20–21, 23, 29, 58, 63, 71, 73, 89, 91, 109, 113, 116, 120–1, 124–30, 131, 151, 159, 164, 172, 184, 211–13
    Natural law. *See* "Natural Law"
    Obligation 2, 3, 9–10, 16, 19, 25–6, 31, 33–4, 39–40, 43–4, 46–7, 55, 59, 67, 71–3, 77, 83, 93, 97–9, 102–4, 105–6, 108–14, 118, 122, 126–9, 131, 138–40, 145, 147, 149, 151, 157, 168, 184–5, 203–5, 210–11, 217
    Property 10, 20, 24, 102, 114, 125, 132, 143–7, 213, 217
    Revolution 18, 102–3, 158, 168
    State of nature 45, 47, 97–101, 125–6
    Toleration (or "religious freedom") 18, 25, 28, 33, 36, 38–9, 41–2, 44–9, 51–6, 59, 63–4, 66–7, 71, 74, 104, 109, 129, 132, 137–8, 147–9, 151, 164, 168, 170, 172–3, 178, 180, 198, 215, 218
Protestantism 47, 57, 66, 138, 163, 180
Puritanism. (*See also* Calvinism) 24, 51–3, 64, 172

Rationalism 22, 62, 69–70, 108, 166, 208
Reformation, the 22, 120
Reformed theology. See Calvinism
Religious argumentation in public 36–9
Religious experience (or "enthusiasm") 5, 10, 30, 51, 68, 70, 74, 136–8, 150, 152, 164, 171
Religious freedom. *See* Political philosophy, Toleration
Religious (re)turn 15–28
    and Tate's challenge 31–9
Remonstrant 58, 147
Roman Catholicism 46–7, 55–7, 64, 129, 148, 172–3, 179
Royal Society 55–6, 184

Scholasticism 15, 18, 27, 53, 55, 82, 90, 160, 172
Scripture. *See* Theology, Revelation in Christian scripture
Socinianism 26, 63, 78–80, 157, 163–4, 178, 187

Theology
    Christology 93–4, 102–3, 138–41
    Covenantal theology 120–1
    Creation 105–30
        *Creatio continua* 119–20
        *Creatio ex nihilo* 9, 85, 89–92, 116–20, 193–95
        Doctrine of creation 115–16
        and human equality (*see also* Political philosophy, equality) 121–4
        and human freedom (*see also* Religious Freedom) 125–30
        and natural law (*see* Natural Law)
    Eschatology 102–3
    God 82–104
        Basis of moral behavior 95–7
        Basis of obligation 97–9, 168, 184–5, 203
        Existence of God 82–5
        Model for legal punishment 99–102
        Nature and Attributes of God
            Good 85–9
            Judge 92–3
            Personal 85–9
            Revealing 85–9
        Trinity 77–82
        True idea of God 9, 10, 29, 71, 74, 77–8, 80, 88, 93, 104, 131, 151
    Judgment 102–3
    Pneumatology 7, 64, 78–80, 119, 136–7

Revelation in Christian scripture
131–50
  and authority 10, 30, 59–60, 65, 67, 131–50
  and the basis for toleration 44, 54, 147–9
  Christian scripture as revelation 1, 10, 89, 104, 131–50, 151–2
  and the Constitution as model 131–2
  and inspiration/infallibility/veracity 16, 59–60, 68, 103, 131–50, 213
  and Locke's concept of God 3, 9, 10, 16, 29, 30, 50, 69, 77–8, 80, 85–104, 151–2
  and Locke's concept of natural law 9, 16, 50, 89, 91, 93, 112, 117, 151–2
  and Locke's doctrine of charity 143–7
  Locke's high view of scripture 10, 16, 30, 59–60, 73–4, 79, 131–50, 151–2, 213
  Locke's theology of scripture 1, 10, 30, 60, 61, 81, 89, 104, 134–6, 151–2
  and Locke's use of political arguments 27–8, 77, 93, 104, 121–30, 143–50
  need for revelation 138–43
  and reason 10, 85, 87, 131–50
  Locke's use of scripture 3, 4, 20, 27, 30, 40, 45, 50, 57, 77, 79–81, 93, 112, 117, 126, 131–50, 196, 213
  and political philosophy 3–5, 151–2

Soteriology 6, 32, 37–9, 42, 68, 113–14, 126–8, 130, 132, 137, 143, 164, 170, 175

Three-fold foundation 2, 151–2

# Locke's Works Index

**Writings on Epistemology**

*Draft A* [1671] 57, 154, 174, 222
*Draft B* [1671] 57, 174
*Understanding* [1677] 93, 196
*An Early Draft of Locke's Essay* [1681] 174, 178, 183, 185, 192
*An Essay Concerning Human Understanding* (E) [1689] 2, 5, 10–11, 18, 23, 25, 57, 59–60, 69–71, 73, 80, 83–4, 87, 88, 90–2, 95–6, 98, 111, 118–19, 121–2, 125–6, 131, 133–4, 136, 138, 140, 145–6, 154, 166, 168–70, 175–6, 183–4, 189–97, 200–13, 215–17

**Writings on Government**

*First Tract on Government* [1660] 166, 168, 172–3
*Second Tract on Government* [1662] 173
*The Fundamental Constitutions of Carolina* [1669] 56, 173–4
*First Treatise of Government* (1$^{st}$ T) [1690] 117, 118, 146, 147, 207, 211, 217–18
*Second Treatise of Government* (2$^{nd}$ T) [1690] 3, 25, 40, 66–7, 71–2, 86, 93–4, 97, 100, 102, 105, 109, 117, 118, 123–4, 133–4, 143–6, 154, 157, 166–7, 175, 179, 184, 193–4, 196–8, 200–3, 207, 209–14, 217

**Writings on the Law of Nature**

*Essays on the Law of Nature* (LN) [1664] 11, 22–3, 55, 73, 156, 161, 168–9, 185, 191, 193, 194–9, 200–2, 206
*Questions Concerning the Law of Nature* (QLN) [1664] 11, 22–3, 77, 85–6, 90, 97, 106, 107, 109, 115, 153, 156, 185, 192, 197, 201–3

**Writings on Religion**

*Ecclesia* [1682] 178, 180
*The Reasonableness of Christianity* (RC) [1689] 5, 8, 10–11, 27–8, 42–3, 46, 48, 50, 58, 60, 67, 71–3, 79, 86–7, 94, 107, 110–13, 126, 131, 134–5, 139, 141–2, 145, 147, 155, 182–5, 168–9, 171, 184–5, 187, 192–3, 196–208, 210–12, 214–18
*A Vindication of the Reasonableness of Christianity* [1695] 47, 60, 67, 163, 169, 181
*A Second Vindication of the Reasonableness of Christianity* [1697] 60, 66, 137, 181, 189, 215
*A Discourse of Miracles* [1706] 185, 136, 215
*Paraphrase and Notes on the Epistles of St. Paul* [1707] 28, 60, 163–4, 189, 196
*Adversaria Theologica* [1694] 79, 187

**Writings on Education & Ethics**

*Of Ethick in General* [1687] 205, 215–16
*Some Thoughts Concerning Education* (STCE) [1693] viii, 73, 160, 169, 184–5, 187–8, 192–3, 195
*Some Thoughts Concerning Reading and Study for a Gentleman* [1703] 60, 176, 181
*Of the Conduct of the Understanding* [1706] 60, 136, 145, 176, 214–15, 217

**Writings on Toleration**

*An Essay Concerning Toleration* [1667] 56, 173
*Pacific Christians* [1688] 59, 175

*A Letter Concerning Toleration* (LCT) [1689] 5, 155, 157, 166–70, 175, 185, 193, 195, 197, 198, 200–1, 206, 212, 218

*A Second Letter Concerning Toleration* [1690] 166, 169

*A Third Letter for Toleration* [1692] 166

**Correspondence**

*The Correspondence of John Locke* 173–4, 176, 181, 183, 200, 204, 213–14

*First Reply to Stillingfleet* 187

*Second Reply to Stillingfleet* 79, 187

www.ingramcontent.com/pod-product-compliance
Lightning Source LLC
Chambersburg PA
CBHW070031010526
44117CB00011B/1779